The Doctor's Life of Faith

Janet Goodall

Contents

Preface

The seeds for this book were sown at a regional conference of the International Christian Medical and Dental Association (ICMDA) at Schladming, Austria, in 2008. The conference was attended by graduates and students from across Europe, with varying levels of understanding about how the Christian faith should work out in practice. Dr James Tomlinson, then ICMDA's representative for Eurasia, had asked me to lead a seminar about finding God's plan for our lives.

I have thought more about the subject since then. At first glance it suggested a search for God's personal guidance in life. Although not excluding that, there is a bigger picture. God's overall plan goes much wider and deeper than just what happens to me. God has a master plan. It is the same for all who believe and trust in him. Even so, not everyone understands that there is such a plan, or how it may apply to them. Even for committed Christian believers, the individual's route towards God's final goal will involve very different experiences.

This has been true in my own life. My Christian parents hoped to be missionaries but were unable on health grounds to live and work abroad. Instead they entertained many a visiting missionary in our home. At the start of my medical training I thought I too was heading for the mission field, possibly in India. Instead I became a consultant paediatrician, first in Uganda, then for many years in Stoke-on-Trent. As a single woman, and especially since retirement, I have been free to travel and share professional and biblical insights widely in many parts of the world, from Australia to Zululand.

Both aspects of this teaching have been illuminated by the recognition that we are all made in the image of God. An important part of that imagery is other-centred love. This is the kind of love often seen between new babies and parents, but supremely displayed in the life, death and rising again of the Lord Jesus Christ. As we study the word of God further, his astonishing plan becomes clearer. God the Father wants each of his children to become more like his Son Jesus, through the transforming work of his indwelling Spirit.

Over the years since that seminal conference, I have observed that there is great ignorance about the Bible and its story. This is true not only overseas but even among those brought up in once-Christian Britain. A century ago, the Bible was valued and widely taught in our schools as well as in churches. Now a surprising number of British people no longer have a copy of the Bible in their house. Television quiz shows reveal how often otherwise intelligent competitors have minimal biblical knowledge. Even regular churchgoers tend particularly to neglect the Old Testament Scriptures.

People with roots overseas may think that in moving to Britain they are entering a Christian country. This includes a great number of the health professionals who have found work in our National Health Service. Yet they often find many of the advertisements they see culturally offensive. They can be shocked by lax public morality and behaviour. If they judge these to represent Christianity, they are unlikely to take the faith seriously. My hope is to offer a clearer picture of the purpose of the Christian faith and what it offers to the searcher for truth.

It has been a good refresher course for me to think over the Bible's wonderful story of God's plan for his world and the people in it. The Christian Medical Fellowship (CMF) has played an important part in my personal, professional and spiritual development since 1956. Drs John and Peggy Edmunds, senior members of the Fellowship at the time, inspired me with their loving hospitality. I was then a junior doctor on Peggy's paediatric team, and she is still a great supporter in prayer. Ever since that early encouragement, CMF has provided professional wisdom, good friends and an occasional platform for speaking and teaching. I am especially grateful for this opportunity to share more widely some of the fruits of that influence. I want to express my thanks to Dr Peter Saunders (Chief Executive Officer), John Martin (Head of Communications) and Tom Roberts (Communications Coordinator) for reading, editing and agreeing to publish the work.

ICMDA has broadened my experience, providing much-valued fellowship with friends in other countries, as well as glimpses into the problems some of them face. A few have given permission for me to retell their stories and readers will surely be touched and grateful for that. More ideas than I realise must have come from various writers, speakers and friends. My chief source of inspiration, however, has been the word of God, the Holy Bible. It is my hope and prayer that readers of my little book will be encouraged to become students of the Bible's 66 books. It is still the world's overall bestseller. Biblical quotations are from the New International Version. For those who use English as a second language the Good News Bible is recommended as it was produced with these readers in mind.

James Tomlinson has been a real encouragement from the start. Many other friends, too many to be named individually, have prayed for, read or commented on the work in progress and for that I thank them all, especially Anne Beaumont, Garth and Terry Hastings and Valerie MacKay. David Finn helped me over the last hurdle before the publisher's deadline. Roger and Frances Delf have repeatedly provided a quiet haven as needed, and a number of computer experts have intermittently come to my aid. Without the knowhow of Nicholas Harrison, Michael Hopkins and Stephen O'Brien the script would occasionally have been lost in space instead of becoming the volume you now hold in your hand. May its message enter your mind, touch your heart and affect your goal in life.

Above all, of course, I thank my loving heavenly Father for his guidance over so many years – and I acknowledge that he has not finished with me yet! I have written of much that he is still teaching me to put into practice.

Janet Goodall
February 2014

For my good friends Astrit and Elena Rrukaj who, with many others, have come to Britain from afar to serve our national health here.

PART ONE

Chapter 1
Why we need a goal

Early in 2009, an American plane nosedived shortly after take-off from New York having hit a flock of birds causing engine failure. Keeping calm, the pilot brought the plane safely down, but into the Hudson River. The terrified passengers thought their last hour had come, both during the crash and as icy water began to fill the cabin. It became a seven-day wonder that all 155 people on board were rescued. Afterwards, one of the survivors told a reporter how, thinking he was about to die, he had asked himself, 'If this was the end, was I the person I wanted to be all my life?'

Most of us probably start off with at least a few vague ideas about what we would like the future to hold for us. When we were very young, kindly grownups would often ask, 'What do you want to be when you grow up?' to which we usually had some kind of an answer. How much does what we said then match what we are now?

Different ambitions

Today's children may reply, 'I want to be a spaceman', 'a pop singer', or perhaps, 'a brain surgeon'. I once met a very junior American medical student who hoped to become a specialist in electro-encephalography. I afterwards lost track of him, so I don't know whether he expanded his ideas before graduation. Others of us have perhaps had times of uncertainty about what to do at all. Or we cling on to some long-held ambition.

Dense fog once grounded the plane I needed to catch to attend an important interview. I was left feeling very let down and uncertain which door to knock on next. Many others must have known that kind of experience.

Is anyone out there and is he interested?

It is often when our plans run into the ground, whatever the cause, that questions start to arise: 'Am I what I wanted to be?' 'Am I on the right track?' 'What's life all about anyway?' Perhaps the advice of our seniors doesn't inspire, and can even upset us. One of my doctor friends, having failed a higher medical examination, was asked by her consultant if she had ever thought of going in for nursing. She had a great respect for the nursing profession, but had worked so hard to get to where she was in medicine that his suggestion greatly offended her. She therefore made even greater efforts to do well in her chosen career and was eventually successful.

Discouragement makes many of us start to wonder who to go to for help. Could that friend be right who says there is a God who is bothered about my plans and prospects? The rescued American passenger might have asked himself, 'Am I the sort of person *God* intended me to be?' We could argue, 'If God exists at all, he has a universe to run, so why should he trouble about me?' Yet if God really is the one who made us, then he is likely to be interested in how we live the lives he created.

Someone else may attempt a kind of personal league table, adding up good deeds or high scores and seeing how they compare with those of other people. Surely a brain surgeon would come out higher than a pop star, whatever their respective earnings. Isn't it better to save lives than to entertain people? Like a good manager, if God comes into this at all, he must surely want me to get to the highest possible place in my career. Successful competition is surely what it's all about. Yet a young pop singer could argue along the same lines, hoping to reach the top of the charts – if not actually saving lives on the way, then at least making life more enjoyable for a lot of people.

Worldly-wise can be unwise

Is professional success God's goal for everyone? Is he not interested in life's 'little people'? Clearly, if we all came out at the top there would be no difference between bosses and workers, interns and consultants. In George Orwell's novel, *Animal Farm*, the ambitious pig Napoleon tells the other farm animals that 'All animals are equal', before adding 'But some animals are more equal than others'. He secretly intended that all others in the farmyard should do as he said. Is this how humans should think and behave? That some of them do so does not make that right. A young friend of mine, brought up in a closed country under the tight rule of a dictator, had thought that Orwell's book must be about her homeland.

Wanting to stand over others, or simply to win their admiration, are poor goals. Once, I was with a fellow student when a passing motorist stopped and asked for directions. My companion so quickly told him which way to go that I later expressed surprise, admiring his knowledge of the route. 'I don't really know where he wanted to go', he admitted, 'But the driver would think I did.' Self-serving hinders us from being of true service to other people.

This is confirmed by lessons from history. By the time of Christ, Imperial Rome had come to rule over many countries and a series of emperors climbed in turn to the top of the Roman tree. Most of them became so proud, greedy and corrupt that the whole empire suffered and finally fell apart.

A better alternative

The Roman Empire was still flourishing when Paul, an early Christian and Roman citizen, wrote to his fellow believers living in Rome:

> 'Do not conform to the pattern of this world, but be transformed by the renewing of your mind. Then you will be able to test and approve what God's will is – his good, pleasing and perfect will.' [1]

Part of Paul's meaning here is that they must rid their minds of the common Roman attitudes of self-interest and self-serving. Instead, they should link up with God's perfect wisdom, even if this went against the norms of the majority. To rely on human reason alone would in the end prove fatal to national survival, but how amazing to be offered access to God's own mind.

It is not popular to think that God often chooses to do his work through little people, instead of using those who are full of their own importance. Paul therefore warned the Greeks of Corinth against ignoring God's wisdom and going instead to ask advice of a few people with big names. [2] There is a true story about a group of disabled children competing in an important race when one of them fell. Without hesitation, the others stopped to help the one who was down. The faster ones then kept in step with their slower companions until they all arrived at the finishing tape together, to receive a standing ovation. The crowd in the stadium had witnessed a greater victory than is usually seen in competitive sport. Weak in the eyes of the rest of the world, and in some places thought of as total misfits, these youngsters had publicly underlined an important principle. We are here to help each other, not to benefit from someone else's downfall.

If this is the sort of person God wants me to be, I clearly need to look at a different set of standards from those commonly held. Perhaps God is more interested in our running the race well than being first past the post. He may be less concerned about my aim for a successful career than whether I tune in to him to be guided by his wisdom in helping others. If this should still bring success, the thanks would first go to him.

Where to start

When about to travel to an unknown place we will look at a map and perhaps talk to others who have been that way before. Should we be any less thoughtful about considering our journey through life? What difference does it make to believe that God, in his wisdom, will guide and direct the paths of those who trust him? If, as Paul wrote, there is a 'good, pleasing and perfect will' for each of us, how do we find it? This is an all-important question if we are to live our lives to the full.

Are we willing to be told what to do and how to do it?

There are successful people who claim with some pride that they have arrived where they are by their own efforts. Yet many of them never stop to ask where their inborn intelligence and drive have come from.

This can be true even for those in the caring professions. Many began by doing better than others at school, before going on to university or medical school. Over the years they have constantly been treated as rather special by family and friends, until they begin to think that they are indeed very special. Whether applied to physicians or surgeons, pop stars or footballers, climbing high can become a matter of personal pride. Films sometimes joke about surgeons who throw their instruments about and swear a lot, but jokes sometimes tell us a few home truths. We should all take warning from this, and when perplexed about the best course should consult others further along the road, avoiding those who would simply say what we want to hear.

Guidance needed

I once knew a surgeon who for a time had to work alone at a mission hospital. He sometimes felt that the operations he had to do were beyond him. He had an old surgical textbook and at such times he would read up first what he should do. How he would have loved to have the author of that textbook looking over his shoulder and telling him the next move!

In the same way, as we look for guidance in planning either surgical operations or journeys, so we need to find directions for our journey through life. God has provided all the directions we need in his inspired guidebook, the Bible. It does not give us many obvious job descriptions, but it can come as a surprise to find repeated assurances that God cares for us with unfailing love, and that he has a good plan for each of us. He promises to lead those of us who are ready to consult, trust and obey him throughout our journey. He offers many assurances that he will not leave us on our own if things get tough. [3] He does not simply act as a critical observer, but offers us his wisdom – wisdom that is completely dependable. [4] He even said to his chosen people that if they carefully obeyed him he would 'set [them] high above all the nations on earth' and they would 'always be at the top, never at the bottom'. [5] Sadly, we have seen the alternative verified in the history of certain once God-fearing peoples. He longs for us to pay attention to him and so find the best way to live.

As we go on to consider this further, readers who are already walking in God's ways are asked to be patient for the sake of those who are still just looking, and perhaps give them a helping hand. In any case, a refresher course could be a good thing, even for you!

For further thought:

- What are you aiming at?
- How do you plan to arrive there? Do you need any help?

References

1. Romans 12:2
2. 1 Corinthians 1:11-14
3. eg Deuteronomy 31:8; Psalm 23:4; Romans 8:38-39
4. Proverbs 3:5-6
5. Deuteronomy 28:1, 13

Chapter 2
Looking back before looking forward

We are given a lot of information nowadays about how to keep fit. We can be informed by the media of a well-known person's careful diet, or be treated to a photo of some senior minister going to work on his bicycle. No doubt many less well-known citizens take great care to eat properly and go for a run before work. In Britain many elderly people do a daily crossword puzzle to help them to stay mentally alert. Yet how many in a population give much thought to their spiritual health?

It is 100% certain that physical death lies ahead for all of us. On the way, many will know failing physical and mental powers or emotional upset. If life is lived in a spiritually unhealthy way, we need to understand how this will affect the survival of 'the real me' – the essential person. Probably most of us know someone with a physical disorder and are good at suspecting somebody's mental or emotional illness, although not everyone understands that spiritual ill health is equally serious. Perhaps doctors and patients alike would be better off to think more about the need for soul-medicine than of the more usual prescriptions for high blood pressure or depression.

Looking for the Maker's instructions

When we get a new piece of unfamiliar equipment, we probably look inside the box to find the maker's instructions for use. There are, of course, people who think they know how to put it all together without being told. Some even throw away the box with the advice still inside it. Then, if the machine doesn't work, or goes wrong later, they struggle for a long time to put it right by themselves. Some kind friend may then repeat the old saying, 'If all else fails, read the instructions', but by now these are lost. The hope is that they will be found or that someone who knows this particular model will come to the rescue.

Thankfully, when we want to find help for our spiritual lives, there is an unfailing source of information and help waiting to guide and teach us all we need to know. A visit to the doctor usually starts with questions and answers about the history of the complaint and what the patient has tried. As we think of spiritual ill health and its remedy, it will help to look at an outline of the history of God's dealings with humanity. His purposes are recorded in the Bible and we'll consider how for centuries people have tried or failed to meet standards given as the Maker's instructions. All too often people have ignored or lost them. By choosing to go our own way, the result has been the chaos and unhappiness found in much of the world throughout the ages.

Missing the mark

Ecclesiastes is a book of the Bible that, if set to music, would be in a minor key. It starts with the author's thoughts on the meaninglessness of life. It is significant that in the first 44 verses, the word 'I' occurs 38 times! We do not find meaning in life by depending on our own wisdom or possessions. Perhaps it is appropriate that the middle letter of the word 'sin' is 'i'. ''Sin' is an old expression for 'missing the mark'. When we offend God by ignoring his standards and so missing his mark, we sin. So much sin comes from disobeying God by being self-willed, with 'I' kept firmly at the centre but an easy target for temptation.

Whether we speak of a driver breaking the speed limit, or someone whose blood level of alcohol, sugar or cholesterol exceeds the safe limit (to miss the accepted 'mark'), is to take risks and face undesirable consequences. A visit to an Accident and Emergency department or a medical outpatient clinic will demonstrate what some of these consequences are. There are also standards to be kept to ensure our spiritual health. Failing to keep them has equally serious consequences.

One of my friends is an expert at the game of bowls and wins trophies for her skill. This requires excellent judgment, for in doing so well she has dealt with a big problem. For those unfamiliar with this ancient game, a 'bowl' (or 'wood') is a heavy round wooden ball that is rolled across a grass lawn, aiming to hit the 'jack', a small white ball already on the green. This may sound easy enough to a novice, but the problem is that the bowl has bias and it rolls in a curve. For centuries, this has been deliberately supplemented by embedding a piece of metal at the heart of the wood. Inexperienced players find it very hard to get at all close to the jack.

All of us, young and old, have an inborn bias; we have a tendency to curve in on ourselves, deflecting us even from meeting our *own* standards. The unaided skill of the best of us will never overcome the 'I' embedded in our hearts, stopping us from going straight.

The two testaments

As we go on to read of what the result of mankind's disobedience, and what God has done about it, our source book will again be the Bible. It is in two parts, the first known as the Old Testament and the second the New Testament. Both give us important and inter-related messages today. These books are not simply textbooks, to read as we read for exams. We need to listen with our spiritual ears to the messages they give and be open to hearing God's voice through them. We don't need to read very far to find serious human failure to honour God and keep his standards. Our newspaper headlines today tell the same story, so we would do well to learn how to avoid such failures.

A 'Last Will and Testament' records someone's final wishes about what to do with remaining possessions after that person dies. Sometimes the person making a will attaches certain conditions, but to die without making a will leaves a lot of problems. In the Bible, the word 'testament' has a deeper meaning, for it is an inspired record of God's will.

Why speak of the Bible as inspired?

Some who are unfamiliar with what the Bible says may find it strange that others believe it to have been divinely inspired. They perhaps view such a notion with scepticism, whilst students of literature may enjoy the language of the old Authorised Version and read it as appreciatively as they would a play by Shakespeare. To offer more insight we need to think more deeply about the origins of the Bible and how it is still such a significant resource for many seekers after meaning and purpose in their lives.

In his book *The Contemporary Christian*, John Stott unpacks the topic with customary clarity. He explains how God has revealed himself to humanity by 'speaking to and through the biblical authors'. He has not acted like a remote radio transmitter, intending his messages to be mechanically recorded and relayed by selected listeners. Rather he has chosen writers whose existing interests and aptitudes have prepared their minds and wills to co-operate with his. Some of them were by inclination historians, some theologians, some enjoyed literary composition, and God 'spoke through them in such a way that the words spoken [and written] were simultaneously and equally his and theirs'. Although produced in very different times from ours we can study the records to determine what principles the original accounts intended to convey, whatever their chosen subject. The worship of man-made idols in the past was a serious insult to a faithful God, and a punishable offence, but today nations and individuals risk the same consequences when something (or someone) takes God's place as an object of worship.

To apply the meaning and message of those old writings to our present day lives will mean assessing the mood and mentality of our surrounding culture. Dr Stott says, 'Only then shall we be able to discern how the unchanging word speaks to the changing world.' He calls this the discipline of 'double listening', that is, 'listening humbly to the Scripture and critically to modernity in order to relate the one to the other'. Clearly this calls for us to make balanced judgements, being neither so immersed in our holy huddles that we neglect the needs of the world about us nor so preoccupied with worldly affairs that we fail to apply to them the revealed wisdom of God. The Bible does not give us many obvious job descriptions, but offers guiding principles as we look for direction in all our ways.

The Old Testament

In the Bible, God expresses his will as an agreement, or covenant – his 'testament' to which his people should agree. This covenant was established by God's grace with people who had rejected him. Instead of bringing judgment on them, he graciously chose to redeem a people for himself, and gave them rules for life which, if accepted and obeyed would allow a continued relationship between them and God. For people to fail in their side of the agreement would break trust and take them towards death and destruction, not life and growth. [1]

Jewish and Christian traditions name Moses as author of the first five books of the Bible, the Pentateuch (excluding the account of his death at the end of Deuteronomy). Some experts suggest 1446-1406 BC as the likely date for these writings, whereas others disagree about both this and the authorship. A basic difference in approach is that the critics are more interested in trying to clarify what cannot now be clarified, but traditional Jews and Christians see the books as a reliably recorded history, with many lessons still to be applied today. This is the line I shall follow.

In *Genesis* we are told the story of creation, including that of human beings. Centuries after the first humans rebelled against God, he called a man named Abraham to follow him. He promised to make Abraham's children into a great nation, and to give them the land of Canaan to live in and to grow as God's people, so that they would become a blessing to the whole world. This promise was repeated to Abraham's descendants, Isaac and Jacob (later renamed 'Israel' by God). Israel's children were rescued from starvation by one of their brothers, Joseph. Earlier he had been betrayed by his older brothers and so began a long and painful story that finally took him to be prime minister of Egypt, where he was in a position to save the lives of all his family. Years passed, the children of Israel multiplied, but were later enslaved by the Egyptians. The books of *Exodus* and *Numbers* tell how God remembered his promises, raising up Moses to lead the people to freedom. On Mount Sinai, God gave his law and told Moses some of the offerings they had to make to God in worship, and as an atonement for their sins. Between these two books comes *Leviticus*, which outlines the sacrifices and offerings that were required to deal with sin, along with many laws for living distinctively as God's people.

The history of the Hebrews under Moses' successor is recorded in a book bearing his name, *Joshua*. It describes how he finally led them into Canaan. After Joshua's death came a series of leaders, recorded in the book of *Judges*. Few of them measured up to God's standards; they gave poor leadership and the people lost direction. Finally God sent them a new leader – Samuel. He was both priest and prophet and ruled wisely and well. Even so, the people rebelled and because they wanted to be like other nations, they asked for a king. God directed Samuel to anoint the disappointing Saul and after him the distinguished David, as their kings.

King David made the holy city of Jerusalem his capital and penned many contributions to the book of *Psalms*. The two books of *Samuel* record the histories of Samuel, Saul and David. Next are the books of *Kings*, containing the account of David's son, King Solomon, his (mostly ungodly) successors, and after his death the division of the kingdom into northern Israel and southern Judah. Solomon built a magnificent temple in Jerusalem, dedicating it to the worship of God, as told in the two books of *Chronicles*. He had God-given wisdom, some shown in the 'wisdom literature' – the books of *Proverbs*, *Ecclesiastes* (warning how empty life is without God) and the love song, *Song of Songs*.

The kingdoms of both Israel and Judah disobeyed God, not least by worshipping idols, and despite many warnings by the prophets (their names making a roll-call for over a third of the books of the Old Testament) first Israel and then Judah were invaded and their people taken into exile. Jerusalem was destroyed by King Nebuchadnezzar of Babylon. It was only after Babylon had been defeated by Cyrus, the king of Persia, that permission was given for the Jews to return home. Efforts at rebuilding the city of Jerusalem and its temple were encouraged by *Ezra* and *Nehemiah*.

Among the other stories the books named for them tell of two significant women, *Ruth* and *Esther*. Matthew mentions Ruth in the family tree of Jesus [2] and Esther, Jewish wife of the king of Persia, was able to save her people from slaughter. God used each of these women to work out his purposes in history.

Last in the long series of prophets came *Malachi*. His book warns of a coming curse instead of blessing if on-going peace talks set up by God with his people should end in failure. Yet among the many forecasts of trouble ahead there had also been some hints about a Saviour, or Messiah, who would finally come to the rescue. The biblical record is then silent for four hundred years.

The New Testament

This part of the Bible starts more hopefully, with the coming of Jesus as the long-promised deliverer. He came very quietly, and we'll be thinking more about this later, but he fulfilled the prophecies about the coming Messiah in many remarkable ways. The aim of his life's work and the events around his death and resurrection offered a new covenant that would no longer be primarily for the Jews, but for people of all nations. He would become the Saviour of the world.

The old covenant had shown that people could not keep God's laws by their own efforts, but Jesus would bring in a new covenant, based on his death and resurrection. Christ's self-giving death and obedient love would cover all that the law required. [3] Through faith in Jesus, people would receive new life and a new heart, given by the Holy Spirit. This astonishing gift of God's Spirit, working alongside and within them, would transform them, helping them to live lives pleasing to God. [4] This new life would be characterised by love for God and for one another. [5, 6, 7]

Attitudes to these Scriptures

The 39 books of the Old Testament are still revered by orthodox Jews and have echoes in the Qur'an. Jewish, Muslim and Christian readers all recognise the importance of great men of faith such as Abraham and value the lessons to be drawn from their lives.

Some modern scholars suggest that the Old Testament describes a very different, warlike God from the loving one we meet in the New Testament. It is true that looking back to the early period of biblical history raises thought-provoking questions with few easy answers. Historical research makes clear, however, that the peoples of Canaan were corrupt and evil: their idol worship was accompanied by child sacrifice, prostitution, and sexual orgies. Like an aggressive cancer, such evil had to be eradicated, however painfully. Some changed their ways in time, put their trust in the one true God and found mercy. [8] This can still happen today.

Many of the prophets longed for peace but they knew it would only come by people repenting of wrongdoing, not tolerating or co-operating with it. There will always be casualties when the good and godly resist the forces of evil. But the Bible offers hope. It makes it clear that God's Son will finally return. Then there will be no more death, mourning or pain and all will be made new. [9]

Traditionally Christians have believed that both Testaments, as originally given, were (and remain) the authentic word of God, his mind and purpose being shared with writers inspired by his Spirit to make them reliable messengers. The Old Testament includes many pointers to the coming of the Christ (or Messiah), bringer of salvation, and the New Testament identifies this person as Jesus, God-made-man and central to the Christian faith.

A few years ago I gave an English New Testament to a Hungarian Christian who at once complained, 'Why have you only given me half a Bible?' It was a good question, for long ago in the first century Augustine, a great Christian thinker, said that in the Old Testament the New was concealed, and in the New the Old was revealed. The two go together.

BC and AD

Before the coming of Christ most of the people described in the Old Testament failed to remain faithful to God, rejecting him and turning to idols time and time again. It seemed as though this pattern would continue forever. Then the coming of Christ changed history. We refer to the time before his birth as BC (Before Christ), but the years since are referred to as Anno Domini (AD) – Latin for 'in the year of our Lord'. To use BCE (Before the Common Era) and CE (Common Era) fails to observe the significance of Christ's entry into the world.

We are likely to find ourselves mirrored in the Bible's account of how humanity has either rejected or responded to God's love in action, with important personal and social consequences in each case. As we start to think about whether this is still happening today, could it be true that a lot of personal and national troubles are caused by what has been called 'a God-shaped gap' in people's lives? Taking no time to get to know him is at the root of much spiritual ill health. If this is really so, it is time to find ways to repair that gap.

Although it is now over two thousand years since the birth of the Christ child in Bethlehem, the story of God's creative love started many centuries before that. To trace his plan for humanity, and that includes each of us today, we will first look back at the Old Testament record as it unfolded and see how well or otherwise people cooperated with the truth God shared with them. How did people learn to recognise God's will and way for living their lives in those long ago days? After that we will look at the New Testament, telling how his plans matured so that his people, too, can gradually become more mature. His aim is to restore us to the image in which we were created.

For further thought

- Would you be happy to follow guidance about how to live well?
- Had you thought of the link between living well and spiritual health?
- Did you realise that God gave us the Scriptures as a 'keep fit manual'?

Further resources

- Wenham G. The Pentateuch in Carson DA ed. *New Bible commentary 21st edition*. Leicester: Inter-Varsity Press, 1994
- Stott J. *The contemporary Christian*. Leicester: Inter-Varsity Press, 1992
- Jones J. *With my whole heart: reflections on the heart of the Psalms*. London: SPCK Publishing, 2012
- Stott J. *Favourite Psalms*. Milton Keynes: Word Publishing, 1988

References

1. Deuteronomy 30:15-18
2. Matthew 1:5
3. Romans 8:1-4
4. John 14:15-16; Romans 8:5-17
5. Micah 6:8
6. John 13:34-35
7. Mark 12:28-31
8. Joshua 2:11-12, 6:23
9. Revelation 21:3-5

Chapter 3
God's timing is not like ours

There is an African poem, its title and authorship now forgotten, describing the difference it made to the pace of village life when an alarm clock took the place of a cockerel's cry as the daily wake-up call. The owner of the clock had to arrive on time for his job in the city so he needed to make an early start. He set off in smart suit with briefcase in one hand and umbrella in the other – and of course, someone else would probably have got up even earlier to carry water or make a meal for him before he left. I once saw someone very like the subject of the poem as he walked back home through a Ugandan forest, his smart city clothes oddly out of place among the wild greenery of that lovely countryside.

This all made me wonder how much longer it would be before others in that village followed his example and became like workers in the West for whom it is all 'go, go, go'. Whatever our occupation, so many working hours tend to be spent hurrying from one kind of appointment to the next and any free time is filled with as much action as we have energy for. We certainly need some kind of time-keeper, whether a simple wrist watch or something more advanced, to help us make sure that we get through the plans for the day. Yet to look back at the early history of God's chosen people is to find that our Maker has not been in such a hurry.

The old, old story

The story begins in the first two chapters of the book of Genesis with a concentrated account of God's creative work as he produced our world, the 'days' spoken of being his idea of time, not our 24 hours. [1] The climax of his work was the creation of man ('Adam') and later woman ('Eve'). He made these human beings 'in his own image', telling them to 'fill the earth and subdue it'. [2] To start with he put them into a beautiful garden where he walked and talked with them to their shared enjoyment.

We must remember that like all the other books of the Bible, Genesis makes no claim to be a scientific textbook. Its first chapter tells us not so much the precise *how* of creation as the *why* of it – why God created a universe at all and then produced living organisms to live on the earth and in the air and sea. It tells us about *God*, the Creator, the authority and power of his word, his pleasure in making something good, his separation of light from darkness and plants from people, providing for all the needs of his creatures before he finally asked human beings to take care of his creation. He had a plan for humanity and, in broad terms, conveyed from the beginning what it was, making it clearer over the centuries that followed. The often forgotten but all-important fact is that God first designed human beings to be like him, 'in his image'.

Each one of us is intended to enjoy a loving relationship with God and with other people, and to take care of his world. Later we'll look more closely at what this could mean, but for now let's not get hung up on whether we should take the account literally or as a poetic description. As you read the story, remember that its purpose is to tell us more about God himself, why he acted as he did and how human doubt and disobedience broke up his intention for an on-going loving relationship.

Not good to be alone

Very early on, the Bible story introduces the importance of companionship. Before God made Eve for Adam, he had said, 'It is not good for man to be alone'. [3] This is borne out by psychologists and psychiatrists today as well as being true of personal experience. Prolonged solitary confinement is a form of torture. Frail old people or abandoned babies can quickly deteriorate when they are parted from former families or a settled home. Loneliness and boredom can lead to depression and even death, something I have seen in badly resourced orphanages overseas. In one of them, half the children I saw were expected to die every year. In an atheistic culture, they had a degree of physical care but a great shortage of loving personal interaction.

Fortunately, genuine personal care can prevent such deprivation. All age groups thrive by finding people who love them and provide them with interest. We come into being through and for relationships, both between one another and, supremely, with our Father God. Even those who live alone can be rich in friendship, a blessing not to be overlooked or neglected even if, like all close relationships, it has to be nourished to stay strong. Some of the sad little children in one of the deprived institutions I visited were transformed into happy, smiling little people simply by regular stimulation and care from an understanding and loving woman. Before she came they had suffered a love-deficiency. Made in the image of a God of love, we have been well designed to supply each other's needs.

A good start that ended in tears

Looking back on mankind's early days in Eden's lovely garden, communication between the Creator and his human creatures was unclouded and personal. After an unspecified time this special relationship was spoiled by doubt and disobedience on the part of Eve and Adam. They had been free to enjoy all that was in the garden, except for the fruit of two particular trees – one would give them the knowledge of good and evil and to eat its fruit would lead to death. They had so far only ever known good. [4] Then, like so many others ever since, they yielded to the temptation presented by Satan, the enemy of souls, and took what had been forbidden. [5]

The man had been first to be warned of the fatal consequences of disobedience if he took fruit from that particular tree, and he must have repeated this to the woman. Later she was strongly tempted to doubt what God had said, so she tried a bite of the fruit, liked it and persuaded Adam to have some, too. The results affected their own relationship, but worst of all they lost that previous precious closeness with God. In turn he could no longer trust them to honour and obey him. So he sent them out of his garden, to experience hard labour, painful parenthood and the previously unknown prospect of death. This dramatic change in their lives is known as 'the Fall'. Later, the families and communities they founded would display the same fractured relationships and the same rejection of their Creator. One act of disobedience, based as it was on doubting God's word, brought disaster to the entire human race.

'Me, me, me' often hurts 'you, you and you'

Even those who choose not to accept the story as given must surely see how true it is for all of us, that from childhood onwards, we have an inborn tendency to rebel and go our own way. The childish cries of 'I want' and 'me first' indicate attitudes that do not always mature with the years. I suspect that they are still active around the committee tables of hospitals or big businesses – as grown up people, whether politely or not, compete for funds for their own little empire. Wherever it is found, self-will, by lacking thought for others, is likely to cause lasting pain.

Often, one false step can cause trouble for more than just the one who took it. Sometimes those about to take such a step, like young children, are not in full possession of the facts and need more explanation. A little boy I had cared for all his life needed to take regular medication, but at seven years old decided that he would instead hide or throw it away. As he said later, 'Nobody else has to take this stuff with his food'. His parents were worried by his subsequent ill health, but when he admitted what he had done it was clear that he had grown old enough to understand a fuller explanation about why he needed regular treatment to stay well. He saw the point, faithfully took his treatment, and recovered.

On a larger scale, disobedience to God's revealed laws is not the private affair we may imagine it to be, even if it matches the way everyone else behaves. It produces spiritual sickness in individuals and social disturbance around them. Yet, like the child's medication, God's laws are for our own good. We each need to study them to help us understand and keep them, for the benefit of all.

History is still repeated

There is a traceable, though often unacknowledged, connection between a national turning away from God and the rise in poverty, debt, divorce, illegitimacy, crime and even ill health. Many of the Old Testament prophets made this kind of connection, but their warnings fell on deaf ears. In the surgeries of general practitioners and psychiatric or other clinics, many presenting symptoms could be traced back to spiritual disorder if only those heading the teams would consider this possibility. Lack of forgiveness alone can cause such bitterness of spirit that serious physical symptoms can follow. Any associated anger may explode into high blood pressure or worse, hurting more people than the one who is angry. Internationally, such embitterment produces war and bloodshed.

I used to think that the warning about the sins of the fathers being visited on subsequent generations of children was rather unjust. [6] Why should their descendants suffer for parental sin? The fact is that they do. Recently I met a small boy some years after his father had left for his homeland, leaving the child and his loving mother to cope alone. He was hurt that the father rarely kept arrangements made to phone him, and other children never hear from an absentee parent at all.

There must be many such in our society who are scarred by someone else's lack of faithfulness. This not only confirms God's warnings about what will follow wrongdoing, but it should also turn us round to consider his great faithfulness and willingness to forgive us our failures. God has a heart of love that will last forever. [7] He longs to bring people back to walk in step with him, spiritually healthy again and at peace with each other. He is full of long-suffering and patience. He gives time for his disobedient people to repent. [8, 9]

For further thought

- Does the connection between spiritual and social health make sense?
- Would you be surprised if your doctor asked about the state of your spiritual life? What 'soul-medicine' would you prescribe to keep someone spiritually fit?

References

1. 2 Peter 3:8
2. Genesis 1:27-28
3. Genesis 2:18
4. Genesis 2:16-17
5. Genesis 3:6
6. Numbers 14:18
7. Jeremiah 31:3
8. 2 Peter 3:9
9. Romans 2:4

Chapter 4
A few significant case-histories

When medical students are learning about pathology, they are taught to think about the microscopic and anatomical causes of an illness and their usual effects. If they can meet and examine someone affected by a particular disease, the subject is then fixed more firmly in the mind. From this early stage of my education I still remember the name of the first patient I met and wrote up. Many years before, she had caught scarlet fever and was now in heart failure due to a damaged mitral valve. I had only just started seeing sick patients in hospital but the encounter literally brought to life a condition that might otherwise have been remembered as just one more lecture or anatomy demonstration.

Having thought about the background and possible symptoms of spiritual ill health, it is now time to think about how it affected a few famous people of old, and what happened as a result. It will be better still if we learn to apply the lessons they offer.

God's chosen people have to learn to trust and obey

Generations came and went after the Fall, with more highs and lows in the Genesis report, until the sudden arrival of a married couple in Ur of the Chaldeans (probably today's Southern Iraq) – Abraham and Sarah. Abraham heard the voice of God personally, calling him out of his homeland and repeatedly promising that he would become the founder of a great nation. Indeed, through him would come many nations and great blessing to the world. This would be despite the great age of both the man and his wife and their chronic state of childlessness. Scripture records that Abraham 'believed the Lord and he credited it to him as righteousness.' [1,2] Centuries later, his simple faith in the promises of God would become an example for others to follow. [3]

As years went by with no sign of pregnancy, Sarah stopped trusting what God had said, just as Eve had done before her. She urged

Abraham to father a child through her Egyptian maid, Hagar, as her surrogate. There was no suggestion that they asked God about it. Perhaps Abraham argued that even if he were to father a new nation as God had promised, his wife Sarah had not been clearly identified as the mother. It is all too easy to misinterpret God's will without double-checking. Sarah, not God, suggested the union with Hagar. From that was born Ishmael, who years later would father the Arab races. It was many years more before the promised son, Isaac, was born to Sarah. By then they were very aged parents indeed.

As an outward sign of a renewed covenant with God, both boys and their father were circumcised. This was to be a constant reminder of God's promise to be with them if they walked in his ways. Yet the two mothers fell out. Sarah sent away Hagar and Ishmael. The young man still bore the sign of the covenant, as do his Arab descendants, but this split between the two sons of Abraham would finally end up as the Arab-Israeli conflict of today.

These stories are not just history but are also recorded for our learning. The lesson for us is that to doubt God's word and run ahead of his purposes is a form of disobedience. We must learn from Abraham's experience to trust God's promises and wait patiently for his perfect timing in keeping them. Otherwise the results can be big trouble that will affect others for a long time to come.

Total commitment can mean great personal cost

It is not clear how old Isaac was when Abraham faced the crisis recorded in Genesis 22. He believed that God was asking him to sacrifice this long promised, dearly beloved son. Although human sacrifice was not unusual in that culture, it would later be forbidden for God's people, so this seems a very strange request. By now, though, Abraham knew and trusted the voice of his God and at once set out to obey. At the last moment a male sheep was provided and sacrificed to take Isaac's place – but not before Abraham had clearly shown his desire to obey God, whatever the cost. Today we find this a strange story, interpreted by Jonathan Sacks (a Jewish former Chief Rabbi) as the way that Abraham had to learn that Isaac was not his property, but God's gift to him (and still the proper attitude to be held towards all children). Another message to Abraham, and now to us, is that however much we treasure someone or something, the first place in our hearts belongs to God, the giver of all good things.

After this God renewed the promise to Abraham that it would indeed be through Isaac that blessing would finally come to the world. Here was a hint, centuries beforehand, that God intended great blessing to come to all people through his only Son, our Lord Jesus Christ. Both Abraham and Isaac (but not Ishmael) feature in Jesus' family tree as recorded by Dr Luke. [4] We shall consider later what cost this blessing would involve. The story of the ram that took Isaac's place on the altar foreshadows how God's own Son would finally pay an even greater price to save the world from spiritual death.

God's ways can perplex us but he has purpose in them

Isaac and his wife eventually had twin boys, Esau and Jacob. Jacob was later known as Israel. God's original promise was renewed to and through him. His twelve sons became founders of the twelve tribes of Israel. Joseph, Jacob's favourite, was undoubtedly rather conceited and tactless, causing his older brothers to hate and almost murder him. Instead, they sold him into slavery and he was taken away from Canaan to Egypt, a miserable change of status for him in every way.

Yet God was faithful to Joseph. Despite a false accusation leading to many years in prison, he finally became premier of Egypt; a long, slow process that transformed a self-important teenager into a wise and generous statesman. He had learned humility, but only through times of much hardship and delay. As prime minister, Joseph was able to move his father and brothers from a famine in Canaan to Egypt where, thanks to God-given wisdom, he had stored up plentiful supplies of life-saving grain.

The book of Genesis ends after Joseph had graciously expressed forgiveness towards his brothers, themselves now very sorry for their part in his sufferings. God had overruled and in the plenty of Egypt had saved them all. Yet the old promise to their forefathers that God would establish his chosen people in the land of Canaan was now on indefinite hold.

Like Joseph, a Christian known to me is enduring a long sentence in a foreign prison. He, too, was declared guilty of crimes he had not done. Joseph's story can be an encouragement to him and others whose faith is tried by different kinds of long and painful constraint.

Many people in training have had their career prospects cut short or permanently cut off, perhaps by political interference, false rumours, personal illness or family responsibilities. Sometimes they have simply failed to be appointed to a much-desired job and felt badly let down. For any of us, a big disappointment can fill our minds with gloom. But God is often painting a much brighter picture that may later be made clear. Our part is to make up our minds to trust to his timing. Perhaps, like Joseph, this confusing experience will help us to develop more patience and humility.

Disappointment can lead to God's appointment

When our lives seem to be going out of control, perhaps through no fault of our own, they are never out of God's control. As with Joseph, a good end can in time follow a bad beginning. Later, as we look back on an unhappy experience, we may realise that the time of waiting on God was part of our training, possibly to prepare us for greater responsibilities ahead, but certainly to encourage our spiritual growth. We will then be able to say with Joseph, 'God intended it for good'. [5] To have learned that means that the time of waiting was not time wasted.

A Christian doctor I knew spent years only one step away from a senior post yet application after application for a consultant post failed. He did not complain or give up, but spent the waiting time getting more experience and sharing his wisdom both with junior doctors and young people in his local church. In due course he was appointed to what became a chair in a university city. He had the honour of becoming physician to royalty when the reigning monarch visited his adopted country. In the years that he had waited faithfully on God, this position was being prepared for him and he learned the truth of the old statement, 'God was thinking yesterday of your tomorrow.' Many others, from Old Testament days onwards, have looked back and seen how true this is and that God honours our faithful trust.

For further thought

- It has been said that the answer to 'Why?' is 'Wait'.
- Good things can follow even after a long time of unwanted waiting.
- Have you had any personal experience of this, or seen it happen to others?

Further resources

- Sacks J. *The great partnership*. London: Hodder and Stoughton, 1991
- Kendall RT. *God meant it for good*. Fort Mill: Morning Star Publishers, 2001

References

1. Genesis 12:1-3
2. Genesis 15:3-6
3. Galatians 3:6-9
4. Luke 3:21-23, 33
5. Genesis 50:20

Chapter 5
Tests of faith

Perhaps many of us have had times when we privately thought that if God is there and cares about us at all, he had got it wrong. His promises seem to have been put on hold for so long that we begin to think that our hopes were based on no more than a vivid imagination.

Jacob's descendants felt like that. They had moved to Egypt from Canaan, the land God had promised to give their forefathers, at a time when to stay there might have meant death by starvation. Joseph's important position and his coming to their rescue had seemed miraculous, but now many years had passed, Joseph had died and his influence had died with him. They were still in Egypt and even worse, they were being abused as slaves instead of being free to go back to their original homeland. It is not surprising that they grumbled, but what about God's repeated promises to make of them a great and blessed nation, based on far away Canaan? Again they had to learn to wait for God's perfect timing, as all of us need to do.

Waiting for God's good time

Today, displaced or trafficked people in different parts of the world share the same kind of misery as that of the captive Hebrew slaves. The story of their eventual liberation may inspire hope for other sufferers. The second book in the Bible is named Exodus because it tells the story of Israel's final departure, or exodus, from Egypt. After all, God had not forgotten his promises to bless them. Their miraculous story must encourage other downtrodden people not to lose faith in him, even when greatly tempted to do so.

We have already seen in Abraham's life story the difficulties that followed when he stopped trusting God's promises and tried to hurry things along by himself. The whole nation of Israel was about to learn Abraham's lesson, for learning to wait on God is the recurrent experience of all who continue to believe in his care.

Release from slavery

In the end, the desperate prayers of the Hebrew slaves were heard above their persistent grumbling and God answered by sending them a man named Moses. He would become a great leader, but is introduced to us as a child at risk of being murdered. He was the baby of a Hebrew woman and cleverly hidden away from a cruel despot only to be discovered and brought up by that despot's daughter. To outward appearances he became an Egyptian of the royal household, but grew up holding to his ethnic origins, going so far as to kill an Egyptian who was beating up a Hebrew slave. To escape further trouble he fled the country. He was in exile for 40 years before God spoke clearly to him – another lesson in patience – and what he heard came as a huge surprise.

Moses and his brother Aaron were told to go together and ask Pharaoh, ruler of Egypt, to release all the Hebrew slaves. What a job description! Understandably, Pharaoh immediately refused to send off his whole workforce. Instead he made the slaves work even harder, so adding to their misery. Yet all of them reckoned without the love and power of God to free his people. Nine plagues troubled the Egyptians but spared the Hebrews. Although each followed naturally on the others, their timing and increasing impact were miraculously under God's control. Professor Sir Colin Humphreys, a distinguished scientist, explains the natural sequence of the ten plagues without any doubt about God's orchestration of them on behalf of his people. [1]

The ten plagues

In obedience to God's instruction, the first plague came when Aaron's staff was raised over the River Nile. The water instantly became polluted with either a surge of blood-red earth or a scum of red algae, killing the fish and causing hundreds of frogs to escape to land. They even invaded Egyptian bedrooms and beds before they died, when heaps of their decaying bodies attracted plagues of gnats and flies. They were likely to carry infections that next affected animals and humans in turn. After those five plagues came three more: a violent hailstorm, a huge swarm of locusts and possibly a severe dust storm producing thick darkness. All these nine plagues affected the Egyptians but spared God's people. Although Pharaoh almost gave in several times, he hardened his heart again between plagues, firmly refusing to let the Israelites go until hit by the last and worst plague of all.

Before sending this tenth affliction, the Lord had directed all Hebrew families to sacrifice a spotless lamb and paint some of its blood on their doorposts. Then, safely indoors, they were to eat a hot meal of roast lamb while dressed for travel. That night the Lord would see the bloodstains and pass over their homes, but the eldest sons of Egyptian families would all die in their unmarked houses. The name 'Passover' is still used by Jews for the annual remembrance of that extraordinary night and the exodus that followed. Pharaoh sent for Moses and Aaron in the night, and ordered them to take the whole company of Hebrews out of Egypt.

The events of the Passover are a picture of Christ's sacrificial death to bring about our salvation. [2, 3] More on that later, but for now it is worth reading in the first chapters of Exodus the whole drama of the release of the Hebrew slaves, led by Moses and Aaron. Parts of the story are upsetting because it is hard for us to think of so much suffering, until we see that it tells how God is able to release his people from enslavement and deal with cruel and godless oppressors. He will not tolerate evil forever. Even as the slaves were escaping, Pharaoh's army went after them as far as the Red Sea, intending to bring them back to Egypt. Instead, the waters withdrew (as they do before a tsunami) allowing the Hebrews to cross on relatively dry land before the returning wave drowned all the pursuing Egyptians.

From gratitude to grumbling

The excited slaves went on their way, led by Moses and Aaron. Moses had lived in the desert but relied on God to direct the way they were to go. He did this by providing a cloud that moved before them by day and a column of fire by night. They moved on as the cloud and fire moved and stopped when they stood still. Stage by slow stage they went on through the wilderness. Their supplies ran out but God delivered daily a fresh but very basic supply of strange sweet food called manna and he led them to sources of water.

Yet only a few weeks after leaving Egypt, the people started to grumble. The discontent was directed at Moses but was really rebellion against God. They forgot about the slave labour, the cruelty, the miracles of timing that had led to their escape and the way that God was still guiding and providing. They spoke of longing to be back in Egypt to have a better diet. They even missed their garlic! [4]

Grumbling can be infectious and it spread throughout the community. Their endless ingratitude must have hurt Moses, who was doing his best to obey God and lead them on a journey that was very hard for him, too. The people's discontent finally boiled over into threats to kill him, all his patient care ignored.

Questioning God's care

The excitement of the exodus was over and life no longer had an ordered pattern, however harsh it had been before. In our own lives, things can sometimes change overnight and the way ahead is no longer as clear as it was. Even after knowing a good life we, too, can undergo a wilderness experience of discomfort, doubt and dryness. Psalm 23 reminds us that after enjoying green pastures we may arrive in dark valleys. But the Psalmist assures us that we are never alone, for God's presence and comfort will help us to come through. We are not left in the dark forever if our trust is in him. It is all too easy to grumble when the way is hard, forgetting that earlier good times were not ours by right, but God's gift.

The fact of human suffering prompts many people today to doubt that God cares – or that he exists at all. There is no easy answer to the cry, 'Why, if there is an almighty God, does he allow so much pain?' The question sometimes opens up a search for God, while those who know him gradually learn to hold on to him in trust in spite of natural distress, later to find that he had supported them throughout.

Blaming God for human suffering

Most people in the developed world never experience the serious suffering that is often an everyday part of life for so many elsewhere.

Those better off may never stop to think or to thank. When trouble comes they too readily blame someone else, from the doctor who missed a diagnosis, to the God who could have arranged things better.

It has to be admitted that on a world scale, much suffering still follows the neglect by a few of the needs of the many. We could cite the armed conflicts that kill or injure civilians as often as those on the front line of battle. The widespread destruction of rainforests may create wealth for some, but drought, desert and even death for others. Much domestic, national and even international grief is man-made. Closer to home, we can hurt ourselves and depress others by constantly grumbling over smaller issues.

Failure to link cause and effect

It is known to the medical world that some serious disorders of health are likely to be self-induced, often (but not always) following an unhealthy lifestyle. I recall an autopsy demonstration in Uganda when the extensive cholesterol plaques in the large arteries of an American tourist were in striking contrast to the smooth aortic lining of a Ugandan of similar age. Their past diet and levels of stressful activity had been very different and probably their blood pressure levels, too. One had died on safari of a heart attack and the other of the blood disorder, sickle cell disease.

In extreme cases, obese or chesty people have been refused surgery until they lost weight or stopped smoking. We should not blame God when we have ourselves to blame. Yet behind the compulsive eating or smoking can be the deeper problem of an unhappy life.

Of course, painful questions remain. Why should a beloved young child be killed in a road accident, or why should the mother of a large family develop a neurological disease that stops her being able to care for them all? There are no easy answers, but we can be sure that God's love is still there to give relief and strength to those who turn to him. [5] We can never say that does not care when we recall that by his death his Son took upon himself the burden of our sicknesses and sorrows as well as our sins. [6]

Unrecognised spiritual illness

Not frequently diagnosed, though equally widespread, is the spiritual malaise experienced in modern as well as ancient societies. This was at the root of the Hebrews' problem – they were not living according to the Maker's instructions in the trustful and loving relationship with him for which he had made them. Today, as then, this sickness of the soul can present with emotional or physical symptoms. Someone with deep understanding may be able to identify the basic problem and point the way to forgiveness and health.

A junior doctor with this gift of insight was able to help two of his women patients by taking a detailed history. He then noted the coincidence for each of them that the onset of symptoms coincided with the date of a previous abortion. One had suffered years of depression before attempting suicide and the other suffered from chronic joint pain but, in answer to a sensitive question, each believed that the abortion had been the start of her troubles. Each woman needed to know release from her burden of guilt. Sadly, the hospital's fast turnover meant that they were lost to follow up by that very busy doctor. Perhaps experiencing his understanding had helped them to recognise and voice the connection and so been therapeutic. In addition, though, they needed to know forgiveness and complete healing of their inner wounds.

Just as putting a sticky plaster over a deep cut is likely to hide but not heal it, so to try and control symptoms by repeated prescriptions can cover up the deeper nature of a problem. Someone I know took his mother to see a specialist about a new onset of back pain. As well as examining her for other causes, the wise doctor asked if she had recently had any personal trouble. In fact she had lost her husband only a few weeks before and was carrying new burdens. Body, mind and spirit are so inter-related that when one suffers, all suffer. It is good when doctors are able to recognise this and practise what has been called 'medicine of the whole person'.

Finding strength to go on

Later on in their journey, the Hebrews would repent and turn back to

God, even if they still tended to return to their own wilful ways again and again when things got difficult. Without neglecting the root cause of a problem, we are also invited to keep trusting the pain of it to God. It may not go away, but he will help us to bear it.

The husband of a woman known to me has a degenerative neurological disease and is slowly deteriorating mentally. He is unable to do much for himself and no longer able to speak, though not evidently unhappy. His wife told me how sometimes she sits and weeps but added, 'Underneath it all I can feel the love of God closer than ever before'. She often finds this love channelled through the kindness of others who help to support them in the suffering.

The Hebrew wanderers would have found less to worry them if they had only resolved to keep on trusting the God who had freed them from slavery. In Exodus 19 and Deuteronomy 5, the record tells how through Moses, the Lord called the whole company to a solemn public meeting at the foot of Mount Sinai. They obeyed, but were scared by the smoke, fire and trumpet blast, which God used to signify his presence. They did not see God but heard his voice announcing his first Ten Commandments. By this time they were so frightened, that although God had more to say he sent them back to their tents. Only Moses would hear the rest.

Instead of remembering that Moses' leadership depended on God's leading him, the people lost heart when he was called to climb further up Mount Sinai. They had no idea when, if ever, he would return. Unknown to them Moses had gone to meet God and hear more of his rules for life. Because they had not yet learned patience, they decided to look for a different leader. Big trouble would follow that decision.

For further thought

- Are you learning to think that illness may have other causes than are obvious?
- Is it easier to complain than to remember good things and be thankful for them?
- What lessons can we learn from the Old Testament stories we have thought about?

Further resources

- Tournier P. *Guilt and Grace*. Crowborough: Highland Books, 1986.

References

1. Humphreys CJ. *The miracles of Exodus*. London: Harper Collins UK, 1974
2. 1 Peter 1:18-19
3. 1 Corinthians 5:7b
4. Numbers 11:4-6
5. 2 Corinthians 12:7-10
6. Isaiah 53:4-5

Chapter 6
Going for gold or contented with glitter?

A friend of mine worked as receptionist for a group of doctors. She told me how worried she was that they were becoming less concerned about spending time with their patients than about running a successful business. It turned into such an unhappy practice that after doing her best, she finally expressed her concern and left. Cost cutting had destroyed the unseen asset of goodwill. As an author of ancient times put it, there is nothing new under the sun. [1] In contrast, she also told me how one of the richest men in Britain took time to visit a new widow, threatened with loss of the farm on his estate that was tied to her husband's job. Out of a kind and generous heart he offered to help her find a new home, allowing her to stay put until it was ready.

Going for gold instead of waiting on God

At the end of the last chapter, we left the people of Israel running out of patience because Moses had disappeared and was completely out of touch for nearly six weeks. God had called Moses to give him two large pieces of stone on which he had written out the ten instructions he had spoken to the assembled company and to tell him more about his rules for their lives. When Moses finally returned to the Hebrew camp, he found to his dismay that the people and even his brother Aaron, his deputy, had given up waiting for him. Worse still, they had turned from worshipping the true (though invisible) God and made themselves a false god, made out of their own glittering gold. It was cast in the form of a calf, perhaps like some of the nature gods they had known in Egypt.

In his shocked anger, Moses threw down the two stones inscribed with God's commands, smashing them. Their leader's reappearance and his reaction produced guilty embarrassment among the people who gave poor excuses for their behaviour. The truth was that by giving up hope of Moses' return, they were mistrusting and rejecting the love of God whose guidance, through him, had brought them safely so far. By going their own way, they headed straight for an experience of severe discipline. The calf was destroyed and many of them lost their lives as well. [2]

How true to modern experience is this episode. Unwilling to either want or wait for a message from God, humanity still turns to the worship of gold in all its forms. In some cultures, including those who think themselves superior, offerings are still made to some kind of nature-god. Some hold particular animals sacred, while some worship 'the Earth Mother'. Any form of idolatry goes against God's wise instruction and risks spiritual death. For many, the greatest idol of all is the pursuit of gold itself. Centuries later, greed is on a list of idols possibly being worshipped then, as it can be now. [3] Jesus once said 'Where your treasure is, there will your heart be also...You cannot serve both God and Money'. [4] If the heart's desire is for material treasure only, that will not last. If instead our hope is in God he richly provides everything we need for our enjoyment, including enough to share with others as well. [5, 6]

Money-making, money-spending

As with the worship of the golden calf long ago, many people today have moneymaking as their priority in life, even if it means acting dishonestly. Gradually they learn to silence their inner God-given conscience. Money is, of course, necessary but it should be a servant, not a master. That place rightly belongs to the God who made us. In societies obsessed with the ups and downs of the money market, and dedicated either to collecting wealth or struggling to make ends meet, it is not surprising that thoughts of the true God may never enter the mind. As a friend sometimes says, 'No sooner do we make ends meet than somebody moves the ends!' Yet Jesus taught that by putting God first and trusting him, we will be able to put aside our worries for he knows exactly what we need. [7] He can provide enough for us to share cheerfully (not grudgingly) with others whose needs are greater. [8]

The early days of most periods of training concentrate on getting through the workload and learning on the job. Later, many workers, such as doctors, are driven to spend more time earning extra money, for example in private practice. In many cases, this is said to be for the survival or education of the family. For others it produces more wealth than is really needed. The goal can be to buy yet another status symbol such as a bigger house, a faster car or even the latest piece of equipment for personal or professional use. It is easy to fall into the trap of thinking, 'Everybody who is somebody has one of these', when in reality *wants* are overriding *needs*.

In a recent broadcast, someone who had pioneered the introduction of communication technology now faced the fact that it had gone far beyond his intentions. He realised that what had started off as helpful tools now risk getting in the way of face to face communication. Concert goers are usually reminded to switch off their mobile phones before the performance but other gatherings can be disrupted by someone's repeated texting or phoning, regardless of company. Unless on call, or genuinely needing to exchange important news, could this say something about a change of priorities? The supposedly urgent can squeeze out the important. Some sensible families ban computers from the shared living space. This proves particularly important when parents and young people need an undistracted opportunity to listen to each other.

Members of staff in intensive care units have had to learn to respect relationships as well as the monitors. Intricate pieces of machinery threaten to separate patients from the voices or touch of their dear ones. Yet we now know that part of good 'intensive' care is to allow patients (and relatives) much closer contact. For anyone unconscious, hearing is the last sense to switch off, so familiar voices may still be comforting.

Making wise use of money

Those who live in a 'spend, spend, spend' culture often find themselves in debt. Shopaholics perhaps need as much help as alcoholics. Trained counsellors, or wise grandparents, may be ready to advise young people how to manage a limited income if they are willing to listen. After such advice one young couple reported happily, 'We've learned that we don't have to buy everything we like the look of'. Perhaps we all need to stay alert to the difference between need and greed.

In contrast, many do give sacrificially. In the nineteenth century, a certain Dr Thomas Barnado gave up his intended medical career to found his famous children's homes. In our own times, doctors and others have dedicated much of their time, talents and bank balances to help those too poor or sick to help themselves. To be able to give more will mean taking an honest look at our personal expense accounts and spending less on ourselves. It is embarrassing that it is often poorer people who act with remarkable generosity.

Self-promotion or self-giving?

I recently read the confession of a hard working Christian doctor who had applied for a new and wonderful position with a salary to dream of. The interview had gone well and he was offered the job. The post would give him a more comfortable life as well as providing more wealth to share with the needy. Surely, this must be a good thing – and for some it might have been so. Each has to decide personally about such offers. Yet as this particular man was about to sign the agreement he developed a most uncomfortable feeling and prayerfully searched his heart. Was he simply chasing money? Would he still find time or inclination to keep a close relationship with God and to help others to know him? Was this a post that would satisfy his professional ambition but could damage his spiritual life? At the last minute he sent a different message to those waiting for his answer. He was withdrawing his application. He realised that he had been setting his heart on the wrong kind of wealth. Only by trusting and obeying God would he find lasting spiritual riches, much more precious than anything else. To share that with others would be to multiply, not reduce it. This whole episode had helped him to sort out his priorities though, of course, many others might have thought that he was a fool to turn down such an opportunity.

Despite the great benefits to be found in walking God's way, there is a possible cost to be counted. As with many other projects we may plan for, it is wise to take time to consider costs-versus-benefits before making a clear commitment to following his ways. [9] If riches increase, we are not to set our hearts on them. If instead poverty threatens, God is a loving heavenly Father who knows all about it and has promised to supply everything we need. Yet to do so he may rely on those who have more than they need to come to the aid of those with much less. [10]

Costly distractions

When Moses came down from the mountain he found not only idolatry. The people were eating and drinking before getting up 'to indulge in revelry' and have one big party. In the western world today, where obesity is already a big risk to health even among children, we are offered a stream of television programmes dealing with the variety, preparation and enjoyment of food. For entertainment many young (and older) people drink more alcohol than is wise, or go too far in other ways when enjoying themselves. To such distractions the prophet Amos added the early equivalent of a pop concert! [11] We are likely to recognise in our own lives what diverts attention from feeding our souls. It may be overdoing such good activities as studying or working hard, as well as others less worthy. Yet studies, work or serious sport will be more fruitful and fulfilling when we seek God's help in planning the use of our time.

Because of so many possible time-consuming activities, including the more serious ones, there is a risk of deeper thought becoming increasingly rare. Just as paying attention to committed personal relationships can be sadly neglected, so any idea of looking for a relationship with God can be pushed out altogether. Richer nations are not the only ones to be caught up in chasing wealth or entertainment and before spiritual appetite is quite lost we all need to take time out for some quiet thought about our priorities.

Wisdom needed

Among all the possibilities we have been thinking about, we need to remember that we are not intended to go around with long faces or become known as killjoys. For our enjoyment, God gives us what we need (not necessarily all that we would like). It is love of money, not money itself, that lies at the root of so many of the world's evils and it is a matter for each of us to decide whether we are going for lasting gold or have a secret preference for short term glitter. God's gold really shines and sparkles, and so do those who treasure it.

This was the reputation of a man named Eric Liddell, a competitor in the Olympic Games of 1924, held in Paris. He is the hero of the film *Chariots of Fire* and was an unusual and humble athlete as he believed that running well was God's gift to him. He was given a gold medal for his world record in the 400-metre race and commented, 'When I run, I feel God's pleasure'. He rarely spoke of being a gold medallist but instead spent his life running a different kind of race as a missionary in China, his eyes fixed on Jesus. [12] He died in a concentration camp, known there as someone who was ever ready to help others in the dreadful conditions they experienced. His priority was to provide as much physical and spiritual support as he could to others and so became worth his weight in gold. Some of this century's athletes also praise God for his gifts to them, as do many other people who find strength in the joy of the Lord. [13]

Little did Moses think as he descended the mountain into the middle of all that unfaithfulness that just the same errors would cause trouble for centuries still to come, and would call for the same solution. He knew that the wrongdoing had to be recognised, repented of and dealt with. He also asked God to teach him more about his ways – a good prayer for each of us to echo. [14]

For further thought

- It is tempting to idolise money. If you had more how would you use it?
- When you give to a good cause is it gladly or reluctantly?
- What distractions interfere with your search for God?

Further resources

- Wilson J. *Complete surrender: A biography of Eric Liddell.* Milton Keynes: Authentic Media, 2012

References

1. Ecclesiastes 1:9
2. Exodus 32:1-35
3. Ephesians 5:3
4. Matthew 6:19- 21, 24
5. 1 Timothy 6:7-10
6. Philippians 4:15-19
7. Matthew 6:31-34
8. 2 Corinthians 9:7-11
9. Luke 14:27-33
10. 1 Timothy 6:17-18
11. Amos 6:3-6
12. Hebrews 12:1-2
13. Nehemiah 8:10
14. Exodus 33:13

Chapter 7
Pointing forward to a new way

Our daily news bulletins tell of more and more acts of lawlessness at home and abroad. There must be good things happening in the world, but the headlines always seem to focus on some individual, business or nation found to have broken the accepted rules of behaviour. Where have these rules and expectations come from?

Rules for the good life

We have seen how when Moses disappeared up the mountain he had been called by God to receive his commandments for living the best kind of life. It seems that over 600 were given verbally, some of them similar to edicts going back as far as the days of Abraham. The important stone tablets that Moses brought back were inscribed with the list of Ten Commandments, often called the 'ten words'. As God troubled to produce a second edition when the first set was ruined, we need to think more about them, for God said that they formed the basis of how the Israelites were to live as his people. [1]

The first four of the Ten Commandments name the one God as their giver and describe the humble and reverent attitude his people should have towards him. They must worship him only, never misuse his name and keep one day in the week set apart for him. The next six commands spell out the expected behaviour towards other people in general, in particular giving honour to parents and respecting neighbours without coveting their wives or belongings. [2] Today we may find all ten words written as two lists at the front of some churches. For centuries they formed the basis of British (and some other) legal systems but our lawmakers no longer make all of them legally binding. This is not to say that they no longer matter. Love and obedience towards God will always affect our treatment of others.

Besides these ten, Moses was given hundreds more edicts and laws, recorded at intervals from the second half of Exodus through to

Deuteronomy. Broadly speaking, some were *public health laws* to be applied to a vast company of desert wanderers, living with limited water and poor sanitation. Long before bacteria or antibiotics were discovered, rules were given about the isolation of postpartum mothers, quarantine for specific infections, or exclusion of potential contaminants from the diet, for example in pork or shellfish. Many of these were forerunners of today's guidelines in preventive medicine.

Others were *social rules* to help people in such a large travelling community to care for each other by not putting their own interests first. Many of these rules stressed justice and the need for fair play between haves and have-nots. When harvesting, workers should leave grain at the edges of the fields and not strip off every grape from the vines so that the needy could have a share, an attitude still very relevant in our own times. There was some overlap between God's social and his *moral rules*. His standards were so very different from the immoral behaviour his people would eventually find among the conquered Canaanites. Already weak-willed, they were warned in advance against letting themselves be influenced by the idolatry and widespread corruption they would find, including fraudulent business deals, child abuse, rape, human sacrifice and trafficking, and more. Mention is made of these and many other evils that still go on across the world, although God's word warns so sternly against them.

The various *religious and ceremonial laws* given to Moses further specified ways for his people to honour and worship their holy God. A variety of ceremonies and sacrifices are outlined in *Leviticus*, blood sacrifices being essential for the forgiveness of sins.

The basis of the old agreement

Out of all the edicts brought back by Moses, God made the Ten Commandments the basis of his renewed agreement, or covenant, with Israel. If they put love of God first, they should then remember to keep the other rules as an expression of their love for him and for others. His covenant with them was that if they obeyed him, their lives would be satisfied and blessed but if they disobeyed, death and disaster would follow. The choice was theirs. 'Choose life', urged Moses. [3]

God's longing was for his people to be blessed, not cursed. As he set out these two alternatives, the Lord said that he had not loved and chosen them because they were a great people, for they were only a small people. No, he loved them because he loved them! [4] He longed for their love in return, to be shown by willing obedience to his laws. These had not been given to show them who was boss, but were entirely inspired by his love and intended only for their good. Would they be able to keep their part of the bargain? Sadly, they had made a poor start in the worship of their golden calf.

A place set apart for God

In order to focus his people's minds on the need to reverence and put him first in their lives, God gave Moses a detailed plan for a mobile Tent of Meeting, or tabernacle, to be set apart for his worship, right in the middle of each new campsite. Its construction, furnishings and intended use, including the varied sacrifices to be offered there, are fully described in the four books from Exodus to Deuteronomy. Everything about it was to be carefully and beautifully put together and everything going on there done with great care and reverence. As worshippers went in, they would proceed to one of two areas, an outer court for non-Jews and an inner court for Jews and beyond them was a third area, housing the altar and accessible only to the priests. At the far end was God's personal dwelling place, the Most Holy Place, or Holy of Holies and there only the high priest could go in. The finished tent would stand at the very centre of their lives and its splendour should speak of the glory of God and the privilege it was that he should live among them.

The Ark of the Covenant, symbol of God's presence

As a reminder of the Israelites' covenant to honour and obey God and so receive his blessings, God's presence would be especially focused above the most important item in the tent, the Ark of the Covenant, kept separate in the Most Holy Place. This was a beautifully crafted box in which would be kept a few reminders of God's past and continuing love: the two stone tablets of the law given to Moses, a jar of the manna that had saved their lives in the wilderness, and a remarkable rod, or staff, provided by Aaron. This rod had signalled the first of the ten plagues in Egypt and its miraculous budding and fruiting later stopped a rebellion, so confirming Aaron's role as priest and guardian of the care and concerns of the tabernacle. [5] Covered in pure gold the lid of the Ark incorporated two golden cherubs placed face to face, their arched wings guarding the area sometimes known as the mercy seat, God's own special place. Significantly, immediately below this, inside the Ark lay the original stone tablets inscribed with the commandments, reminding them that God's presence was linked to their keeping the covenant made between him and them, although he would show mercy to those who repented of breaking it. It was at the mercy seat that he would meet and speak with their representative. [6]

The whole Ark was so special that it was normally kept behind a curtain and only the high priest was allowed into the Most Holy Place to go near and touch it. Aaron was the first to be set apart for this role and he would go in to meet with God to worship him, learn his will for his people, and carry out annual atonement for all their sins.

The Day of Atonement

Once a year an especially solemn day was kept by all the assembled people. On it the high priest, freshly bathed and cleanly dressed, approached the holy God. He was to offer blood sacrifices, first to atone for his own and his household's sins and then for those committed by the people during the past year. It is all described in detail in Leviticus 16 and was very labour-intensive, time-consuming and, to our eyes, messy. The different areas of the tabernacle were presented back to God after being sprinkled with the blood of the sacrifices. Blood was even applied to the sacred Ark as the people waited outside the tent. The high priest acted as the go-between, mediating with God by using the sacrificial blood to make atonement ('at-one-ment' with God) for their having sinfully disregarded his covenant. They were all guilty.

On behalf of the waiting people outside, the high priest also sacrificed one of a pair of goats as an extra offering for their sins. Then, with his hands on the head of the other goat, he confessed all the wicked things the people had done that year. This 'scapegoat' was then taken into the wilderness and let loose, making doubly sure that the burden of sin was carried well away. With a final burnt offering for each family, the great day was over, and a year later the same ceremonies would have to be performed all over again.

The importance of keeping close to God

At times of crisis the Ark of the Covenant, symbol of God's presence, was ceremonially carried before the people to remind them that he was leading the way. As told in Joshua 3-8 this happened when crossing the River Jordan as they finally entered the Promised Land, and again on the march round Jericho, the first Canaanite city to fall to them. Further invasion was held up by one man's disobedience, a theft that needed to be exposed and punished. Afterwards Joshua gathered everyone together beside the Ark to renew their covenant with God at Mount Ebal and they then went on to victory. In this we, too, are reminded that when we fail to keep to God's way our spiritual progress is held up until repentance for the wrongdoing has secured his forgiveness, confirming our desire to be faithful as he is faithful. He will then strengthen us for the next challenge.

After Joshua's death and during the days of the judges the Ark was cared for by Aaron's grandson in Bethel and there the Israelites used to go to seek wisdom from God. [7] As told in 1 Samuel 3:1-7:2, the Ark was in the temple at Shiloh when the young prophet-to-be, Samuel, lay asleep there. God's voice woke him with a message warning of trouble ahead, a prophecy fulfilled when the Israelites too casually took the sacred Ark into battle, almost treating it as an insurance policy. It was captured by the Philistines who in turn suffered badly for treating it disrespectfully so, frightened by God's response to their offence, they put inside it a rather odd guilt offering and sent it back to the Israelites. Curiosity got the better of some of them and, breaking the 'no touch' rule, they lifted the lid, with lethal results.

Much sobered, the Israelites hurried the Ark away to a respectful, quiet home at Kiriath Jearim where it blessed that family for decades until King David decided that it was now safe to take it to Jerusalem.

With due ceremony and celebration, the historic token of God's presence entered the holy city and later came to rest once again in the Most Holy Place, by then in the glorious temple built by King Solomon. Three centuries later, after enemy vandals had damaged the temple, young King Josiah began to repair it, revived the worship and returned the Ark to its proper place. Sadly, only a few years later he was killed and in the last chapter of 2 Chronicles we read how the temple was destroyed and its valuables stolen by Babylonian invaders. From then on, the Old Testament makes no more mention of the Ark of the Covenant. It had been symbolic of the presence of God and although its loss did not mean that he was lost with it, such disrespectful handling came on the heels of the detestable things done by Josiah's successor. Not only was the Ark lost but the covenant was broken. Seventy years of desolation followed.

Essential difference between the old and new covenants

The Old Testament tells us how the old agreement between God and man was made, broken and only temporarily restored by keeping various ceremonial laws involving daily and annual sacrifices. A holy God must not be treated casually or carelessly, or his authority disregarded by those still claiming to be his people.

So what has all this to do with us today? The New Testament tells of the contrast that came with God's new covenant, when the crucified Jesus gave himself as the only atoning sacrifice never again to be needed. At his death, the curtain that had separated off the most holy part of the Jerusalem temple was ripped apart from top to bottom, allowing free access to God's holy presence. From then on, sin could be confessed and forgiven at any time, not in a special place, by a special person on a special day, once in the year. Jesus rose from his grave to return to his Father and now lives again, the highest of high priests, to be our everlasting mediator with God once and for all.

The book of Hebrews makes clear the great difference between the burdensome nature of sacrifices in the Old Testament and the freedom of spirit known to those who rely on that final offering made by Jesus. [8] We shall think more about this later, but parts of the New Testament will be better understood when we have read the Old Testament and grasped the significance of some of the ways it points to the Lord Jesus Christ, our sacrifice and mediator combined. God gave his people plenty of opportunities to live in harmony with him but they kept choosing to go their own way. Many still do.

Displeasing God by self-rule

In Moses' lifetime the people continued their ups and downs. Joshua, his godly successor, struggled to call the people to obedience when they reached the Promised Land. Most of the judges who followed him had even less success. The gradual occupation of Canaan was an outward victory but a spiritual defeat as, regardless of many warnings, God's people began to make forbidden marriages with the immoral people they had conquered, some taking on foreign gods with the foreign wives. Such disobedience limited God's blessing and the book of Judges ends on a dark note, for 'everyone did as he saw fit'.

After the judges came a series of prophets to remind God's people of their broken covenant with him. Prophets are not to be confused with fortune-tellers. True prophets have heard God's voice and announce his warnings about personal and national disobedience, along with the good news that the way to restored blessing is repentance and renewed obedience. Many godly prophets were killed by those who objected to their warnings. Some, like Samuel, had years of influential leadership.

Samuel's life story is told in the two Old Testament books that bear his name. After learning to respond to God's voice as a child, he urged the people to do so, too. Instead, they rebelliously asked Samuel to find them a king, wanting to be like the ungodly nations around them. The old prophet anointed the first two kings but foretold trouble ahead as a result. After disobedient King Saul, God-fearing King David and his wise son, King Solomon, the next generation tore the nation into two parts, Israel and Judah, each with a separate king. Eventually each kingdom broke faith by turning to idol worship, lost God's help and suffered enemy occupation or transportation to foreign lands. Samuel's prophecies came true.

Some of these stories not only preserve history but should also make us think seriously about the reasons for national success or failure and ask whether these could still apply today. For example, we read how 'Hezekiah...held fast to the Lord and did not cease to follow him... And the Lord was with him; he was successful in whatever he undertook.' [9] Quite the opposite had been Ahab, 'who sold himself to do evil in the eyes of the Lord, urged on by Jezebel his wife. He behaved in the vilest manner by going after idols...' [10] He had chosen to be advised by false instead of true prophets who told him what he wanted to hear, thereby sending him straight to his death in battle. The whole unhappy story makes its own point.

Idolatry

We are left with a warning and a sad comment on the price of disobedience. Many kings of Israel and Judah in those distant times were at best half-hearted about keeping God's standards. Time and again the major barrier to their obedience was idolatry, putting something else ahead of faithfulness to God. If kings, supposedly in top jobs, needed to keep God's instructions in order to stay on their thrones, how much more do the rest of us with poorer resources need his wisdom to guide us through life. Today the worship of other gods is often expressed by putting first a love of power, money, fame or other forms of self-interest. Such idolatry steers lives away from dedication to the one who created us to be in his image, trying instead to fit in with the image of the surrounding culture. [11] However wealthy or poor a nation, this is a constant risk.

In that earlier era the intended harmony between God and mankind was not fully regained as his people became increasingly self-satisfied. Some still practised a few religious ceremonies from habit, but their hearts were disobedient and they set up lesser gods, forgetting God's anger over that first golden calf. Prophets repeatedly warned that such unfaithfulness would only end in trouble, but few people listened. God's standards had been given to them for their benefit, not his, because he loved them and wanted to guide them to have good and healthful lives, but he was regularly ignored. Their disobedience was punished by being taken into exile. As then, so now, it is dangerous to ignore or neglect God's commandments.

Up-to-date warnings

We can learn lessons from men and women of old but similar stories continue today. The neglect of spiritual education, including Bible knowledge, has produced a generation without clear moral standards. In August 2011, a series of riots took place across England. Violent crowds roamed round some towns and cities, bringing destruction wherever they went. Some simply joined in with the crowd, but all damaged other people's property and businesses, breaking the law and spoiling relationships within their communities. It only takes attention to daily news bulletins, or even a visit to a general practitioner's surgery, to see the impact of damaged relationships within families, communities and between nations.

Broken relationships

The book of Malachi comes right at the end of the Old Testament. His name means 'my messenger' and his last message from God was that someone would eventually come who would aim to restore broken families but if he failed to get a response, said the Lord Almighty, 'I will come and strike the land with a curse'. Under his loving rule God has evidently planned for united families to be the strength of a nation.

The truth of Malachi's warning is borne out in today's headlines. The media love to make a public show of reputations damaged and families divided by inappropriate sexual desire or excessive hunger for money and possessions. For others, the lowering of standards can be less dramatic but is often based on a rising desire to seek personal satisfaction above all else, including honour or wealth. Instead hope should be fixed on God. [12, 13] People who had once stood tall can slowly crumble and fall, their past good standing lost.

In 2009, the British nation was shocked to learn of some surprising expenses claimed by certain Members of Parliament, not all arising from their parliamentary duties. Personal reputations were damaged, but so was the trust that many had placed in Parliament as a whole. Since then, crooked dealings have been exposed in other prominent individuals and national institutions both in Britain and further afield. Like the effect of one bad apple in a bagful, corruption spreads once it starts and betrays trustful relationships. There is serious neglect of the moral biblical teaching that once was the norm in British schools.

There is an old popular song that refers to the 'white cliffs of Dover', the chalk walls so clearly visible to ships approaching the south coast of England. However, chalk does not wear well in wind and waves, and lumps of it suddenly break off without warning. People tempted to build a house on the cliff top by the lovely view, have had to move inland when, either suddenly or slowly, the once clearly marked cliff edge has fallen into the sea. Without urgent action, such owners will lose everything.

Like slow erosion by the waves of the sea, personal standards can be worn away, swiftly or slowly, by an incoming tide of popular opinion or winds of change that promote biased views opposed to God's standards. We need to keep refreshing our memories about the true standards, being warned about how easily we could let them slip.

For further thought

- Are you conscious that wanting your own way often upsets other people?
- Do you make an idol of whatever, or whoever, comes first in your life?
- Are you tempted to ask advice from those who will say what you want them to say?

References

1. Deuteronomy 4:13-14
2. Exodus 20:1-17
3. Deuteronomy 30:15-20
4. Deuteronomy 7:7-8
5. Numbers 17:1-18:5
6. Exodus 25:22
7. Judges 20:27-28
8. Hebrews 9:15, 24-26
9. 2 Kings 18:5-7
10. 1 Kings 21:25-26
11. 1 John 2:15-17
12. Jeremiah 45:5
13. Romans 15:13

Chapter 8
Hope on the horizon

T hose who try to heal the fractured societies spoken of in the last verse of the Old Testament do so at a cost, but it is more costly to resist change. [1] A curse does fall when personal preferences ignore those of others, damaging or breaking up healthy relationships. Yet at source, there can be a hunger for love.

A report on the radio reported how shocked a mother was to find that her son had joined a local gang that threatened violence and robbery. Because she loved him, she asked him to bring all the gang members home, cooked for them and showed them motherly care. As a result, the group broke up and a past member said, 'She gave us what we had been wanting but had never had before.' He was not just talking about the hot dinners, but of the selfless love with which she had served them despite all the risks she had taken in the process. What had evidently been her costly Christian love had worked the miracle.

Are rebellion and breakup inevitable in our societies? Or may someone like that mother come to the rescue, caring enough to bring healing to damaged communities and peace of mind and heart to those who had none? Here and there, the Old Testament prophets gave a few glimpses of such hope.

Hints of relief ahead

Many of us will have heard or perhaps sung in Handel's famous oratorio *Messiah* and been stirred both by its music and the quotations from Isaiah's prophecy, looking ahead to the birth of a special child. The choir sings with obvious joy, 'The government shall be upon his shoulder' and proclaims how the child would be known as 'Wonderful Counsellor, Mighty God, Everlasting Father, Prince of Peace'. [2] Little wonder that many Jews interpreted this passage to mean that the future Messiah would come as a mighty freedom fighter to restore peace and power to the kingdom of Israel. Yet Isaiah also described one who would come as a man of sorrows, to be 'led like a lamb to the slaughter', bearing 'the sin of many.' [3] We are reminded of the sacrificial lambs of the Old Testament and it later became clear that Isaiah's description found perfect fulfilment in the person of Jesus. He came to earth as that long- promised child but was also the long-awaited Messiah, the anointed one, also known as the Christ. [4] Later to be called the Lord Jesus Christ, his arrival came centuries after it was foretold in those ancient prophecies.

So what about the promises God had made to bless all nations, for example through Abraham? [5] Abraham, Isaac, Jacob and then Moses had made covenants with God by which their trust and obedience would find his blessing in return. This choice was then offered to the whole nation, with the unhappy consequences we have seen as they repeatedly failed to keep their part of the agreement. Failure to love God and neighbour has always spoiled the intended harmony between God and humankind.

The old covenant had not been a hopeless error of judgment on God's part, but it became a lost opportunity for the nation to flourish under his loving rule. It also gives us a prolonged demonstration that none of us will ever be able to keep God's laws in our own strength. Yet looking at the hints in Isaiah, there is a glimmer of hope that help was on the way. It took a long time for that light to get stronger, but once more we find that times of waiting are times for God's purposes to mature. There were good reasons for his biding his time.

Hope for a fresh start repeatedly disappointed

Acts of heroism or generosity impress us, as when soldiers under fire go into dangerous territory to rescue a wounded friend, or a relative is willing to donate a kidney for someone who would die without it. We may feel more critical if, in our judgment, those at the receiving end did not deserve such sacrifices.

Let us for a moment imagine how this could work out. Suppose that an overweight family had been prescribed a diet necessary to keep them fit and well, but time and again they gave it up. They were warned that serious heart or lung problems and even an early death could lie ahead, but they took no notice and kept on eating what they liked. Their slim and healthy dietician may give them an excellent model for aiming at a balanced diet and taking exercise, but all in vain. At this point some would give up trying to help, but not our dedicated dietician.

She knows the risks they are running and decides that the only way to keep this fat family healthy would be for her to move in with them, empty their cupboards and supply them with good food, paying for it all herself. She may also fund the entrance fee to a sports club but then would need to stay alongside to keep encouraging them to hold to her regime. What a commitment! Yet they could still give it all up and sneak off to the fish and chip shop when her back was turned. Had she lacked judgment even to try, or been moved by the best of motives? Many would think her a little mad.

This unlikely story parallels the repeated failure of God's people to keep his rules for life, despite the warning note with which the Old Testament ends. After that for hundreds of years we have no record of any more words from God. Does this silence mean that he had washed his hands of such rebellious people and left them to die in their sins? Or do the hints made by Isaiah suggest that God, like that imaginary dietician, had already considered moving in with fallen humanity to show them how to live, and to save them from spiritual death? The time was coming for him to act. [6, 7]

An amazing volunteer

Let's now go back to listen in to a theoretical consultation between God the Father and his only Son. At the start it must be stressed that this is an entirely imaginary conversation, yet no doubt something was agreed between them, for Paul tells us that the gracious divine plan to grant eternal life was made 'before the beginning of time'. [8, 9]

Suppose God had said, 'My Son, we have designed a beautiful universe and plan to create a people to live on the planet that will sustain life, on planet Earth. They will be so much like us that our image in them will be easy to see and we'll really enjoy each other's company.'

'That's a great idea,' said the Son. 'We'll put them in a garden where there will be food for their bodies and beautiful plants and animals for them to enjoy. Let's start with a man and then give him a wife, visiting them every day so that they grow wise and spiritually strong in our company. When they have children they'll be able to hand on to them what they have learned from us.'

'It will be good for the children to get to know us for themselves, too' said the Father, but added, 'There is one snag. We must design them free to choose whether this is the kind of life they'd like or instead want to go their own way. It will be up to them whether they stay close to us or fall out with us, in which case they'd wither away without our care. They must choose with open eyes so we'll need to tell them that early on.'

'Yes, we must take the risk of letting them choose', agreed the Son. 'Otherwise they'll just be robots with a built-in automated programme. As well as walking and talking with them in the garden, let's prepare a handbook that will tell them how to behave. If they no longer agree with us and have to leave the garden, the book would explain how to bring our relationship back to life again.'

'Before the whole book is ready' said the Father, 'we'll recruit and train prophets to take them the message about our love and concern but also warning them what will happen if they stay out of contact with us. We'll ask the prophets to write parts of the book.'

'Yes', replied the Son, 'But what if people don't want to listen to us, or for that matter, the prophets? Some will respond, but others may get angry about being told what to do, and anger in the heart would end with blood on their hands. In fact, for them to do anything wrong will spoil our image in them, their spirits will be damaged and die and, in time, their bodies too.' 'We don't want them to die cut off from us', sad the Father thoughtfully, 'so we must work out how to save them from that. I have had an idea...'

'...I know what we could do', the Son said quickly, 'How about if I go and live with them? Because you and I are so completely at one,

I could show them the best way to live, loving each other just like we do. Because we also love them so much, this would be a great way to show it.'

'True', replied his Father, 'but then you'd be taking another big risk. Just think what it would mean for you to leave here to live among them on our so far beautiful earth. Although still my Son, you'd need to start off as a baby in a human family but grow up thinking and behaving very differently from everyone else. If you were to go with the radiance we share now, people would be blinded and scared. You'd have to put that aside.'

'I can see all that, but if I become one of them it gives them the chance to listen better to what we want to say. To join in their life would be much better than just staying here and watching them go wrong.'

'Even so', said the Father thoughtfully, 'Because you'll still be speaking with our authority, some religious leaders among them will feel threatened, especially when people choose to listen to you more than they listen to them. They could even want to kill you when you speak of me as Father. That would be a big price for you to pay.'

'That's all the more reason to keep on loving them and give them a chance to turn back to us. In any case, you'll be with me all the time. We'd be in this together.' replied the Son.

'And suppose most of them don't listen to you and do kill you? Their attitudes and actions will already have taken them so far away from us that their spirits would die. There's only one way we could turn this around...'

'...and that would be for my death to be in their place,' said the Son, warming to his subject. 'If they realised that our love for them is truly without limits, surely some of them would see why I am willing to offer myself to clear their record and repair our broken relationship. If they accept that and ask for forgiveness they could have a fresh start. We'd share our Spirit with them to help them stay close to us again.'

The Father looked very serious for a few moments. Then he said. 'We'd certainly be in it together, but your sacrifice would have to be once and for all – our last offer.'

The Son responded, 'When they see what we mean by it, surely at least some of them will be sorry and ask to be forgiven for turning their backs on us. Then we'll be able to welcome them back and love them just as much as you and I love each other.'

'That is certainly what we would have been wanting for them from the start,' replied the Father, 'In fact, I would like them all to become just like you!'

'Then I'll go if you say so,' said his Son, 'I'll go down and show them how to live our way, whatever it costs.'

'Go then, my Son. We are agreed. I'll see you off, we'll be in constant touch, and after your work is done, we'll surprise them'.

This imaginary conversation is not without foundation for it is true that Jesus Christ, Son of God, did agree to come and live on earth as God-made-man and was killed by – and for – those who rejected his love. Having offered himself to restore the broken relationship between God and man, his Father brought him to life again – the big surprise. Before that happened, Jesus had said:

'The reason my Father loves me is that I lay down my life – only to take it up again. No one takes it from me, but I lay it down of my own accord. I have authority to lay it down and authority to take it up again. This command I received from my Father.' [10]

The inside story

When he was on earth, Jesus gave more glimpses of the inside story. He taught that his coming to earth had been the result of God's love [11] and that he and his Father were one. [12] Their union was so close that although he was free to choose, even as he faced the horror of a cruel death, he accepted that he had come to give his life in this way. [13]

Right to the end of his time on earth he deliberately lined up his will with his Father's. [14] He always chose to obey his Father. [15] Instead of those Old Testament sacrifices, he was going to pay the ransom that would free those who believed from their impending spiritual death. [16]

An early Christian hymn, quoted by Paul completes the story of how God raised Jesus from the grave and took him back to his side once more, mission accomplished. One day everyone will confess that he is Lord and glorify his Father for such a wonderful plan:

> 'Therefore God exalted him to the highest place
>   and gave him the name that is above every name,
> that at the name of Jesus every knee should bow,
>   in heaven and on earth and under the earth,
> and every tongue acknowledge that Jesus Christ is Lord,
>   to the glory of God the Father.' [17]

Jesus has promised to come back one day to take home with him those who have learned to love him. [18]

The whole story of the Bible shows how Jesus came to be the blessing to all nations that God had first promised to Abraham. The ritual sacrifices of the old covenant would never be needed again. [19] Instead, Jesus offered himself to take away the sins of the world, once and for all, and each of us is included in that offer. Before accepting such generous grace, we need to know more about the one who offers it. It is time to introduce you in more detail to the Saviour of the world, God-made-man, whose name is Jesus. In the New Testament we have first-hand evidence: those who knew him during his time on earth tell his story. We'll go on to consider this next.

For further thought

- Have you had the experience of making, then breaking, a resolution?
- Have you become concerned about the disordered state of the society you live in?
- Are you a little clearer about why God stepped in and Jesus came?

Further resources

Inter-Varsity Press (Leicester) has produced many commentaries in their *Bible Speaks Today* series:

- Old Testament commentaries: Editor, Motyer A.
- New Testament commentaries: Editor, Stott J.

References

1. Malachi 4:6
2. Isaiah 9:6
3. Isaiah 53:7-12
4. John 1:41-42
5. Genesis 12:2-3
6. Galatians 4:4
7. Ephesians 1:9-10
8. 2 Timothy 1:8-10
9. Titus 1:2
10. John 10:17-18
11. John 3:16-18
12. John 10:30
13. Mark 8:31
14. Luke 22:42
15. John 15:10
16. Matthew 20:28
17. Philippians 2:5-11
18. John 14:2-3
19. Hebrews 8:13

Chapter 9
Show me the evidence

When faced with a new idea it is right to ask about the evidence on which it is based. The prescriptions of the earliest physicians were often based on tradition, or a 'try it and see' attitude. The same can hold in some cultures still. In many places there used to be strong but misplaced faith in repeated blood-letting, and in Uganda about 40 years ago I saw a child with cerebral palsy who had multiple cigarette burns on his back. The pain had produced involuntary movements that he could not make on his own so this treatment, probably advised by a witch doctor, was thought to be a good thing. Today's medical teams expect clear evidence before they accept new theories or therapies.

Yet in other areas, the tidy results of analysis may overlook matters of great importance. Thus, economists may find it more cost-effective to send certain patients to centres of excellence for treatment, even if far from their homes. Long known to paediatricians, there is now a lot of evidence that older people, too, recover better when supported by familiar people. They can be worried about the loss of time and money when visitors have to travel a long way, yet make slower progress without them. Cost-benefit analyses should explore such personal as well as cash costs. It is significant that most of the (limited) research literature is in nursing journals.

Evidence for costs that are hard to measure

Some years ago, when deliberate child abuse was a new concern, a two year old with a bruised face was admitted to hospital on suspicion of this being non-accidental injury. Was the father's story of a genuine accident to be believed? The child stayed in hospital until the matter could be settled by the magistrates, but he became depressed and unresponsive until his parents came round the ward door. He immediately leapt up, reached out to them and, safely back in their arms, became their happy little boy again. The before and after scenes were caught on camera and said what the child could not have said for himself. The eyewitness record convinced the court to let him go home, and careful follow up showed this to have been the right thing to do.

When discussing matters of belief we also need trustworthy evidence. Changed behaviour backs up the story of changed beliefs, making the new believer's story much more acceptable. This is why some of Christ's earliest followers taught and wrote up the story of his life, death, resurrection and ascension. Their histories have such a ring of truth that over the centuries, millions who never knew the authors have since believed their evidence, to find their own lives changed as a result. [1]

The Bible as reference book

In this exploration I shall use the Bible as our textbook. In a few parts it can be hard to understand but unlike some modern sceptics I accept that the Scriptures, as originally given, provide us with a record inspired by the Holy Spirit of God. This belief is supported not only by the writers themselves [2, 3] but by respected biblical scholars. Mine will not be an academic study, but hopefully most of us can gain access to one of the many translations of the Bible, either as a book by our bedside or online.

As we carefully and prayerfully read his word, God helps us to understand it, not just speaking to our minds but also getting through to hearts and spirits.

We looked earlier at the repeated sacrifices recorded in the Old Testament, designed as they were to make a sinful people temporarily right with God again. As we turn to the good news told in the New Testament we find that, in his Son, God fulfilled many of the prophecies that spoke of a coming Messiah who would open up a permanent way for mankind to know peace with God. Some who had observed Jesus for themselves wrote up their observations, confirming that he truly fitted this identity. Jesus often quoted from those old books himself, claiming to be the one they had described all those years ago. What he did backed up the gracious things he said.

We cannot dismiss the Old Testament as being past its use-by date, or the New Testament records as just a made up story. They are both very much up-to-date and have been preserved to be believed and acted on.

Books of the New Testament

The 27 New Testament documents together provide us with unique and reliable evidence about Jesus' life, death, resurrection and ascension. They record and apply his teaching. The Gospels alone give many first-hand details of his wonderful works and words while many of the other books deal with how we should follow him faithfully in this life, looking forward to being made fully like him in the next. If the stories were made up, they would not have the unexpected outcome that many of them do have. They not only give us Jesus' life story but record his life-purpose and, if we open our inner ears, will come as the very word of God to our hearts, minds and consciences.

The value of eyewitness records

One of those who had kept company with Jesus later sent a letter warning against false teaching about him. In it he said, 'We did not follow cleverly invented stories when we told you about the power and coming of our Lord Jesus Christ, but we were eye-witnesses of his majesty'. [4] There is little more convincing than such witnesses.

Some friends of mine got on very well with another couple, both doctors, but thought it odd that they openly held Christian beliefs. Then the Christian husband developed a malignant melanoma, unresponsive to treatment. He and his wife knew what was happening, but the friends were amazed at the way they faced his death. The patient seemed positively excited, for he knew that he was on the way to meet his Lord. The obvious peace and joy in his life at a time when they would have felt the opposite, convinced those who had never met this before to seek and find such faith for themselves. It added to their friend's joy that before he died he was able to help them to enjoy a personal relationship with the Lord Jesus Christ. The evidence of his inner security was what had started their search and their own lives were transformed by this new relationship, even when they lost the old one.

The New Testament authors: who's who

There are certain theologians, sometimes called higher critics, who question the traditional view that the Gospel stories are accurate, dismissing sections that they disagree with or genuinely doubt. However, many other scholars of repute have carefully studied evidence gained from research and believe that the accounts we have are authentic. (See also chapter 2). We are favoured to have more than one record of the unique person and work of the Lord Jesus Christ.

The first three Gospels Matthew, Mark and Luke are based on eyewitness accounts (the so-called Synoptic Gospels). Unlike the others, Luke had not met Jesus. He composed his report from information given by those who had enjoyed knowing him. The fourth record, by John, was not so much the straightforward life story of Jesus that the other three gave, but a more thoughtful commentary on the meaning of his life, his miracles and his teaching. Like Luke, John probably wrote his book after a longer interval than the others. Between the four of them, they describe Jesus' matchless life from different angles and each gives most space to the final chapters of his earthly life, followed by his amazing resurrection and ascension. In truth, they were expert witnesses.

To get at the truth it is always helpful to hear more than one viewpoint, which is why legal trials call for a variety of witnesses. Different stories can be like pieces of a puzzle that, when fitted together, give a clearer picture of what really happened. Witnesses, as at Jesus' own final trial, do not always agree, but the stories told by our four gospellers are complementary, not contradictory.

Matthew had been a tax collector, called out of what was then a much-despised occupation to follow Jesus. His record simply states that Jesus saw him, sitting at his tax collector's booth. 'Follow me', he said, and Matthew got up and followed him. Even if he had already heard or even seen Jesus before, it says much for Jesus' magnetic appeal that a man making his living from money matters responded so promptly to his invitation to leave everything and follow. [5] Perhaps he was more used to being scorned, first because he worked for the Romans and then because most tax collectors were suspected of helping themselves to some of the cash they collected. Whatever he was like when called, he followed Jesus to become one of his inner circle of twelve men known as apostles, or simply as the Twelve.

Probably writing with a Jewish readership in mind and with a professional interest in making things add up, Matthew particularly loved to use quotations from the Old Testament. He introduced them with remarks like, 'This took place to fulfil what was spoken of through the prophet...' or, about Jesus' cousin John the Baptist, 'This is he who was spoken of through the prophet Isaiah.' This John was to be the herald Isaiah had spoken of who would prepare the way for the coming of the Lord.

Before enlisting Matthew, Jesus had also called Simon Peter, his brother Andrew, James and *John*, another Gospel writer. [6] These four were fishermen and possibly not as worldly-wise as Matthew, yet they, too, promptly gave up their work when Jesus called them to follow him. According to the account in John's Gospel, John the Baptist, the herald, had already pointed out Jesus to Andrew who, with his brother Simon, had then met Jesus and recognised that he was possibly the promised Messiah. When he called them to follow him they were therefore ready.

We are not told whether James and John had met Jesus before, but as members of the fishing community they would know that other fishermen had gone after him. When Jesus called them personally they immediately left their father to carry on the business with his other helpers. Later, Jesus would call James and John 'sons of thunder', hinting at their impetuous and possibly fiery disposition [7] but by the time he wrote his Gospel, the ageing John had become calmer and more reflective.

Mark does not feature by name in his Gospel and was probably much younger than the other gospellers. Believers used to meet at his mother's house in Jerusalem and they sometimes knew him as John. [8] That could be how he met Peter, whose memories he is thought to have drawn on later to write his shorter book, for at the end of his first letter Peter speaks of Mark as being like a son to him. It is possible that Mark's account was the first and that other gospellers used his story as a help in writing theirs. Be that as it may, Mark's is the only Gospel to tell of a young man who escaped arrest in the Garden of Gethsemane when the crowd came by night to arrest Jesus. It is generally supposed that this is an autobiographical incident.

The final meal Jesus shared with his disciples took place in an upstairs room, conceivably one at the home where Mark lived with his mother. If so, as a curious teenager he might well have slipped out of bed to eavesdrop and when the party left for the garden he followed them, still in his nightshirt. His Gospel records how the linen garment was lost when someone tried to arrest the unnamed youth and the frightened boy ran off without it, by now in a big hurry to get safely back to his nice warm bed.

In his Gospel, Mark still comes over as a man in a hurry, eager to get down all that Peter was telling him. He writes with the galloping speed of someone bursting to tell all that he knows. The first three chapters of his Gospel are likely to leave the reader breathless, with his many mentions of 'at once', 'without delay', 'very early in the morning'. In the same space he mentions about ten times how the crowds followed Jesus about so that he had no time even to eat. It was a hectic schedule.

John became one of Jesus' closest friends and his Gospel differs from those of the other three, being more reflective and thoughtful about the events he describes. He starts by speaking of Jesus as 'the Word' who came to bring God's message of light and love to a dark world and to convey his majesty and glory. John the Baptist had announced his coming and called people to show by their baptism that they repented of their sins. Early on he identified Jesus as the Lamb of God, superior to one of the old sacrificial lambs because the atonement for sin that he offered would be once and for all, no longer necessary every year as in times past. John writes in his Gospel that those who receive Jesus will be welcomed as his children into the family of God, though only a few would do so during his time on earth.

John selects seven of Jesus' miracles as signs of his divinity when he showed his authority over the natural world, human disease and even death. As part of the whole person healing that was his ministry, when he cured people's illnesses he often spoke of forgiving their sins, changing their cries for help into praise of God, his Father.

John gives us the fullest record of the last teaching session when Jesus sat with the Twelve around the table for the annual Passover feast. This was (and by Jewish families still is) a reminder of the meal eaten before the exodus from Egypt. John leaves it to the other three Gospel writers to describe the new meaning that Jesus gave to this meal. From then on, Christians remember how he matched the bread and wine of the Passover meal with his own body and blood, so soon to be broken and poured out for us. He offered himself as a ransom for sin, replacing the sacrificial Passover lamb. Whether called Holy Communion, the Eucharist or simply the Lord's Supper, each simple service now reminds us of all that Jesus suffered for us and in thanksgiving we give ourselves back to him.

John is the only one to describe the humility of Jesus as he washed the feet of his friends, a courtesy they had all neglected before that final Passover meal. Afterwards, apart from Judas who had left to betray him, the disciples went with Jesus to a favourite place of theirs on the Mount of Olives known as the Garden of Gethsemane.

John remembers how Jesus still had important things to say before he left them. He spoke of how a vine will only produce fruit if the sap is free to flow and, in the same way, if they were to live fruitful lives they would need to stay connected to the infusion of new life he would give them. John quotes a long prayer later made by Jesus to his Father with requests for himself, his disciples and finally for those in the future who would come to believe in him. It was not long before Judas arrived with an armed gang and Jesus was arrested, most of the disciples deserting him.

From a modest reference it seems that John was known to the high priest, and could get in to his courtyard, hence his full report of the mock-trial that happened next and his knowledge of all that followed.

Although not named, he was probably the disciple asked by the dying Jesus to take his mother, Mary, and care for her like another son. [9]

Jesus' last days on earth

The Gospel writers go into great detail about Jesus' arrest, trial, crucifixion and resurrection. Between them, Matthew and Mark (also Luke) give most detail of the last hours spent in the garden. Jesus was in agony as he asked his Father to confirm that he must go through with the terrible ordeal about to happen. The late hour and the meal together sent his dearest friends to sleep just when Jesus most needed their support. One of them must have woken up enough to overhear and record some of his agonised prayers before he was given angelic comfort so that when the crowd arrived to arrest him he was again calm and trustful.

The Gospel writers had become convinced enough of Jesus' uniqueness to record their observations of his self-giving life, his miraculous works and, as it seemed to them at the time, the disappointments of his arrest, trial and death. Later they had such astonishing encounters with his resurrected person, changed but still recognisable, that when they saw him again they had no doubt about believing John's cry of, 'It is the Lord!' [10] Weeks later, Jesus returned to his Father, no doubt after days of revision, explanation and more teaching as he prepared them for his departure. He would send his comforting Spirit to help them to remember his teaching as they spread the good news of salvation, made disciples and wrote their books. [11]

Matthew and Mark end their Gospels with an account of Jesus' ascension after he had given his closest followers what is known as the Great Commission. They were to preach the good news across the world, making and baptising more disciples. Yet that was not to be the end of the story, for early in Luke's book of *Acts*, he describes Jesus' ascension but also describes the astonishing descent of the Holy Spirit at Pentecost, to inspire and energise the disciples' own spirits. [12]

You haven't yet been properly introduced to Dr. Luke, but we'll be hearing more from him later.

For further thought

- It is easy to have fixed ideas about the Christian faith without ever having studied it. The best place to start looking further would be to read one or more of the gospels.

Further resources

- Bruce FF. *The New Testament documents – Are they reliable?* Downers Grove, IL: Inter-Varsity Press, 1981
- Bauckman R. *Jesus and the eyewitnesses*. Cambridge UK: William B Eerdmans Publishing, 2006.

References

1. 2 Corinthians 5:16-17
2. John 21:24
3. 2 Timothy 3:16-17
4. 2 Peter 1:16
5. Matthew 9:9
6. Matthew 4:18-22
7. Mark 3:17
8. Acts 12:12
9. John 19:26-27
10. John 21:7
11. John 14:16, 25-26
12. Acts 2:1-41

Chapter 10
The greatest story ever told

The Gideons International is an organisation that distributes free Bibles, for example to hotels and hospitals. I was once present when a senior member of hospital administration was given his own attractive copy. 'Thank you', he said politely as he took the gift, adding, 'I'll put it safely in the cupboard with my other Bible.'

I hope that he would easily be able to take one out to read. Although the Bible is still a world bestseller, many people never pick one up or read it attentively. I recently heard of a young woman, English to the core, whose daughter had to do a school project on the Good Samaritan. This story told by Jesus described the practical kindness of a Samaritan towards a man he would not normally have mixed with, but found half dead on the road after being beaten up. The stranger had stopped to help and then paid for the victim's care and accommodation. The girl's mother had looked in vain on the internet for information to help her daughter. When someone suggested that it would be easier to read the story in the Bible [1] she admitted that she did not own one.

This would once have been unheard of in Britain and it seems likely that there will be many others, including many from overseas, who do not know the Bible's good news. Perhaps some newcomers think of the Christian faith as a foreigners' religion, but know little about the person of Jesus and do not often meet people to enlighten them. If you have a Bible, I hope that it does not stay safely shut up in a cupboard and, if you don't have one, that you'll find a way to read the story for yourself. The internet may help if there are none immediately available, or cultural tradition makes it unsafe to be found with a copy. Yet it has rightly been called the word of God and, as he speaks, his voice can still be heard by those with ears ready to listen.

The importance of a detailed history

I once attended the funeral of a doctor friend who was in her eighties, and long since retired from practice. As we heard about her former achievements, some of us learned things about her unknown to us before and would have been interested to discuss with her in person. It need not be so with Jesus, for his is surely the greatest story ever told, and much of it is fully recorded for us to learn from. Even better, if we ask him, we are promised that his Spirit will be with us and will help us to understand it.

Like someone reading the news, I have so far given a few headlines concerning the person of Jesus as told by those who wrote about him, but we'll now go into more detail. We shall look more carefully at the reason for his coming to earth and how he steadily pursued that purpose. The amazing events that followed his death complete the story, changing it from a seeming tragedy to an amazing triumph. Best of all, we are promised that one day he will return to claim his faithful people and bring peace to our troubled world. This story has been preserved to tell us who Jesus was and how he explained God's purposes for mankind – so let's look at it more closely.

The coming of Jesus

Two of Jesus' historians, Matthew and Luke, start their Gospels with the antenatal record of Mary, a pure young village girl living in Nazareth, who found that she was pregnant. Her fiancé, Joseph the local carpenter, knew that this could not be his child but the tale she told him about the pregnancy was very strange indeed. She spoke of a visit from an angel who had said that she would conceive through an act of God, that the child would be called the ('the', not 'a') Son of God and that he would save his people from their sins. She knew what a great privilege this would be and had humbly responded, 'May it be to me as you have said'.

Joseph was faced with a big problem. He loved the girl and did not want her to be publicly disgraced, as an unmarried girl would be in their Jewish culture. Even so, he wondered whether he ought to break off the engagement. Perhaps he should send her away to have the baby somewhere else, well away from those who knew them. Thankfully abortion was not an option in those days.

For a time Mary chose to go away to the hill country of Judea to visit her elderly cousin Elizabeth. This must have been a lonely and difficult journey for a young girl, but she found Elizabeth also rejoicing in a remarkable pregnancy. Today, as an elderly woman pregnant for the first time, she would be given close antenatal care. Yet she was sure that as God had given this baby to her and her aged husband Zechariah, he could be trusted to care for them all. The promise had been that the child would be forerunner to the Lord [2, 3] and she understood at once that young Mary's miraculous pregnancy identified her as the mother of this Lord, their long-awaited Messiah. According to Luke's timetable, Mary could even have greeted the infant John before she went back home, now certain of her own pregnancy.

By then Joseph had experienced a strange dream, confirming to him that the father of Mary's child was truly the Spirit of God, not another man, and that he should not wait to marry the girl. By now she would be well over three months pregnant, and he was to take care of her as husband in name only until the baby was born. They were to give him the name 'Jesus,' meaning 'the Lord saves', for he would save his people from their sins. Through the activity of his Spirit in Mary, God was coming to be with them in human form as this special child. [4] It is hard for our limited understanding to grasp, but this child would be both fully God and fully human, united in one person. He came to earth through the Spirit, in form a human being while also sharing the nature of his Father, God. [5]

His birth and infancy

Jesus' birth took place in Bethlehem. His parents had come to take part in a census but the city was already so overcrowded that they could only find a most unsuitable place for Mary to give birth. Yet in the second chapter of both their gospels Matthew and Luke record amazing events happening there. The first visitors were humble shepherds who had been given a remarkable message about this special baby. Probably much later, wise men arrived with kingly gifts for him. On the way they had not so wisely called on King Herod in Jerusalem. By innocently asking him the way to find one born 'to be King of the Jews' they made Herod so worried about a possible rival that he gave orders for all the infants in the same age-group as Jesus to be killed. An angel warned Joseph to escape to Egypt so the little family left that same night.

By then Jesus was probably around two years old. We can imagine him, perhaps travelling wide-eyed under a starry sky and safely held by Joseph or Mary on their donkey, or in the cool of the day holding onto a parent's hand as he toddled alongside to stretch his legs. It was a long journey, in the opposite direction from the route taken out of Egypt by Moses and the Israelites. The child would not yet know that important piece of national history, and had no idea of the cruel infanticide left behind in Judah. Like so many today, the little family lived as refugees until it was safe to leave Egypt and return to their homeland. They resettled in Nazareth where Joseph set up business as a carpenter. As Jesus grew up he would hear the Old Testament Scriptures regularly read in the local synagogue, no doubt reinforcing lessons learned at his mother's knee.

Growing up

The years passed and the boy grew up. Luke describes an episode when he was twelve years old. With a crowd of other worshippers, he and his family had gone to celebrate Passover in Jerusalem. On the way back home, his alarmed parents realised that Jesus was missing and looked desperately for him for three whole days. He was then found back in the temple at Jerusalem in thoughtful conversation with the religious teachers there. He explained to his mother that he was 'in my Father's house'. This is the only clue we have of his early awareness of a close relationship with God, and the only recorded episode from the days of his youth. We are told that he had other brothers and sisters [6] but otherwise we know very little of Jesus' early life. It is clear from his teaching, however, that during these years he immersed himself in the Scriptures. His baptism by John in the Jordan River marked the beginning of his public ministry. By then he would have been about 30 years old.

Outwardly Jesus would have looked like any other Jewish young man, and certainly was not the blue-eyed blond portrayed by many western artists. If he had helped Joseph, the carpenter, he is likely to have been physically strong. Hands sensitive enough to feel imperfections in wood would later bring healing and comfort to many sick people. Although carpentry was a valued craft, his was not a wealthy home. We know this because when his parents had first presented the infant Jesus in the temple, they took the least expensive offering allowed. There were times in his adult life when he was without ready cash. Although he was brought up as a working man, people would later find him gracious in speech and astonishing in what he said and did. [7] In the days before loud speakers or microphones he must have had a good strong voice, sometimes heard by thousands at once. His growing popularity with ordinary people (and possibly his north-country accent) upset the religious leaders. Especially in southern Judea, they became jealous and plotted against him.

Leaving home and being baptised

We do not know how much Mary and Elizabeth had told their sons about the unusual circumstances of their birth. Perhaps at some stage the boys would compare notes and wonder about their future lives, until gradually each of them accepted his calling and they possibly drifted apart. By the time Jesus left home, his cousin John the Baptist, although only a few months older, was by now probably orphaned and had gone to live in the wilderness, aware by now that he was forerunner to the Messiah. He was very eccentric in dress and lifestyle, which was perhaps how he attracted the attention of so many people. [8] He told them to repent, baptising those who did so, explaining that a mightier one than he was on the way.

When Jesus joined the queue for baptism, John knew that he was that expected mighty one and was therefore reluctant to baptise him. Jesus insisted that he should do so, although he had no need to repent. In this way he showed his identification with humanity and his total consecration to God. As Jesus came up out of the water, what looked like a dove came and landed on him and the voice of God was heard identifying him as his beloved Son. The 'dove' represented the Spirit of

God, preparing Jesus to take up his lifework. Once again Father, Son and Holy Spirit came together at the start of his public life. [9]

The Spirit next led him to the wilderness where he fasted for over six weeks. When at his weakest, the devil arrived to test him with temptations directed at body, mind and spirit. He suggested that he turned stones into bread to satisfy his hunger, that he throw himself from a high place to prove that God would save him and finally urged him to worship the devil and be rewarded for it with great kingdoms (not, of course, Satan's to give!). Jesus found perfect answers in the words of Scripture to overcome each of these attempts to throw him off course. [10]

By this Jesus not only silenced the enemy but also showed us the importance of hiding God's word in the heart, to be drawn on for guidance and strength during all kinds of testing times. It follows that we need to read and learn the Scriptures ourselves if we are to find appropriate thoughts popping into our minds when under spiritual attack, or to learn that a verse quoted to a needy friend had hit just the right spot. Jesus knew exactly what passages to repeat to overcome all temptation by the enemy of souls and we can learn to do the same.

Jesus' relationship with God affected all that he did

As we read the life of Christ, recorded in all four Gospels, the characteristic that stands out is his practice of selfless love. Jesus went about doing only what was good. He especially cared for the sick, weak and needy, including untouchables such as lepers. By mixing with others seen by the super-religious as outcasts, he turned upside down the accepted order of things. It is not surprising that by keeping company with those whom many others despised, the 'tax collectors and sinners', he upset those who thought such people were beneath them. Instead Jesus took note of their needs and showed them great understanding. We need to recall his example when tempted by today's emphasis on status symbols. We'll look next at some of the people he helped by showing love in action whatever their social standing. He was no snob!

For further thought

- The Bible tells us all we need to know about the life of Jesus.
- It is better to read it than to rely entirely on someone else's opinion about him.
- In Jesus we will find a good model, but he offers even more than that.

Further resources

- May P. *The greatest person*. London: Christian Medical Fellowship, 1996
- Stott J. *The incomparable Christ*. Leicester: Inter-Varsity Press, 2001.
- Yancey P. *The Jesus I never knew*. Grand Rapids, Michigan: Zondervan, 2002.

References

1. Luke 10:25-37
2. Isaiah 40:3
3. Luke 1:17, 76
4. Matthew 1:18-23
5. John 10:30
6. Matthew 13:53-56
7. Luke 4:22
8. Matthew 3:4-5
9. Matthew 3:13-17
10. Matthew 4:1-12

Chapter 11
Jesus brought new life and health

During my second post as a junior doctor I was asked to go out to an ambulance to certify a death. This was long before ambulance crews knew how to set about resuscitation as paramedics do now. It was unknown for them to perform an electrocardiogram and death was certified by absence of breath and pulse. If no mist appeared on a mirror held over the mouth, that person was thought to be dead. As this was state of the art at the time, I accepted what I had been told by the ambulance crew and went out, death certificate book at the ready.

The patient was a woman, and although not obviously breathing, the important thing was that she was blue and not yet showing the extreme pallor of death. As I listened in there was a faint heartbeat, so we rushed her to the ward and put up an intravenous drip. (There were no intensive care units then either!) Our patient eventually regained consciousness, not at all pleased that her attempt at suicide had failed. She had been resuscitated but not fully healed.

Today the ABC of emergency resuscitation is widely taught even to school children. Some might learn to recite, 'A for checking the airway; B for artificial breathing and C for cardiac massage', and know how to do it all. By using this ABC, a friend of mine saved the life of a young woman who had suddenly collapsed, unconscious, at their place of work. Yet Jesus did even greater things than these.

Jesus' miracles of healing

As well as his famous feeding of five thousand with a boy's picnic lunch and afterwards illustrating his power over the forces of nature, [1] the Gospels tell of over two dozen miracles of healing, including three people whom Jesus raised from the dead. Only one of the three lay on her deathbed; one was being carried to his funeral and the third was already buried. These were no mere acts of resuscitation. [2,3,4]

Jesus asked some of the other needy people he helped whether they believed in him before he worked the miracle and strengthened that faith. [5] One or two were healed at a distance, at someone else's request. [6, 7] Not all were told that their sins were forgiven, but this was so with a paralysed man whose friends had lowered him down through the roof to lie in front of Jesus in a very crowded room. He was still paralysed even after hearing the words of forgiveness, but in response to those who thought it had been easy enough to say that, Jesus proved his authority both to forgive and to heal by telling the man to get up and go home. To the amazement of all, that is what he did. [8] When Jesus healed, he attended to mind, will and spirit as well as to a sick body. The carpenter's son might even have helped to mend the roof!

Someone previously paralysed and dependant on others, who suddenly got up and walked unaided, gave a dramatic demonstration of healing without need for any more proof of Jesus' authority and power. This was also true for a man known to have been born blind – after trusting in Jesus, he could see. [9] As a rule, these acts of healing needed no one else's involvement to complete them, although a healed leper was told to show himself to a priest. [10] Unlike advanced leprosy, the early stages would be less obviously cured, but for a priest to say that this was so would allow the man back into a society freed of worry about his earlier infection.

Ward rounds with Jesus

David Stevens, an American doctor, wrote a book asking how we would feel if when we went to the doctor the brass plate on the office door said, 'Jesus, MD'. Jesus is sometimes called the Great Physician, and for good reasons. Chapter five of Mark's Gospel is rather like a PowerPoint presentation, illustrating some of his miracles. As a child I was told that the stories were like those of patients seen on different hospital wards. They give examples of the different kinds of people Jesus helped: the demented, the diseased and desperate, the dying – and even the dead. He included men and, less commonly for those days, women and children in his acts of healing. Let's follow his visits to the different 'wards' and take note of what happened there.

The men's ward

Here we find an apparently mad man (Matthew's account describes two of them). In those days – and perhaps in our own – such severely disturbed people were very much feared and shunned. I am reminded that my first training post included being on call for a psychiatric hospital full of mentally ill people. I was the lowest member of a surgical team in the nearby hospital and was sent for when a surgical opinion was needed. Feeling very inadequate, I would arrive at the other hospital to be met by a warder carrying a big bunch of keys who then took me to see the patient. Every door we came to on the way was locked, explaining the need for so many keys, and when we finally reached the right ward I was shown in and the door securely locked behind us. Few patients were really violent, but had all been declared insane, so the authorities played safe by keeping them securely shut up. On the whole, those needing my humble opinion were harmless enough, simply out of touch with reality, but suffering from something like an abscess, or bleeding from a laceration or burn. With better drug therapy most patients later went home and the hospital was closed.

The man Jesus visited was insanely violent, but was not safely locked away in a hospital. He had once been caught and chained up by others who were strong and brave enough to catch him, but with unnatural strength he had torn off the chains (and his clothes) and run away from them to live in a cemetery. There he roamed restlessly round among the tombs. He was as wild as wild could be and no one ever came near him, as he was thought to be possessed by demons. He often cut himself with stones, so what might he do to a visitor? People kept well away from him.

It must therefore have been a great surprise for him to see a boat arrive one day, and a man he had never seen before step ashore. Despite the madman's rush at him, the stranger kept walking fearlessly towards him. It was obvious that, unusually, his wild behaviour was not frightening this visitor away. When the spirits possessing him announced that this was 'Jesus, Son of the Most High God', he knelt at Jesus' feet. He was miraculously released from his wild behaviour as Jesus allowed his demons to leave him to take up residence in a herd of pigs.

The immediate change in him was amazing. Back in his right mind, and his clothes, he was happy to sit quietly, wanting to stay with his kind deliverer. Instead, Jesus told him to go home and share with others the wonderful story of how this great change had happened to him.

The women's ward

The patient was a sad woman who had suffered for twelve long years from serious blood loss (probably persistent menorrhagia). Despite spending all her savings on many and varied medical opinions, she was poorer in health as well as in purse. By now she must have been terribly anaemic and weak. The old public health and safety laws said that women like her should be considered unclean and untouchable, and among other taboos she would have been kept out of the synagogue. [11] Presumably the original precaution had to do with avoiding any cross-infection as the close knit community of Hebrews travelled through the wilderness. Instead, religious hardliners had since turned it into a permanent policy.

The children's ward

Mark cleverly interweaves the woman's story with that of a desperate man, hurrying to Jesus, straight from his child's bedside. The man, Jairus, was a leader of the synagogue and father of a dying twelve year old. He came to beg Jesus to come home with him and heal her. During the years that he had been taking pride in his little girl's growing strength and development, the sick woman had gradually been getting weaker. Jairus had possibly been the main person to keep her out of his synagogue. Then, horror of horrors, as he set off to take Jesus to his daughter, he saw this very woman creep up behind him and touch the edge of his garment. Now the robe would be technically unclean, yet he urgently wanted Jesus to come home with him.

Jesus had felt power go out from him as the woman touched his robe, and Jairus must have watched as the woman stepped shyly forward to explain herself. His dilemma now was whether he, as a kind of religious policeman, should ask Jesus to go and change his outer garment before bringing the woman's uncleanness into his house.

If he were to be especially strict, he could ask Jesus to stay apart for a whole day because in order to change the robe he would have had to handle it. More than one student in an operating theatre has been embarrassed by accidentally touching the surgeon's gown with an unsterile hand. The operation has then had to wait until the surgeon changed his gown. Is that what Jesus should have done?

Jairus must have decided that his fatherly concern should override any legal scruples, but as he and Jesus set off for his home, the news came that the little girl had died. Here was a final dilemma. According to another of those old health and safety rules, to visit or touch a dead person would require a period of quarantine. [12] Would Jesus still come? In fact, the story has a happy ending. Jesus did go to the bereaved home and went straight to the child's bedside. He deliberately took her hand in his and said, 'Little girl, get up.' She opened her eyes and he told her delighted parents to find her something to eat. Any contamination would cleansed with the healing. If Jairus eventually learned the truth about Jesus' self-giving life and death, he would realise that his own decision to put love before law for his daughter's sake had been a godly one after all, for such other-centred love is the fulfilment of the law. [13]

What about today?

In all that he did Jesus gave his own energy on behalf of others. The fast pace of his life over the three years of healing, teaching, and travelling across the country on foot must sometimes have left him exhausted. [14] In his humanity he experienced suffering of body, mind and spirit and this was the price he paid for healing the sicknesses and sorrows of others. Any who have similar on call rotas, such as junior doctors or young mothers, will know a little of their draining effects, but can claim his promise to be renewed by the energy that he still gives. [15]

The demon-possessed man, the chronically sick woman and the dead child all responded to Jesus' words of loving authority because he was who he said he was, the Son of God. They represent the types of people that many still find it hard to deal with, doctors sometimes calling them 'heart-sink' patients because of their often slow response to treatment. Others sometimes use labels that are even more unpleasant, but Jesus showed care to all without discrimination.

The original man, woman and child of the Gospel account were isolated behind different kinds of barriers. They needed more than drugs to put them right and so, too, do today's mentally or chronically ill people. They so often feel isolated and find few health professionals really dedicated to their care. Thankfully the hospice movement has brought better understanding of the needs of dying or bereaved adults and more recently those of children. Many health professionals are learning that illness and disability are not only physical problems but people have deeper needs that must not be ignored. Those who recognise this should help others to think about how much better any of us would feel for someone's tender loving care, whatever our physical or mental state.

It was as he drew closer to them that Jesus, moved by compassion, challenged prejudice as he calmed the disturbed, cheered the downhearted, comforted the desperate and cared about those dying and bereaved. Such loving care can bring inner healing for sufferers and encouragement for their supporters, professional or otherwise. This is especially so when, as with Jesus, it is God's love at work, channelled through devoted hands.

A mother once came to see me with her boy of about ten years old who was quite clearly much delayed in his mental development. His mother obviously loved him dearly and he was smiling happily. Interested in how such children affect their families I asked if I could take his photo to use in my talks. As she agreed, his mother added, 'When you show his picture, tell them he's brought a lot of love'. Her own evident love for him was being returned with interest. In time, to keep on loving selflessly can promote affectionate two-way traffic.

For further thought

- Do you know anyone with dementia, a disability or who is dying or bereaved? What, or who, do you think may help them most?
- Would you consider taking a more active interest in their welfare?

Further resources

- Stevens D. *Jesus MD*. Grand Rapids Michigan: Zondervan, 2001.

References

1. Mark 6:45-51
2. Mark 5:22-24, 35-43
3. Luke 7:11-15
4. John 11:17-44
5. Matthew 9:27-30
6. John 4:46-53
7. Matthew 15:22-28
8. Luke 5:17-26
9. John 9:1-2, 6-11
10. Matthew 8:1-4
11. Leviticus 15:25-30
12. Numbers 19:11
13. Romans 13:10
14. Mark 4:37-38
15. 2 Corinthians 12:9

Chapter 12
What Jesus taught and how he was received

I well remember the insistent ring of my telephone during the night. I had to get out of bed to answer it, in the hope that by then I would be sufficiently awake to respond to whatever the call was about. Since then, rules have been introduced to limit (at least officially) the number of hours that most British doctors are on duty, but even now it would seem very odd for someone on call to walk away and go somewhere else.

Jesus' on call rota

At the start of Mark's Gospel we read how a long queue of people kept Jesus busy until late at night as he miraculously healed them of many and varied diseases. Next morning he got up while it was still dark and went out to pray, presumably needing both renewed strength and much wisdom for the day ahead (and giving us an example to follow in our own busy lives). When he was told that everyone was out looking for him, probably hoping for more miracles, he said, 'Let's go somewhere else.' This was a surprising response from such a caring man, but he explained that his priority was to teach. [1] He still performed miracles but not to the exclusion of the spoken word. Why?

It is important to be clear that the reason Jesus had come was to share wonderfully good news. He lived in an occupied country, with rulers in constant fear of an uprising. Jesus was not the first person to gain a following and then be arrested and silenced. His time for that still lay ahead, but what was it that he needed to tell people so urgently before attracting unwelcome attention? The miracles had shown his great love for others and his special power over disease, but why else had he come?

Jesus' message

Most of us will know how those hoping to become national leaders set out a manifesto of their aims and how they plan to fulfil them.

They may appear on television or, as election time draws near, climb up on the back of a lorry and use a loud speaker to broadcast their intentions. Jesus had no such political ambitions. In contrast to modern politicians, what has become known as Jesus' manifesto was delivered quietly, during a morning service at the small synagogue in his home town of Nazareth. Perhaps not many would remember the old story of how he had been conceived there by an unmarried girl. They simply knew him now as the local carpenter's son and gave him their full attention when he stood up to read from the book of Isaiah. He had chosen a passage traditionally interpreted as the action plan of the future Messiah, the one anointed by God and expected for centuries:

> *'The Spirit of the Sovereign Lord is on me, because the Lord has anointed me to preach good news to the poor. He has sent me to bind up the broken-hearted, to proclaim freedom to the captives and release from darkness for the prisoners, to proclaim the year of the Lord's favour and the day of vengeance of our God, to comfort all who mourn...'* [2]

Instead of the phrase about release from darkness, Jesus specified 'recovery of sight to the blind' but stopped reading after mentioning the Lord's favour, leaving out the bit about God's coming judgment. He ended by saying, 'Today this Scripture is fulfilled in your hearing'. Isaiah's messianic prophecy was being fulfilled in him. He would provide a way of escape from the Lord's vengeance.

His audience already knew that he had been doing some of the merciful deeds foretold by Isaiah and had perhaps started to wonder whether he was a prophet. Yet he went on to give examples of how Gentiles, not Jews, had believed the prophets of old and suggested that his Jewish audience was equally unlikely to listen to him. His point was proved by their reaction. The idea that non-Jews might also be among God's chosen people angered them so much that instead of welcoming Jesus as their Messiah they tried to kill him there and then. He somehow managed to walk through the murderous crowd and get away, although their hostility did not silence him. [3]

The Sermon on the Mount

This is the name given to one of Jesus' most famous teaching sessions as recorded in Matthew 5-7 with a shorter version in Luke 6. In the sermon he explained how he had not come to get rid of God's laws but to fulfil them. Yes, murder and adultery are wrong, but so are the hostile or lustful thoughts that became intentions and led to the deeds. The mistake of the religious leaders was to think and teach that to keep the commandments to the letter would win them favour with God. But they are not a checklist; they are God's guidance for life at its best. To make an idol of formal religious observance and external show was to miss the heart of the matter, namely humble, obedient and selfless worship of God and self-giving love for others.

The super-religious Jews of Jesus' day were not humble. They made a great show of their religion, praying long prayers at street corners for everyone to see. They had made religion their god instead of truly worshipping God. Jesus' teaching went much deeper than that. He said that prayer was important but should be privately directed to the Father in heaven, not turned into a public display. [4] Giving to charity should be a private matter, not done to impress others. [5] He even said that enemies and oppressors should be forgiven and prayed for. [6] This was revolutionary teaching unheard of before, and even today it is hard to follow.

I once visited a wonderful hospital in Jerusalem where the walls were covered in small tiles, each bearing the names of people who had contributed generously to the work. No doubt this was the hospital's way of saying 'Thank you' but was scarcely keeping the gifts private and could have risked excessive pride and self-satisfaction in the givers.

The two greatest commandments

When a legal expert asked Jesus, 'Teacher, which is the greatest commandment in the law?' the answer surprised the man. Jesus put first 'Love the Lord your God with all your heart and with all your soul and with all your mind'. Linked with that was the command to 'Love your neighbour as yourself'. [7]

These two commands sum up the whole law. God has said that with the new covenant he would engrave his laws into minds and hearts, not on tablets of stone like the originals. [8] His Spirit would be given to his people, to help them make their first response to any new challenge one prompted by love, not just duty. Someone has said that love stops the 'hardening of the oughteries' that produces a merely dutiful observance of a rule, sometimes with a pat on one's own back for it. Instead Jesus turned on its head the idea that keeping the rules is the way to earn favour with God. That would be the religion of a well-informed head, not of a loving and responsive heart. The head and the heart can be separated by the stiff neck of pride and hypocrisy, including self-deceit. Old attitudes need to be faced and hearts changed if God is really to be pleased.

To hear such new teaching from Jesus was good news to people oppressed by religious leaders who had added a few rules of their own to the hundreds we know about which they were proud to have learned and kept. They despised those who broke them because their own 'oughteries' were particularly hardened. They had turned the intended two-way relationship with God into a formal ritual. Yet Jesus' teaching also challenged his hearers to pray that their own hearts would be made receptive and obedient.

The word 'neighbour' does not simply mean the people who live next door, but includes every other member of the human race, who need our love. The people who listened to Jesus had to rethink (repent of) previous attitudes and learn how to treat others as they themselves would like to be treated. Before them was a living model of someone who practised what he preached. They were used to dry sermons full of even drier quotations from their religious leaders, but Jesus spoke so freshly with the clear authority of God that people were amazed and delighted.

Jesus, Son of Man and Son of God

A traditional title for the expected Messiah was 'Son of Man' and this is a name Jesus applied to himself 81 times as a reminder of his humanity. He claimed it, for example, after forgiving and healing a paralysed man, [9] when speaking of his future betrayal and suffering [10] and also of his final return. [11] Child of Mary in his humanity through the Holy Spirit of God, he was also Son of God in his divinity. Difficult as we may find this to grasp, in him his humanity and his deity were indivisible.

We often hear people say about a young child, 'He's just like his father,' or, 'She has her mother's smile'. Because Jesus was divine as well as human he lived on earth to show us what God, his Father, is like and he did not hesitate to say so. He claimed that anyone who saw him had seen the Father. [12] When people doubted this, he appealed to the evidence of his miracles to prove that God was with him. [13] Some of those who heard him said blasphemously that they had been enacted by demonic powers, [14] yet those who had seen or been changed by the miracles could not deny that they must be the works of God. [15] Some even dared to identify Jesus as being truly the Saviour of the world. [16] He accepted this description, saying that anyone who believed in him would know a very different life, life everlasting, whereas unbelievers would not. [17] As God is love, [18] his acts of love, like those we thought of in the last chapter, are truly God's own love in action. Jesus was just like his Father because they were one.

Bringing in a new kingdom

Traditional Jews, oppressed for centuries, expected the Messiah to come at last to release them. They looked for an obvious conqueror, powerfully riding in to his kingdom to rule over a new and godly regime. In Matthew's account of Jesus' birth, wise men had named him king of the Jews and brought him costly gifts, but Jesus himself spoke quietly of bringing in the kingdom of God by acts of love to the poor and needy, the alien and the prisoner, releasing them as his manifesto had promised. [19] These ideas were foreign to the religious and political leaders of the day who feared that by talking of another kingdom Jesus was going to lead a violent rebellion against them. Instead he said that he was not offering membership of an earthly kingdom. [20] His was a kingdom open to all those who accept him as their Saviour and king. His rule would be marked by loving kindness and peace.

True or false?

Some modern liberal theologians may (and do) suggest that some of the reports about Jesus are inaccurate. They have even colour-coded different sayings of his according to whether they think them true, probably true, doubtful or never said by Jesus at all. Other scholars still hold firmly to the inspired nature of the biblical record as do I, and academic debate is best left to those trained in that field. It is worth noting, though, that archaeologists have found many thousands of ancient fragments and complete copies of the biblical documents. Carbon-dating of these manuscripts shows great textual agreement over many years, indicating they have been reliably carried down to us through the centuries.

Memory can be remarkably accurate in cultures where not everyone can read or keep records, yet verbal messages can still be safely delivered and notable events in national history repeated in songs and stories, fixing them in mind and memory for future generations. My own observations of simple, uneducated people have shown how they can readily commit to memory detailed facts and significant conversations. Although the biblical authors were by no means without learning, this might have been true for some who gave them their information, but in our computer age we forget about earlier ways of remembering things. When I lived in Africa I only had to repeat my shopping list once to someone who could scarcely write his own name and spoke very little English. Yet after repeating what I had said, the faithful Joseph would come back triumphantly from the market with everything on the list. There are, of course, better reasons than that for believing the biblical records, without sharing the doubt and prejudice so often evident in such discussions.

Apart from Luke and Paul, the New Testament reporters had probably not had much higher education, but they had all developed godly wisdom. Jesus' remarkable impact on those who knew him would have burnt into their memories so many details of his unique life and death, words and works. Most important of all, he had assured them that, when he left them, his Spirit would bring all things to their remembrance. [21] The amazing events of the resurrection and the weeks

following are faithfully recalled for us by those who shared them,
and John's Gospel finishes with the solemn assurance that his record
is reliable. [22] As the disciple thought to be closest to Jesus, John would
have treasured all his recollections and recorded them accurately.
As he says, this was so 'that you may believe that Jesus is the Christ,
the Son of God, and that by believing you may have life in his name.' [23]
It would therefore be a great loss not to read what he has written.

The other biblical authors give the same sense of offering true records.
Meeting Jesus, either in the flesh or through his Spirit, had profoundly
changed their lives, and they were eager to share their good news with
all who would read their stories.

If someone today made the claims that Jesus made, we would think
him mad, misled, or up to no good. This is what some people did think
about Jesus at the time. Others believed him enough to follow him,
especially those who could see how wonderfully he was meeting
people's needs. Many others just liked to listen to him because he
spoke so graciously and what he said was so very unlike the kind of
talk they were used to from their religious leaders. Their endless lists
of rules and regulations were slowly weighing others down. [24] Yet this
man said that if they came to him they would find only a light load,
for he would lift their burdens. It is as if someone with a loaded
backpack were to meet a very strong and understanding person who
said, 'Let me take that from you'. What a relief – Jesus called it 'rest
for the soul'. [25] Freedom from bondage at last! [26]

For further thought

- Why would the Jews (and others) fail to accept Jesus' words
  about who he was?
- Had you realised that Jesus was truly God-made-man?
- Do you live by a set of rules, even by self-rule?

Further resources

- Lloyd-Jones M. *Studies in the Sermon on the Mount* (2 vols): Grand Rapids: Eerdmans Publishing, 1959-1960
- Packer JI. *Freedom, Authority and Scripture.* Leicester: Inter-Varsity Press, 1982
- McGrath A. *Jesus: Who he is and why he matters.* Leicester: Inter-Varsity Press, 1994

References

1. Mark 1:33-38
2. Isaiah 61:1-2
3. Luke 4:16-30
4. Matthew 6:5-8
5. Matthew 6:1-4
6. Matthew 5:43-44
7. Matthew 22:34-40
8. Jeremiah 31:33
9. Mark 2:9-12
10. Matthew 20:17-19
11. Matthew 24:30-31
12. John 14:8-11
13. John 10:34-38
14. John 8:48-49
15. John 9:30-38
16. John 4:42
17. John 3:16-18
18. 1 John 4:8
19. Matthew 25:31-40
20. John 18:36
21. John 14:26
22. John 21:24
23. John 20:31
24. Matthew 23:1-4
25. Matthew 11:28-30
26. John 8:36

Chapter 13
Learning to look beneath the surface

Children need to be more mature than we may think before they understand that a familiar word can also have a less than familiar meaning. A classic example is the small girl who stopped stroking her cat after she heard that her grandmother had died of a stroke, afraid that either her furry friend or the one who stroked it may meet the same end. Either way she dared not take the risk. A word like 'holy' may suggest moth-eaten garments to an English-speaking child. A few years later, as vocabulary expands, children (and some adults) enjoy playing with the double meanings of words, finally understanding the inner meaning of proverbs, parables and puns.

Teaching in parables

Jesus often told parables, using earthly stories with heavenly meanings. There had to be a certain level of spiritual understanding to see the point. Even the religious leaders did not always grasp what he meant and neither did his particular trainees and friends. As with his parable of the sower, the Twelve had to question what he had meant by talking of widely scattered seed reaching very different ends according to where it landed. [1] He said that if it fell on the hard path the birds would eat up the seed, or it would quickly die away if it landed on shallow or rocky soil, or was choked by thorns and thistles. Only in a field of good soil does seed take root and produce a plentiful harvest.

Like younger children, these grown men could not see the double meaning until Jesus explained how he had matched the different kinds of soil with the ways that different human hearts deal with his words. Some are hard-hearted, so the word is snatched away immediately. Others at first seem to take in the truth with joy, but their earlier interest becomes choked by opposition and worldly cares and they turn away. What Jesus longed for was for his words to be well received, and to grow up to bear fruit in people's lives. Instead he pointed out the risk of hearing without trying to understand, sometimes known as lack of 'double listening'. This allows many people to read the Bible or hear it read without realising that it brings a message from God. In another parable Jesus described as 'sons of the kingdom' those who accept his word and let it grow and influence their lives. Instead, others allow wrongdoing to take over and spoil God's intention for them. [2]

Parables in action

Earlier, we looked at Jesus' manifesto, where all the categories mentioned there had a double meaning (see Luke 4:18-19).The poor to whom he preached were poor in spirit as well as possessions, prisoners were locked in to lives of hopelessness or bound by sinful habits, the blind could not see who he was and the oppressed were weighed down by circumstances. He had come to liberate them all. Many of Jesus' miracles were acted out parables, such as when blind eyes were made to see, or disabled people healed and enabled, or even the dead brought back to life. Each of these incidents had their inner meaning, for he was also offering clear spiritual vision, restored power in life and spiritual revival.

Today we can still see events that act as parables. In 2010, the roof of a Chilean mine collapsed, trapping 33 mine workers underground. After almost ten weeks of uncertainty and enormous efforts to rescue them, each of them in turn finally stepped into the small chamber lowered down to bring them back to the surface, out of the darkness of the mine. They came out to meet the media headlights and the welcome of their loved ones. 'As we came out of darkness into light', said one of them, 'I understood what babies feel as they are born. It was like being born again.'

Being born again is the telling phrase that Jesus used when speaking of the spiritual rebirth he offers. [3] In fact, among those trapped underground was a Christian believer who encouraged his fellow miners to put their trust in Jesus' offer of loving forgiveness for their past sins. Many of them were 'born again', sure that whatever happened to their bodies they now had new and undying spiritual life. In his day, many of those healed by Jesus would find that they had not only been made whole physically but, by receiving his forgiveness, had also become fully alive spiritually. Not one of those miners refused to get into the rescue chamber, sent down to them at such great cost. To hang back would have been fatal, but to believe that this was their way of escape gave them hope and persuaded them to step inside and be saved. The spiritual application should be clear. We could reject Jesus' costly offer of new life but that would be to choose to die in the dark. Instead, as with the miners, fresh light and new life await those who decide to put their trust in him.

Bread of life

One occasion when Jesus openly pointed to the message within the miracle is recorded in all four gospels. Amazingly, he fed over 5,000 people with a small boy's picnic lunch. Jesus had just heard of the brutal execution of his cousin John the Baptist and taken the Twelve to a remote place for some peace and quiet. Instead, the huge crowd had tracked him down and as they grew hungry he set aside his own grief to attend to their need. Before the coming of fast food stalls or farmers' markets, he miraculously divided the lad's small donation of five small barley loaves and two little fishes to feed everyone, with plenty of leftovers, too. Some picnic! How amazed the boy's mother would be when she heard what had happened to his packed lunch. It is still worth remembering that, placed in Jesus' hands, our little can become much.

In John's Gospel the account of the miracle is followed by Jesus' use of it as a parable. He spoke of the true bread sent by his Father to offer life to the whole world and then claimed to be that source of spiritual nourishment himself:

'I am the bread of life. He who comes to me will never go hungry, and he who believes in me will never go thirsty...
I am the living bread that came down from heaven.
If anyone eats of this bread, he will live forever. This bread is my flesh, which I will give for the life of the world.' [4]

The Jews then, and many other people since, have made the mistake of taking this literally. Yet when Jesus referred to 'eating my flesh' (and later in the passage to 'drinking my blood') he made use of picture language to point forward to his death. It needs 'double listening' to realise that he was not suggesting cannibalism! We have no film of him in action, but can imagine him pointing to his body when he mentioned the bread being his flesh, and stretching out his arms in the pattern of a cross as he spoke of giving his life for the world. His would be the only sacrifice ever needed to forgive the sins of those who understood, repented and accepted his offer. By it Jesus brought in a new covenant with God, doing away with the old sacrifices on the annual Day of Atonement (see chapter 7), which were just shadows pointing to the reality of his perfect sacrifice. [5] His personal offering was once and for all, and by his forgiveness he restores the relationship with God that our sins have spoiled. Yet John reports that it was at this point many of his disciples found it all too hard to accept, and stopped following him. Like many today, they heard his words but did not grasp his meaning.

The bread and wine used during a communion service are not changed into literal flesh and blood, but are again pictures, or symbols, of Jesus' body broken and his blood poured out. Those who have understood this and accept his forgiveness, take this simple meal in thankful remembrance of his offering and the unity it gives with other believers worldwide. One future day he has promised to return, when the symbols will be needed no more. Meanwhile, as we look back with gratitude we also look forward with hope. [6]

Satisfied or dissatisfied?

We sometimes say, 'I'm dying for something to eat' or 'I'm longing for a drink'. It is easy to recognise our physical needs but not everyone identifies their spiritual needs, or that Jesus offers to satisfy both spiritual hunger and thirst. [7] Yet needs must be recognised and admitted to before they can be met.

Travellers on the London underground often hear an announcement saying, 'Mind the gap', as they prepare to step from the train to the platform. Many people have a God-shaped gap in their lives that is responsible for the hunger and thirst they try (and fail) to deal with by drinking too much alcohol, taking drugs, casual sex, money-making or even non-stop hard work. This can all be as dangerous to the spirit as it would be to ignore the warning voice on the train.

I recently heard someone tell how he had tried most of these distractions until, let down by false friends, he ended up in prison. There he was told of the great love of Jesus for the world, and learned that this included him. In responding to this good news, he met the Saviour who had bridged the gap separating him from God. As he accepted God's forgiveness he found the satisfaction he had been searching for all the time.

To learn more about this, let's think further about the story of Jesus.

For further thought

- Do you recognise the symptoms and signs of spiritual hunger in anyone?
- Is it possible that you still have a God-shaped gap in your own life?
- Take heart, there is hope.

References

1. Mark 4:2-20
2. Matthew 13:24-30; 36-38
3. John 3:3-8
4. John 6:35, 51
5. Hebrews 10:1-4, 10, 12
6. 1 Corinthians 11:23-29
7. John 7:37-39

Chapter 14
Execution of an innocent man, and what followed

n recent years parts of the British press have almost seemed to delight in trying to bring down certain important people whose secrets they have discovered and decided to make public. Finally the ceaseless gossip destroys their victims, sometimes after years of useful service. Others, including a few doctors, are found to have committed really serious offences and have to pay the appropriate penalty.

Jesus had no guilty secrets. The baptism of repentance received at the hands of his cousin John the Baptist had not been for sins of his own, for he had none. Instead he was showing his willingness to identify with sinful human beings. After the baptism, he went about preaching, teaching and performing amazing miracles, particularly acts of healing. He had so much more authority and ability than the usual religious leaders that everyone marvelled at him. For one memorable day crowds of people publicly shouted his praises as he rode into Jerusalem on a young donkey. Despite such a humble mode of transport, the people were quite ready to claim him as King of Israel. [1] Then the atmosphere changed completely.

Hostility grows

The day after this remarkable entry into Jerusalem, Jesus went back to visit the temple. There he found moneychangers who were making a quick profit in the house of his Father, God. He drove them out with some force, saying that the 'house of prayer' had been turned into 'a den of robbers'. This statement was sure to upset the religious leaders who had allowed this to go on but now felt threatened by this carpenter's son who said God was his Father. Their pride could neither admit to the truth of his words nor think of making changes. Instead they began to work out how to silence him. Their first move was to stir up the people to reject him, [2] and Jesus knew that it would not be long before he was arrested.

In John 13-17, we read how the Twelve had gathered to celebrate what would be Jesus' last Passover feast with them, to which he gave new meaning. He was going to bring in a new covenant, foreshadowed by the old one. But first he must undergo the sacrificial offering once made by spotless Passover lambs. After he had done that, there would be no more need for such rituals. Peter would later write about 'the precious blood of Christ, a lamb without blemish or defect,' through which the gap between God and mankind had been closed. [3]

After the meal Jesus sent one of them on his way, knowing that this man, Judas, was planning his betrayal. There was a final teaching session with the remaining eleven and a walk to the Garden of Gethsemane where Jesus withdrew to pray. Although he had asked his three closest friends to watch with him it was now late. They had eaten well and instead they fell asleep. He was in agony of spirit, knowing what lay ahead, yet he was able to willingly submit to the plan he and his Father had laid out long before. [4] Someone must have woken up enough to overhear at least part of his prayer to give us the words, 'Not my will, but yours be done'. This acceptance of his Father's will and purpose has inspired many sufferers since to trust the outcome to God.

Soon a violent crowd descended on them and bound Jesus, who from then on was handed from place to place. Earlier he had shown such power and authority that to allow this must have been a conscious choice on his part. First he was taken before the religious court to face largely false accusations. Jewish leaders could not order execution themselves but, furious at Jesus' persistent claim to be the Christ, Son of God (as well as Son of Man) they applied to Pilate to use his Roman authority to pass the death sentence. [5]

Jesus had confirmed his claim to be the Christ when challenged about it by the high priest – something mentioned by all four Gospel writers. A lesser man might have taken it back or denied it, rather than signing his own death warrant in this way. Yet he had known for a long time that the priests and lawyers intended to kill him, unaware that this was what he had been prepared for from the beginning. Even so, they would be included in the offer of forgiveness that his self-sacrifice would bring.

A claim to be Messiah was not itself blasphemous but what had made the religious court even angrier was Jesus' confidence that he would finally go to sit at God's right hand, something carefully recorded by Matthew, Mark and Luke. To his accusers this claimed equality with God, as did calling God his Father. In their eyes both statements were truly blasphemous. Roman law did not recognise blasphemy as an offence; neither Pilate the Roman governor nor Herod, with whom Pilate consulted, could find any fault in Jesus. Certainly they found nothing deserving the death penalty. [6] Yet the people, many of whom had so recently been ready to welcome him as Messiah, were now stirred up to shout, 'Crucify him,' and as Luke later reported, 'their shouts prevailed.' The terrible sentence was passed. [7]

Christ crucified

The agonies of crucifixion would have been bad enough were they limited to the most intense physical and emotional suffering. But Jesus, whose purity had never been spoiled by sin, was to be loaded with all the sins of the world, paying its penalty on behalf of us all. This was what he had dreaded most, for God cannot bear to look on sin; at his time of greatest need, Jesus was about to feel deserted by his Father. Darkness would cover the whole land as his spiritual suffering drew from him the anguished cry, `My God, my God,' (not this time 'my Father') 'why have you forsaken me?' [8] Never before had they for one moment been separated in spirit. We need to realise that when we speak of 'the sins of the world', it means all wrongs ever done by mankind from the beginning until now – including our own.

In those dark hours, was part of Jesus' suffering a kind of horror movie? Were the wickedness and woes of the world – past, present and future – paraded before his inner eye? Was his spirit bowed down when confronted by the death and damage of war, the cruel torture inflicted by one human being on another, the abuse of little children, the neglect of the poor by the rich, or other miseries forced on many lives. Right up to today, increasingly evil imaginations have planned even more unspeakable things. Did he have a preview of all this? We cannot imagine how his soul was revolted, or how even so he took upon himself the full penalty for all those acts of wickedness as though he had done them himself. Beside all that, he was burdened with the less colourful sins of pride and arrogance, even among those with a reputation for being religious, and other secret sins still offensive to his pure soul. Yet to bear all this was the agreement he and his Father had made before creation, because although they hated the sins they still loved the sinners. Undeserving as we all are, repentant sinners can be forgiven and past records wiped out as an act of sheer grace.

Many people in the world are truly ignorant of the saving grace of God the Father and Jesus Christ his Son but even supposedly clever people, past and present, have deliberately turned their back. Some choose other gods and philosophies, thereby adding the extra pain of rejection to his suffering. Isaiah tells us that Jesus bore our sicknesses and sorrows, the grief of centuries. [9] The full cost of the crucifixion remains a dreadful and awesome mystery, while others have thought long and hard about the life and liberty it can mean to us.

Jesus had withstood the tempter after his baptism, when he (falsely) offered to give him the kingdoms of the world in exchange for one act of devil worship. Having resisted him then, perhaps on the cross he was given a glimpse of the world as it would become if generation after generation gave in to Satan's continued efforts to destroy the intended image of God in them. As he suffered the terrible burden of the sins of others, he would know with full force the desperate need of the world for a ransom, a Saviour. In his manifesto, Jesus had offered freedom to the captives and this great act of self-giving would do just that. He provided a way back to God for everyone held captive by the devil, the enemy of souls. No doubt the same enemy had hoped to use the crucifixion as a final attempt to destroy Jesus and defeat God's work through him. The attempt gloriously failed.

Even in the midst of the agony and horror, Jesus evidently kept speaking to his Father and going back to his word as a source of strength. The gospels record seven 'words' Jesus spoke from the cross. The first was a prayer for his Father to forgive those who were executing him (such love!). [10] Two were words of comfort, first for a repentant thief dying on the cross next to his and then for his grieving mother as she watched her son die. [11, 12] Two were quotations from Psalm 22 and two more came as he died, declaring his work of atonement finished. [13, 14] At the end, in a loud voice (not just a feeble gasp) he again named his Father as he committed his spirit into his hands. [15] The ordeal was over, the victory won and their relationship restored.

The ransom paid and hostages freed

Today we hear increasingly about people being taken hostage. A costly ransom is often demanded by their captors before hostages can be freed and until this is handed over the captives' lives are at risk. We can imagine their helpless fear and dread, not knowing what hope they have of release and a safe return home. During a hostage crisis someone often goes as a mediator, hoping to settle the dispute and free the captives. Sometimes someone is killed in an attempted rescue and whether or not the ransom is paid, it is altogether a stressful and costly exercise. Jesus knew the danger of spiritual death for those held captive by sin and he acted as the only acceptable mediator.

He once said that he had come to earth to give his life as the ransom needed to save them, and Paul says the same thing in a letter to Timothy:

> '...God our Saviour ... wants all people to be saved and to come
> to a knowledge of the truth. For there is one God and one
> mediator between God and mankind, the man Christ Jesus,
> who gave himself as a ransom for all people.' [16]

In this way, Jesus still longs to bring back those who are far off from him to enjoy a restored and secure relationship with God. [17] When he yielded up his spirit to his Father, the ransom price had been paid in full and sinners could be set free of their guilty burden. Luke reports how, as a sign of his mediation being accepted, the huge curtain in the temple was ripped apart from top to bottom. Until that moment, only the high priest could go into the Most Holy Place beyond the curtain to make the annual offerings to atone for sin. Now the barrier was down, once and for all, giving free access into God's presence for all who trust and accept Jesus' costly offer of forgiveness and a new life.

If we agree to this wonderful exchange (and what hostage would refuse to be freed?) we have a share in the new covenant that now replaces the old one we considered in chapter 8. [18] By this new agreement, as we confess our personal share in the sins of the world and repent of them, we are offered forgiveness and freedom. We are brought near to the Father again, gradually to regain the lost image of God we were designed for. Surely, our hearts should be full of gratitude and love for the unmerited favour of his grace.

A sorrowful interval

Despite all that he had taught them, this full meaning of Jesus' death had not yet dawned on his disciples. Jesus' body was sealed in a tomb and an armed guard set over it. There was no mistaking that he was dead, and with him the bright hopes of his followers died, too. They had forgotten some of the very important things he had said in his lifetime:

> 'For God so loved the world that he gave his one and only Son, that whoever believes in him shall not perish but have eternal life. For God did not send his Son into the world to condemn the world, but to save the world through him.' [19]

> 'The Son of Man did not come to be served, but to serve, and to give his life as a ransom for many.' [20]

> 'The Son of Man will be delivered over to the chief priests and teachers of the law. They will condemn him to death and will hand him over to the Gentiles, who will mock him and spit on him, flog him and kill him. Three days later he will rise.' [21]

Jesus had clearly known why he had come and what the outcome would be. Matthew, Luke and Mark quote that last statement about his resurrection, given to the Twelve, but forgotten about in their sorrow. Instead, they dwelt on their friend's cruel humiliation, his agonies and final death. They mourned the loss, forgetting that he had spoken of both ransom and resurrection. Perhaps they were still ashamed of their desertion when he was arrested. Peter would feel worst of all. After boldly telling Jesus that he was ready to die for him he had, out of fear, three times denied being part of his company. [22, 23]

The next day was the most miserable day of their lives for Jesus' disciples. They must have kept going over the dreadful events, burning them into their memories as they kept close together behind locked doors. They even forgot how, at his last tutorial with them, Jesus had promised that after he left them his Spirit would come with counsel and comfort, helping them to remember his teaching. [24] This would happen later, ensuring that the Gospel writers gave us a clear and honest record of all the events they so clearly remembered. But for now they had lost hope and felt that life had lost its purpose.

Many people today must feel just like that, some of them after an episode of mob violence and death threats such as happened in the Garden of Gethsemane. Today's victims can know what it is to have had a dear friend killed, or homes and families destroyed. Others experience different kinds of lost hope and often feel so depressed that they don't know what to do or where to go. Yet our Lord Jesus Christ is still able to heal hurting people. The rest of his story has given new hope to many, for it shows how, with God, all things that seemed impossible are possible after all. [25] A miracle was about to happen that would have a worldwide impact, then and for evermore.

For further thought

- Jesus had held such authority, so why did he permit the verdict to go against him?
- Have you ever before thought through what Jesus' crucifixion could mean for you?
- Have you ever lost hope and then been surprised by joy?

Further resources

- Jessup G. *Passover*. London: Olive Press, 1980
- McGrath A. *Making sense of the Cross*. Leicester: Inter-Varsity Press, 1994
- Stott J. *The Cross of Christ (20th anniversary edition)*. Leicester: Inter-VarsityPress, 2006

References

1. John 12:12-15
2. Mark 11:15-18
3. 1 Peter 1:18-21
4. Luke 22:41-44
5. Matthew 26:63-66; 27:1-2
6. Luke 23:13-16
7. Luke 23:20-25
8. Mark 15:33-34
9. Isaiah 53:4
10. 'Father, forgive them, for they do not know what they are doing.' (Luke 23:33-34)
11. 'I tell you the truth, today you will be with me in paradise.' (Luke 23:39-43)
12. 'Dear woman, here is your son,' and to the disciple, 'Here is your mother.' (John 19:25-27)
13. 'My God, my God, why have you forsaken me?' (Matthew 27:45-46), 'I am thirsty.' (John 19:28-29)
14. 'It is finished.' (John 19:30)
15. 'Father, into your hands I commit my spirit.' (Luke 23:45-46)
16. 1 Timothy 2:4-5
17. Ephesians 2:13, 17-22
18. Hebrews 9:15, 24-26
19. John 3:16-17
20. Matthew 20:28
21. Mark 10:33-34
22. John 13:37-38
23. John 18:15-18, 25-27
24. John 14:16-18, 26
25. Luke 18:27

Chapter 15
He's alive!

A good friend of mine, a surgeon, was well-known internationally and served on many committees, at home and overseas. He made valuable contributions to the education of students and graduates, being especially concerned that Christian doctors should have a good understanding of medical ethics. Then he died, quite suddenly, and we were all very shocked. A few months later I had a dream in which a company of Christian professionals were sitting round a committee table when the rest of us noticed that this respected colleague had joined us.

'But he's supposed to be dead', we said to each other, surprised and bewildered. He looked much the same as when we had last seen him, attentive and thoughtful. We were also curious about how he had found things in heaven. So my neighbour nudged me to ask him. After telling us about the lovely music he had heard there, we next dared to ask what the Lord was like, at which point our friend disappeared and I realised that it had just been a dream. Yet I knew that there could be no words to describe the glory of the risen Christ, now seated at the right hand of God. [1]

He lives forever!

One of the first hymns I learned by heart and loved to sing as a child started solemnly and quietly with, 'Low in the grave he lay, Jesus my Saviour'. It then cheered up, getting faster and louder with the joyful chorus, 'Up from the grave he arose, with a mighty triumph o'er his foes … and he lives forever...' It ends with a triumphant cry of, 'Hallelujah! Christ arose.' That hymn was written in the 19th century, inspired by the way the first century disciples had discovered its truth. The gloom following Good Friday was dispelled early on Sunday morning as the women who went to the tomb found its entrance no longer sealed. Inside were grave clothes, but no sign of a body. Mary Magdalene was the first to meet the risen Lord Jesus in the garden.

Then the women hurried to tell the good news to the disciples – and were not believed! Instead, Peter and John ran to see for themselves. As the women had said, they found that Jesus' body had gone. Only the empty grave clothes were left behind, neatly wrapped and laid aside.

Ten of the disciples were finally convinced of the amazing truth that he was alive again, when the risen Lord paid them a personal visit and they were overcome with joy. The eleventh man, Thomas, missed this event and questioned the story – until Jesus came to him in person, when he at once worshipped him as Lord and God. [2] Many other doubters since have followed his lead.

In Jerusalem there is still a garden tomb, open to visitors and set in a lovely garden, as was Jesus' original burial site. It does not matter whether or not it is the exact place of his grave. It does however convey what it must have been like. The burial chamber is rather like a cave. Outside is a heavy round stone, like a millstone, that would roll across the entrance and completely seal it. Part of an inside wall forms a shelf, long and wide enough to hold a body. One Easter morning a party of us visited the garden and found a closed door across the entrance to the tomb. On it was a simple notice saying, 'He is not here: He is risen'. Every time believers celebrate the joy of Easter day, they are reminded how impossible it was for death to keep its hold on Jesus. His Father had seen to that. [3]

Doubts dispelled

For many, the story of the first Easter weekend will already be very familiar. Others are perhaps a bit foggy about the details and a few more may find it completely new. For all of us, it can be hard to imagine even a fraction of the amazed wonder of the disciples as their Lord appeared among them again. Perhaps they, too, at first thought that they were dreaming, but this was no dream. Dead men don't walk. But Jesus walked, talked, made a lakeside barbecue and ate with his disciples, very much alive. He stayed around for weeks. Over 500 people saw him besides the Eleven. [4] During those weeks he came and went in a bodily form that was the same and yet not the same. The scars of crucifixion were still visible, but the risen Lord could now overcome solid and spatial barriers as he visited his old friends. John's Gospel tells us how he spent time with Peter and healed the painful embarrassment he must have felt after those three denials. [5]

There are slight variations in the details given in the four Gospel accounts, but the events were so amazing and the witnesses so different, that this should not hinder belief. Indeed, it would give more cause for suspicion if all the accounts were exactly the same.

Resurrection or resuscitation?

Even though there are still people who say that Jesus was resuscitated, not resurrected, the final thrust of a soldier's spear to his heart had been to make quite sure he was dead. Even without this, a flogged and crucified man would not have survived for three days, loaded with spices and without water. Resurrection differs from resuscitation.

One day during a busy outpatient clinic in Uganda, a junior doctor came to me with distressing news. He said, 'You remember that boy with croup? We put up a drip, but he has died. We have not yet told his father.'

'Croup', or laryngotracheitis, usually affects little children with small airways, easily obstructed by swollen mucus when infected, so it is potentially lethal. Yet the patient was too big for that to have been likely, so I immediately went to look at him. Sure enough, there he lay, quite still on the couch with a sheet over his face and no signs of life. Partly to show the juniors the practice of resuscitation, we cleared his airway, performed cardiac massage and gave artificial respiration. Fairly soon, to our delight he gasped, coughed up a plug of mucus and later sat up and asked for a drink. He had been successfully *resuscitated* but not truly *resurrected*.

Luke reports what must have been one of the Lord's very early appearances after his resurrection. [6] Mary 'the wife of Clopas', had been among the women standing near the foot of the cross and seen Jesus die. [7] Cleopas is probably the same name and it was as a couple that the two were walking home from Jerusalem, very much cast down by disappointed hope and grief. Mrs Cleopas, for one, had seen the terrible trauma of crucifixion and had no doubt that Jesus was dead. When joined by another traveller they did not know who he was. I recently failed to recognise a young man known to me since he was a toddler, but I, too, saw him in unexpected circumstances. I can understand how the couple might naturally have thought that their walking companion was a stranger, not someone known to have died. It was seven miles to Emmaus. Luke tells us that on the journey Jesus had been spelling out to them the Old Testament prophecies concerning the Messiah.

His life and death had been foretold in so many prophecies. For example, he fulfilled the role of the suffering servant foretold by Isaiah. [8] What a wonderful Bible study that must have been! It had warmed their hearts. As it was getting dark when they reached home, they invited him in. The true identity of the stranger only dawned on the couple when he broke bread at their table. Then he left them. Amazed and delighted they went all the way back to Jerusalem to rejoice with the other disciples at such great news.

Over the next few weeks the risen Lord Jesus would doubtless teach the disciples more about why he had died and the meaning of his resurrection. His cousin John the Baptist had first introduced Jesus to others as 'the Lamb of God, who takes away the sin of the world'. [9] Jesus was the perfect and final Passover lamb, who, unlike the sacrificed lambs, willingly chose to shed his blood in order to save others. In saying to the Father, 'Here I am, I have come to do your will,' [10] he committed himself to the greatest self-offering of love ever known. In the previous chapter we saw how, through his death and resurrection, Jesus brought in a new covenant, or agreement, between God and mankind. The old sacrifices are no longer needed, because by accepting his loving payment of the ransom, repentant sinners can be freed, full of grateful love for him.

Justified

Writing to the Romans, Paul said that when God raised Christ from the dead, this completed the possibility of justification. One common way of understanding this word is that it makes me 'just as if I'd never sinned.' This is true, but wonderfully, there is more. Our sin is not just dealt with and the slate wiped clean, leaving us in a 'neutral' state before God; we are also declared to be *positively* righteous in God's sight. In legal terms, the judge of a court justifies people when he dismisses the charges against them, and declares them to be in right standing in the eyes of the law. So we are not only 'just as if I'd never sinned', but also 'just as if I'd kept the law perfectly'.

Our justification is possible because Jesus, the perfectly righteous one, paid the death penalty for sin in our place. On the cross, he took all our sin and the punishment we deserved. In return we are given the gift of all his righteousness and life. The apostle Paul describes it as 'not having a righteousness of my own that comes from the law, but that which is through faith in Christ – the righteousness that comes from God on the basis of faith'. [11] When we repent and confess our sins, trusting his promise to wipe them out completely, the penalty we deserved is lifted and no record is kept. We are free to make a fresh start. The broken relationship with God is restored and peace with him renewed, through our Lord Jesus Christ. [12] God says, 'I will remember their sins no more.' [13] On the cross our sin was condemned, so that 'the righteous requirement of the law might be fully met in us'. [14] This means that Jesus' righteousness is counted as our own and our sin is counted as his, so that in Christ 'there is now no condemnation'. [15]

Let's illustrate this with a modern parable. Those who use computers will know that to speak of 'justification' means to arrange a section of text so the edges are straight. We can send old documents, either temporarily or permanently, into a 'recycling bin', available for review or final deletion. When I first started to use a computer, I did not always understand the handbook and often had to ask Steve-next-door to come and help me. Steve was the expert who had found this particular model for me in the first place and always seemed happy to come to my aid, refusing more reward than my gratitude.
Then he and his lovely family moved away.

Now imagine that, instead of another Steve, the designer himself has given you a wonderful new computer and you start to type an important message on it. At first you can neither write nor spell properly and despite warning messages the whole script ends up off-centre, full of mistakes and unfit for purpose. Then suppose the maker himself comes along, and you shame-facedly confess to having made such a mess. He offers to clear the screen and completely empty out the recycling bin. Past errors are deleted never to be seen again. He then rewrites your work, using all his skill so that you end up with a perfectly formatted document with no errors. The work is all his, but it has your name at the top of the page. And this remarkable maker promises to stay on hand to explain the handbook and give you personal tuition and guidance in future, all with no charge to you. What a relief! Think how you would try to please him by making good progress.

For the messy script, we may think of the life created and entrusted to each of us by God. Trying to live without reference to our Maker is to head for trouble. We need more than our own ideas, or those of other people, if we are not to end up with a sub-standard result. Sadly, far too many of us like to go it alone and continue to live uncontrolled and unsatisfied lives, some more obviously messier than others. Yet through the death and resurrection of God's Son Jesus Christ, the 'screen' is cleared and a perfect document is credited to us. By trusting and accepting his offer of forgiveness and his gift of a righteous status, our past errors (and deliberate sins) are erased. We are justified, or declared to be in line with God's standards, our Maker's instructions, as found in his handbook, the Bible.

Because we cannot fully grasp or keep these new standards on our own, we need someone to come to our aid. Jesus promised that when we believe and trust in him, his Spirit comes in, ready to help and to teach without ever moving away. [16] The Spirit will highlight and explain sections of the Bible that we especially need to apply to our lives. This is not an automatic process, made possible by pressing some heavenly computer key. It is an act of God's love and grace. He asks only for our response. It is not realistic to think we'll never make any more mistakes but to confess them is to find fresh forgiveness. [17] We can learn from our past wrongdoings but we are not to be weighed down with guilt. The recycling bin is empty, 'remembered no more'.

Some who want to learn more about computing skills join up with a class of other interested people. The true church is not a building but a body – the company of all who believe in the resurrected Jesus and own him as their Lord. [18] When we join this company we find a new worldwide family, some wiser in age and experience who would be ready to advise and pray for us. Why struggle on alone? Jesus said, 'So if the Son sets you free, you will be free indeed.' [19] The screen has been cleared, freeing us from the burden of trying to sort it out and we are ready for a new start. The only response needed is to give ourselves back to him in repentance and gratitude for such a priceless and never ending gift.

For further thought

- Have you now got a better idea of why Jesus came and why he died?
- Do you see how important it was that God raised him from the dead?
- Have you believed, said a heartfelt 'Sorry' for the mess, and thanked him for his love in cleaning it all away?

Further resources

- Yancey P. *The Bible Jesus read: Why the Old Testament matters.* Grand Rapids, Michigan: Zondervan, 2002.
- Wright NT. *Justification.* London: SPCK, 2009

References

1. Mark 16:19
2. John 20:24-28
3. Acts 2:24
4. 1 Corinthians 15:6
5. John 21:15-17
6. Luke 24:13-35
7. John 19:25
8. Isaiah 53:3-12
9. John 1:29
10. Hebrews 10:7
11. Philippians 3:9
12. Romans 4:24- 5:2
13. Hebrews 8:12
14. Romans 8:3-4
15. Romans 8:1
16. John 14:16, 26
17. 1 John 1:7-10
18. Romans 10:9, 13
19. John 8:36

Chapter 16
I still have my doubts

For many, the story so far might have been new, unbelievable, or possibly not thought about very deeply before. Some offer reasons for thinking differently, so let's take a closer look at these reasons and how they may be countered.

'I don't believe in God anyway.' This is an increasingly common statement in the West, although not all who profess atheism are as confident as they sound. Their beliefs are often poorly thought through, being influenced by a few authors who hit the headlines. Too many of those who dismiss the Bible's teaching have not always read it properly, offering very poor reasons for their disbelief in a Bible they have never studied.

'I'm not religious.' In the western world this is a very common excuse for thinking no further about things spiritual. In some other cultures, religion can be such a part of the national identity that to change it can even be seen as treason. Yet in the most materialistic cultures, people are still religious even if they don't realise it. The god that is worshipped can be a status symbol. Not far from me lived a man who, every Sunday morning, washed and polished his beautiful car and then sat in it to gaze at his equally beautiful house. Jesus offers a special relationship, not just a form of worship.

'I'm too busy to think about that sort of thing.' It is possible to make such a god of a profession or career that even the needs of the family are neglected and the possibility of an interested God ignored. Doctors, politicians, journalists or clergy can easily let unending work take over their lives, while others simply struggle to survive. It has probably not dawned on many of them that God is a God of love who longs to help them to know his presence and provision.

'I've got where I am by my own efforts and nobody tells me what to do.' People whose god is 'me, me, me' can be strong-minded bosses or

bullies who enjoy being feared. Some powerful people can be proud of what they see as self-made success, without ever thinking that personality and drive may be God's gifts to them.

'*I do the best I can.*' (Even if I don't always practise 'the best'). The results of any wrongdoing, especially if found out, are called mistakes (often those of other people) or just plain bad luck. It can be a game to break the rules and it never registers that there are God-given standards. These people rarely say, 'Sorry, my fault'.

'*We can clean up any mistakes by ourselves.*' This idea is as foolish as though a patient with advanced renal failure had the offer of a perfectly matching kidney but says, 'No thanks, I'm managing quite well on my own.' Similarly, the deadly disease of sin can never be cured by our own efforts. Our Saviour's costly gift of himself wipes out our sins as we repent and ask his forgiveness. As we confess, he forgives. [1]

'*I have different beliefs.*' Atheism and non-Christian religions give no satisfactory answer to the question of guilt. Wrongdoings cannot be cancelled out by doing good works, or paying money to a priest. Some expect failure to result in rebirth as a lower life form. Yet whatever the philosophy, sins will pile up without being washed away.

'*All we need is love.*' I recently met a young woman who claimed this as her belief. Of course, we do all need love, but not just as a sentimental feeling. Love needs a lover and a beloved, best expressed through a sometimes costly relationship. Thus: God (the lover) so loved the world (the beloved) that he gave his one and only Son (the cost). [2] Jesus taught the importance of love for God and neighbour as the two most important rules for life. [3] The love he spoke of and demonstrated was wholly self-giving, not the self-centred or self-seeking kind we often hear of in popular love songs.

'*I'm confused by the way Christians disagree.*' Not everyone who ticks the box 'Christian' as their religion understands what that really means. Different branches of the Christian church vary in tradition and practice, sometimes painfully. A Bible-believing Christian church will teach that Jesus' death was a voluntary sacrifice to pay the price of sin on our behalf. To accept his forgiveness renews a loving relationship with God and, Jesus hoped, unity with other believers. [4] Sadly this is not always so.

Jesus was heard to say that he chose to lay down his life [5] and would die to pay the ransom price for sinners to be forgiven. [6] Yet there are some who claim to be Christians who say that to think in that way is to turn his sacrifice into a cruel act of a vengeful God. Never! It was an act of loving grace shared by Father and Son, who through it offer their shared free gift of forgiveness. [7] Others see Jesus simply as an example we should copy, but our tendency to sin will always stop us being like him on our own. We are assured that forgiven sinners are given the gift of his Holy Spirit to help and to guide them. [8]

'*I can't believe in the resurrection.*' This was such an amazing event that I sympathise with those of a scientific or sceptical outlook who find it difficult to believe something so unique and unlikely. For them, death is only reversible by resuscitation, not resurrection. However, we must not make liars of so many eyewitnesses. Some of them wrote their reports only a few years after the event and many of them were ready to die rather than to deny their story. The clear evidence of Jesus' risen presence in their completely transformed lives was not based on deceit.

For weeks after the discovery of Jesus' empty tomb, a chosen few spent time with him, walking, talking and eating together. During those weeks hundreds more saw him. Finally, a man named Saul had a vision of Jesus that knocked him sideways. [9] His story will be told in our next chapter. Ever afterwards he held an unshakeable belief in Jesus' resurrection and discusses this fully in 1 Corinthians 15 – a chapter to be studied by believers and unbelievers alike, for our faith stands or falls on the fact of Jesus' resurrection.

Years ago, a law graduate called Frank Morison set out to disprove the resurrection of Christ. But as he applied his well-trained powers of deduction to the biblical and contemporary records he became convinced that this unique event had really happened.

'I've been impressed by a friend who believes, but am not sure it's for me.' From the beginning, the most important evidence for the truth that Christ is alive, acting through his Spirit, is that of changed and unashamedly dedicated lives.

The final leap of faith often comes through seeing how believers cope with stress, disappointment or loss, or their readiness to explain and hold to their beliefs despite being teased or experiencing much stronger opposition.

'I've tried it before and it didn't work.' When people refer to a new baby as 'it', they give away that they do not really know the little boy or girl, who is a 'he' or 'she', not an 'it'! Similarly, when speaking of faith as 'it', people often mean religious observance alone, such as going to church or saying their prayers. True faith involves learning to know God – a matter of the heart and will, not just the head, and not only the repetition of a creed, but a real commitment. God knows us by name and loves every one of us, offering us a living relationship, not just a formal religion. Like all relationships, this one needs to be taken care of in order to grow and survive, but God will hold on to us more firmly than we can ever hold on to him. [10]

'I've still got other questions.' Perhaps by now some readers will want to know more and be ready to ask a believing friend, or find and read a Bible for themselves. How is it that Jesus of Nazareth came to be regarded as such a significant historical figure and why does his teaching still apply today? To discover more about him will answer some questions and make others seem less important.

We'll therefore turn next to two more expert witnesses who were convinced that Jesus' claims were true. Although they had not known the earthly Jesus, they had known of those ready to die because they had put their trust in him. Even today, there are many like the first martyr Stephen, who go to their death with a shining face. Like him, they are confident that they are passing from death into new life with their Lord, Jesus Christ. [11] Surely, that is a hope worth sharing – so read on!

For further thought

- Are you inclined to be proud of 'doing it my way'? Does that work? Honestly?
- Remember that so-called reasons for not believing can just be excuses.

Further resources

- Carswell R. *Grill a Christian*. Leyland: 10Publishing, 2013
- Stott J. *Basic Christianity (2nd ed)*. Leicester: Inter-Varsity Press, 1971
- Morison F. *Who moved the stone?* London: Faber and Faber, 2007

References

1. 1 John 1:9
2. John 3:16
3. Matthew 22:36-40
4. John 17:20-21
5. John 10:11, 15, 18
6. Matthew 20:28
7. 2 Corinthians 5:17-19
8. Romans 8:9-11
9. 1 Timothy 1:12-14
10. John 10:29-30
11. Acts 7:55-56, 59

Chapter 17
More expert witnesses

I n a complicated trial, especially when witnesses disagree or there is reason not to believe them, it is common for one or more expert witnesses to be called in. Many senior doctors have had this experience. Their evidence is made more acceptable if they have conducted relevant research with convincing results, and best of all for their evidence to add to that of others. The biblical record is not without its own research workers and it is now time to hear evidence from one of them. Dr Luke, author of the third Gospel, was especially interested in historical research. He was probably Greek and would be familiar with debate and discussion. As a doctor he was well-trained in thinking about a differential diagnosis.

A trained research worker

It seems that Luke never met Jesus personally, but we know of his careful research about him from the introductions to his Gospel and his second book, *The Acts of the Apostles* (more commonly known simply as *Acts*). He addressed both books to his friend Theophilus, with the assurance that he was reporting reliable eye-witness accounts. [1,2] We meet up with Luke in person from Acts chapter 16 onwards, where his use of the word 'we' instead of 'they', suggests the point at which he joined others who were travelling with that great missionary, Paul, during his second long journey. Luke evidently observed and recorded events as they journeyed on together, writing up Paul's activities and teaching in many different cities.

In his medical practice, Luke had probably encountered a wide cross-section of society. For his times, as is reflected in his choice of reports, he was unusually sensitive towards the needs of women, the poor, and outcasts of various kinds. It is thought that parts of Luke's Gospel story had been reported to him by Mary, who was best placed to give him details of her own miraculous pregnancy and that of her elderly cousin, Elizabeth (mother of John the Baptist). Only mentioned in

Luke's Gospel are some of the remarkable events that happened before and after each little boy's birth, possibly also told to him by Mary. At the other end of Jesus' life, she would report how the dying Jesus had asked his beloved disciple, John, to take care of her, which he did in his own home. No doubt John then told her more about what he had witnessed during her son's life of caring and teaching. Heart-sore at the crucifixion, Mary was one of the women who first told of the resurrection.

Luke often spoke of the adult Jesus' prayer life. In Luke 11 he records 'the Lord's prayer'; a prayer addressed to the Father, taught by Jesus to his disciples then and still in regular use today. As a Greek, Luke was careful to mention the inclusion of Gentiles as well as Jews in God's plan for humanity, to be underlined during his travels with Paul. Probably converted in adult life, Luke had no doubts about the truth of the good news he had researched and was now reporting.

The book of Acts starts by repeating Luke's credentials. It then goes on to unfold the history of the early church. Pentecost is still rightly celebrated as the church's birthday, for that was when the Holy Spirit came upon the gathered company of disciples in ways that we shall think more about in chapter 19. They were transformed from being a group of deserters to enthusiastic broadcasters of the truth about the life and death, resurrection and ascension of their Lord and Saviour, Jesus Christ and demonstrating his continuing work in them through his Spirit.

A very surprising witness

Luke eventually became physician to *Paul*, (formerly Saul) a great traveller, preacher and writer who inspired and encouraged a lively faith in Jesus wherever he went, but also aroused much opposition. His surviving letters make up almost half of the books of the New Testament. Both Luke and Paul serve as expert witnesses for the defence when dealing with challenges about the truth of the gospel. Their motive, though, was not so much to defend the gospel as to present it as life-changing good news.

Paul was a surprising witness because his story began when, named Saul after the first Hebrew king, he was a great enemy of new Christians, known as the 'followers of the Way'. He was a brilliant man, much respected as an academic expert in Old Testament law and well-known as unable to tolerate the teaching of the young church. Saul had been brought up to believe that the Old Testament sacrifices were still necessary and that the Messiah had not yet come. However, the new Christians believed that by such a costly offering of himself, Jesus had once and for all cancelled out the need for all other sacrifices and that he was, in fact, the Messiah, whom God had raised from the dead. All this was too much for sceptical Saul. He set out to destroy all the believers he could find, 'being extremely zealous' to guard the old Jewish traditions. [3]

Yet once personally convinced of the truth of the resurrection and the Lordship of Jesus, Saul's well-informed background gave such valuable insight to missionary Paul. He could apply his knowledge of the ancient prophecies about a future Messiah to the ways in which Christ's life, death, resurrection and ascension fulfilled them. Despite his best efforts, just as they had rejected Jesus, his fellow Jews rarely accepted this teaching and several times nearly killed him. In the end he would turn away from them to teach the Gentiles. [4] His story is full of drama.

About turn!

Saul's conversion had been dramatic. He had stood and watched as Stephen, the first Christian martyr, was stoned to death. His inflamed bloodlust then drove him to hunt down believers in Damascus, but on the way he was given a sudden and astonishing personal revelation of the risen and ascended Jesus. He realised that the Lord was speaking to him, asking why Saul was persecuting him and striking Saul temporarily blind. [5] This 'Damascus Road' experience turned Saul right around to become as eager a Christian believer as he had been an opponent. This term is still applied to someone who undergoes a complete change of mind after sudden illumination.

Although this amazing encounter was never to be repeated, Paul first made friends with those he had tried to hunt down and spent a couple of weeks getting to know Peter. [6] It was an act of new humility for the distinguished academic to learn from the old fisherman about Jesus' earthly life and work, his death, resurrection and ascension and his final gift of the Holy Spirit.

We can only imagine the shock to the persecuted church to learn that their chief enemy had now become a believer. Saul's change of loyalty would be as shocking for those early believers as it would be for voters today to find that an enthusiastic party leader had suddenly changed sides, say from Democrat to Republican, and then taken a few tutorials from someone in the former opposition.

From that time on, Saul became better known as Paul, a name more acceptable to Greeks. The pleasure he had previously found in travelling the country to hunt down scattered believers was channelled into adventurous journeys on a very different mission. This demonstrates how God often makes use of natural interests and personalities when they are given over to him. Paul's restlessness and drive were redirected into church planting throughout Asia Minor and parts of Europe. Many of his letters were written to teach and encourage those young churches. When rejected by the Jews, Paul took his message to the Gentiles. After three missionary journeys, his plans to go further westwards were eventually stopped by death threats from the Jewish leaders. At first, for his own safety, he was kept under Roman protection, but later he spent many long years as a prisoner in Rome, with the faithful Dr Luke in attendance. [7] He used much of this enforced confinement for thinking and writing before, according to tradition, he was finally executed for his faith.

Paul's letters

Many of Paul's letters were written during his years of imprisonment, again showing how something good can come out of what had at first seemed so bad. When free to travel he would never have found time to write down his teaching. The letters he sent to the scattered young churches and their leaders contain teaching we can now share, both as challenge and encouragement. As a well-trained Jewish academic, he could apply his detailed knowledge of the Old Testament to explain the meaning of Jesus' death and resurrection to many who had perhaps never made the connection before. He had been specially chosen for that job.

The letter Paul wrote to the Christians in Rome is the longest of his surviving epistles. When he wrote it, he had not visited Rome, though he longed to do so – a hope to be fulfilled only as a prisoner. The Christians in Rome were a mix of Jewish and Gentile believers, some of whom had probably arrived when the early church in Jerusalem met with persecution and was widely scattered, a time known as the *diaspora* (dispersion). Unconverted Jews would still observe the Old Testament law, perhaps expecting Jewish believers to do the same. Roman Gentiles would be expected to be completely loyal to Caesar, the emperor, and to support temples for the worship of Roman gods. Many in the city were openly immoral, so among these many ideas there was much to confuse the young believers living there. They urgently needed Paul's clear teaching.

By giving Jesus the title 'Christ', meaning Messiah, Paul reminded Jewish believers that this is exactly who he was. For others, well aware that Caesar was lording it over his people, to say 'Jesus is Lord', with belief in his resurrection, would be unpopular, if not treasonable. Yet it was by acknowledging Jesus as Lord that both Jews and Gentiles alike would be saved – put right with God. [8] Paul reminded his readers that everyone has sinned, falling well below God's glorious standards, although his grace freely justifies those who have put their trust in the sacrifice of his Son to bring them back to him. [9] Although the payback for sin is death, Paul immediately goes on to say that instead of death, 'the gift of God is eternal life through Jesus Christ our Lord'. [10] Those who accept this gift no longer have the death sentence hanging over them, for there is now no condemnation to dread. [11] What an amazing act of grace, no grudges held, or records kept. Instead of spiritual death, believers will know eternal life, defined by Jesus himself as starting now and never ending. Once entered into it is an on-going relationship with the Father and the Son. [12] All who receive this life also receive the gift of the Holy Spirit of Jesus, who offers to overcome their weakness and helps them live in line with God's will. [13]

Reading Paul's great letter to the Romans transformed the spiritual understanding of some famous Christian leaders such as Augustine of Hippo, Martin Luther and John Wesley. In the 20th century the well-known actor, David Suchet, has told how it convinced him of the truth of Christianity after he had searched through other faiths and traditions. It can still do the same for any who study it today and the whole letter deserves our careful and prayerful attention.

All because of God's grace

It is worth studying how often Paul mentions the *grace* of God in his letters. In fact, he makes more mention of God's grace than any other New Testament writer, perhaps being so grateful for God's grace in working such transformation in his own life. We should take note and be thankful ourselves, for we can receive it too.

Grace is the expression of God's unmerited favour in making and fulfilling his great plan to save us, through his Son Christ Jesus. Offenders who repent and believe are freely restored back into relationship with him, their past sins forgiven and forgotten. There is nothing at all that we can do to earn this forgiveness for ourselves. God adds gifts to gifts through his overflowing grace. [14] We must never allow any familiarity with such good news to take away its impact, or suppress our gratitude.

We are reminded that as such grace has been shown to us, we should also be gracious to others when we are tempted to act ungraciously. Examples Paul gives are for us to 'excel in [the] grace of giving' [15] and for our conversation to be 'full of grace'. [16] Paul must have been a very humble and grateful recipient of such favour, forgiven and transformed from would-be murderer to missionary, becoming an ambassador for Christ. [17] He reminds his readers that justification like this is a free gift of grace, made possible through the atoning sacrifice of Jesus. [18] As the message of such amazing grace reaches more and more people, their hearts will overflow with gratitude to the glory to God. [19] This was Paul's own response to the supply of grace promised him to help bear his (unspecified) thorn in the flesh. [20]

Just as Jesus was full of grace and truth, so should his followers be. [21] We are told to see to it that no one falls short of the grace of God, for it keeps away the bitterness that troubles and spoils. [22] Paul's letters begin and end with a prayer for grace to be with his readers: 'So, may the grace of our Lord Jesus Christ, and the love of God, and the fellowship of the Holy Spirit be with *you* all.' [23]

For further thought

■ How much of the Bible have you read? There is a difference between reading it like a textbook and listening to its message. A good beginning would be to read one of the Gospels, then the book of Acts.

Further resources

■ Pollock J. *Paul the apostle.* Eastbourne: Kingsway Publications, 1999
■ Yancey P. *What's so amazing about grace?* Grand Rapids: Zondervan, 1997

References

1. Luke 1:1-4
2. Acts 1:1-3
3. Galatians 1:13-14
4. Acts 18:6
5. Acts 9:1-22
6. Galatians 1:18
7. 2 Timothy 4:11
8. Romans 10:9-13
9. Romans 3:23
10. Romans 6:23
11. Romans 8:1
12. John 17:2-3
13. Romans 8:9, 26-27
14. Romans 12:6-8
15. 2 Corinthians 8:7
16. Colossians 4:6
17. 2 Corinthians 5:20
18. Romans 3:22-25
19. 2 Corinthians 4:13-15
20. 2 Corinthians 12:7-9
21. John 1:14, 17
22. Hebrews 12:15
23. 2 Corinthians 13:14

Chapter 18
Will you accept or refuse?

When I lived in Uganda I employed someone to look after my garden. Peter was not particularly good at it but he did his best, despite some original ideas. (Do carrot plants really need beanpoles?) As he was very poor he needed the money, but one day he did not appear and I asked his friend where he was.

'He is in prison', Joseph replied.
Shocked, I asked him, 'Why is he in prison?'
'He had no money for poll tax', said Joseph.

I knew that accommodation in our local prison was likely to be very unpleasant and it did not cost me much to send the cash and pay his debt. Peter did not refuse the gift or tell the judge that he would rather stay locked up. Instead, he believed that I meant it, accepted the offer and was quickly released. In the eyes of the law his debt was paid, and by accepting that, he was free. Although the offence would still be on his record he could return to the garden, happy, grateful and even more inventive.

We might sometimes have seen a sad advertisement, offering something for sale as 'an unwanted gift'. How hurt the donor would be to see this and to recognise that something given as a mark of affection had not been wanted and the person it was intended for was so ungrateful that they were trying to get rid of it. Surely we should not hurt the Son of God by saying that we do not want the gift he so longs to give.

Moving from darkness into light

One day as I was writing this book I heard a knock at the door. I answered it and there stood a neatly dressed little lady, carrying a big bag and asking very politely if I would be kind enough to look at what she had to sell. She was a gypsy. The striking thing about Rosie was her courtesy and her shining face. I'd met this before in other gypsies and soon confirmed that, like them, she was a Christian and delighted to come in for a chat, just as two other gypsies, Pearl and Lily, had done before her. I had been intrigued when Pearl told me that they were 'hearing' the book of Exodus until I realised that they could not read. Recently the Bible Society has published a translation of the Gospels in the Romani language, spoken by many gypsies. This will be even more rewarding for them to hear until the full translation of the Bible is ready.

I asked Rosie to tell me her story. Like many in her community, and in common with certain other faiths, she had always believed in God. Yet she had never heard of Jesus until a company of French travellers came over to teach her people. She, along with many others, had gathered their caravans together in a field to hear what the newcomers had to say.

'They told me that Jesus died to be my personal Saviour', she said, 'and I knew, although I hadn't murdered anyone or anything, I was still a sinner. So I believed and trusted him. It was like coming from darkness into light,' she added happily, 'and he is with me all the time now.'

European gypsies, usually known as Roma, or Romanies, are often given a bad name and looked down on or even deported, by the societies around them. Yet for over half a century the love of Jesus has quietly been spreading among them and drawing many to put their trust in him, with consequent changes of behaviour. The same thing is happening among Australia's aboriginal people. Over a similar period, and in different parts of that great country, Christian faith is taking root.

Some years ago I was taken to northern Australia to see where some of these people live. The ground was littered with empty beer cans and the local bar was heavily protected against the frequent drunken assaults. Yet in a different area I glimpsed a tall, erect and handsome Aboriginal man, fit to be a chief among a people now so depraved, but showing what they could have been. I did not know his history, but the revival of spiritual life in both Aborigines and Romanies reminds me of some words in the Bible: 'God chose the foolish things of the world to shame the wise. He chose the weak things ... the lowly ... the despised ...so that no one may boast before him.' [1]

Rosie's open secret was that she had heard about Jesus, believed that he died for her, repented of her sins and knew that she had been forgiven. Her camp is often moved on but she said brightly, 'It doesn't matter, because it gives us a chance to spread the word of God.' Good news is for sharing and now she is sharing it with you.

It is time to decide

Not long ago a young Englishwoman, visiting a Christian family, was puzzled by the way they were speaking about someone she did not know. Finally she asked, 'Who is this Jesus you are all talking about?' If you have read so far, you should not be in her position of ignorance. Thankfully, when she was told what you have been told, she gave her life to Jesus as her Lord and Saviour. This was her grateful response as she realised that he had given his life to clear all possible charges against her.

The record given by so many past and present witnesses is clear and trustworthy. It is time to realise that it applies not only to others but to each of us individually. We have examined God's wonderful gift of a new life and a new lifestyle, offered to all through the mediation of our Lord and Saviour, Jesus Christ. The reality of this gift can no longer be ignored. It is for anyone wanting a fresh start, to be 'just as if' they had never sinned for, unlike Ugandan Peter's record, our sins are remembered no more. Not only is justification on offer but to claim it requires belief, repentance and acceptance, faith in Jesus' full payment of the ransom price then closing the transaction. [2, 3] Life is made new, both for this life and beyond, for although the wages of sin is death, the gift of God is everlasting life through Jesus Christ our Lord. [4] How wonderful is that!

Before we go further, would you stop and think how this applies to you? I hope that by now you have a clearer grasp of the relief this could mean to you as well as giving joy to the great giver himself. Won't you tell him how sorry you are for your part in the sins that took Jesus to the cross? Then accept with heartfelt gratitude his gift of forgiveness now and everlasting spiritual life from now on. Thanks to Jesus' death and resurrection you will be made a new person, set free from the wrongdoing that has held you captive and starting to behave in ways that please him. Any future sins, once admitted, will find forgiveness in the same way. This should also be remembered by any convinced believers who keep on feeling guilty after doing something wrong (or not doing something right) instead of owning up and asking to be forgiven.

To respond to our Saviour's gracious love will be to love him in return and make him Lord of our lives, now and for evermore. Death will be to find him ready to give us a welcome to a new home with him.[5] Yet it is possible to be inwardly moved but still undecided, although not to decide is to decide. Decision is an act of the directed will.

A knock on the door

There is a beautiful painting by the artist Holman Hunt showing the thorn-crowned Jesus knocking on a long closed ivy-covered door. There is no light in the windows but he has a lantern in his hand, ready to illuminate the inner darkness. But first he needs to be invited in. The picture shows no handle on the outside of the door, so the decision to open up rests with the person inside. Perhaps too busy to look outside, or fearful of what might happen when they do open the door, some people prefer to turn a deaf ear. Yet the knocking continues as long as there is hope of a response. On the back of the original painting the artist had written, 'Forgive me, Lord, for keeping you waiting so long'.

In *Revelation*, the last book of the Bible, Jesus says, 'So be earnest and repent. Here I am! I stand at the door and knock. If anyone hears my voice and opens the door, I will come in and eat with that person, and they with me.'[6] He longs to come in to share your life, so will you invite him in to clean you up and bring with him fresh light for your spirit? In the person of his Holy Spirit, he will do just that.

Feelings do not alter facts

After such a decision some people feel joyful that a great load has lifted, while others simply accept his promise without the great emotion that perhaps they had expected. I am reminded of the old story of Mr Fact, Mr Faith and Mr Feeling, three men walking along a high and narrow wall. To let Mr Feeling lead is asking for trouble. One moment he will be jumping for joy and the next looking down, afraid of taking a false step or falling off the narrow wall. Mr Fact should go first, Mr Faith following him, with Mr Feeling still having a place, but well to the back.

We need to have faith in the facts about Jesus' life, death, resurrection and ascension with his offer of justification as recorded in our handbook, the Bible, and put complete faith in him. By asking him to be our Lord we will then look for his help as we learn to walk in his steps every day. Joy and peace are likely to follow as we go on with him [7] but the grace of perseverance is as important. With our eyes fixed firmly on our trustworthy Lord and Saviour, Jesus Christ we walk in step with him and do not lose heart, whatever lies ahead. [8]

What is the alternative?

We are, of course, free to choose. Jesus gave the assurance of everlasting life to those who believe in him but warned of the risk of condemnation for those who do not. [9] We only have word pictures of what that will involve, but in one of Jesus' stories he speaks graphically of the horror of being consciously separated from God. [10] Although he did mention hell many times, it was as warning rather than threat. Certain offences, actions, destinations and desires would lead there but could be voluntarily cut out of our lives and thoughts to avoid that fate. [11] Many of us will have allowed our hands to do unworthy things, our feet to take us to unworthy places and our eyes to watch or read unworthy things. Only as we offer every part of ourselves to God will he supply the needed strength to obey his word. [12,13]

If the idea of hell appals us, it will also appal Jesus that despite his warnings many still choose the path to destruction because they find it less restricting. [14] He spoke much more joyfully about entering the kingdom of heaven than heading for hell, for he gladly offers fullness of life here and now, [15] with the prospect of even greater joys ahead as death takes us out of time into eternity.

Yet we are also told that there will be a day of judgment, when we will have to account to God himself about what we did about his offer of forgiveness and how we have spent our lives. [16, 17] Our future destiny will depend on our response. How much better it will be, if each of us can be confident that Jesus will step forward and claim us as already being washed clean and accepted as members of his family and kingdom.

Don't leave it too late

It is always easy, in a busy life, for the urgent to push out the important. None of us knows how long life will last, but as death is not the end it is urgent as well as important for each of us to consider what we look forward to next. We must not risk that knock on our door falling silent. We must listen out for it and respond. Some who read this may once have responded, but since then worries, wealth or other priorities have edged out the one who would have provided for all your needs. Jesus may be knocking on your door, too, to be invited in again to his rightful place as Lord of your life.

When I was a student a local woman came to the dermatology clinic, her face partly covered by a scarf. We were all terribly shocked when she took this off to reveal a huge malignant ulcer already eroding most of one cheek. It had started small and she hoped it would heal up on its own. Sadly she had come too late to be cured by the limited therapy then available. We cannot heal ourselves of the malignancy of sin that threatens to destroy us. Hear Jesus' knock on your door, and delay no longer to invite him in to heal you and make you fully alive for the rest of this life – and beyond.

Prayer

Lord Jesus, I am truly sorry for keeping you out of my life for so long. I had not realised quite how much you love me, or that you died to save me from past, present and future sins. I ask you to forgive me for holding on to your rightful place for so long and without reserve commit myself to you now. By your Holy Spirit please change me into your likeness and help me to be your loving servant, trusting and obeying you, for the rest of my life. Amen.

Further resources

- Lewis CS. *The great divorce*. London: Geoffrey Bles, 1945.
- Nouwen HJM. *The return of the prodigal son*. London: Darton, Longman and Todd, 1994.

References

1. 1 Corinthians 1:26-31
2. Romans 5:1
3. 1 Timothy 2:3-6
4. Romans 6:23
5. John 14:1-3
6. Revelation 3:19-20
7. Galatians 5:22
8. Hebrews 12:1-3
9. John 3:16-21
10. Luke 16:19-31
11. Mark 9:42-49
12. Romans 12:1
13. 1 Peter 1:5
14. Matthew 7:13-14
15. John 10:10
16. Romans 14:10
17. 1 Corinthians 3:10-15

PART TWO

Chapter 19
Is that all there is? Turning on the power

We broke off from thinking about the meaning of Jesus' death, resurrection and ascension to invite you to become a whole-hearted disciple. With those of the first century we are about to find that even more good news awaits us. Although to them it did not at first seem to be quite so good, we have the benefit of hindsight.

Goodbye (for now)

After almost six weeks of renewed companionship and fresh insights, their Lord gave a last commission to the remaining eleven, saying:

> 'All authority in heaven and on earth has been given to me.
> Therefore go and make disciples of all nations, baptising them
> in the name of the Father and of the Son and of the Holy Spirit,
> and teaching them to obey everything I have commanded you.
> And surely I am with you always, to the very end of the age.' [1]

He was then lost to their sight. So why had he also told them to wait in Jerusalem? Was he going to come back to them there? [2] Until he did so, how could they possibly cope without his reassuring presence?

Do the right thing – if you can

A recent speaker on the radio had only a few minutes to explain his beliefs, but his message seemed to be that assisted willpower is enough to keep us from failure as we attempt to do what is right. It is all to do with attitude. Make up your mind to be strong but humble, tempted but pure, always doing good to others whatever they do to you and, he said, in this way you will find forgiveness and peace. Yet the big problem is how to achieve the right attitude and then have a will strong enough to live up to it.

The disciples had already proved how weak-willed they were when they all deserted Jesus at his arrest. Many of us will identify with the struggle to do the right thing that Paul experienced and wrote about:

> 'For I do not do the good I want to do, but the evil I do not want to do—this I keep on doing. Now if I do what I do not want to do, it is no longer I who do it, but it is sin living in me that does it.'[3]

Further on in that passage, Paul speaks of being held captive by sin and needing to be rescued and freed from it. In his mind (his 'attitude'...) he knew very well what was right but, like many others, kept failing to do it. He finally cried, 'Who will rescue me?'– then answered his own question: 'Thanks be to God, who delivers me through Jesus Christ our Lord.' He had learned the lesson of our last two chapters, that those held captive to sin are only liberated by accepting the mediation of our Saviour, Jesus Christ. We cannot release ourselves by our own efforts.

Their Lord had promised the disciples that when he left them, his Spirit would come to give them power to live his way. This was the gift they were to wait for, bringing all the help they needed. The Spirit would change their attitude and help them keep to the new standards.[4] Yet Jesus had also said that sometime he would come back, a promise repeated by other witnesses of his ascension,[5, 6] so perhaps the disciples hoped that this would happen very soon. Instead of his bodily return, though, they had not long to wait before experiencing the arrival of Jesus' own Spirit, rightly called the Holy Spirit.

A neglected person and an unrecognised provision

Our three-in-one God is one God existing as three persons: Father, Son and Holy Spirit. This three-person God is referred to as a 'trinity' from 'tri' meaning three and 'unity'– God is three-in-one. This is not the same as three separate gods as some mistakenly assume. The concept of unity in trinity is difficult for human minds to grasp, although music lovers know that when three separate notes from the same key are played as a chord they produce one harmonious sound, so much richer than when each is played alone. So it is with the three persons that harmoniously make up the Trinity. For a long time the third person was the most neglected member of the three. Especially in past days when known as the Holy Ghost the impression given was a rather spooky one. For centuries the Bible was not available to the common people, but very early on people recognised that the activities of the Holy Spirit were in complete harmony with those of Jesus, who in turn had shown the world the exact likeness of God the Father. He had foretold the effect of his Spirit being like a stream of living water that would satisfy spiritual thirst forever. [7, 8]

In 2012, the British nation was shocked to learn about the tragic death of a young man after quite straightforward surgery. An earlier brain tumour had needed radiotherapy but left such damage to his pituitary gland that he would need lifelong replacement hormone therapy. Unfortunately the surgical team had not read his previous notes so did not prescribe this post-operatively and his blood sodium level became dangerously high. He repeatedly cried out desperately for a drink of water but was simply thought to be a neurotic nuisance. In despair he even telephoned his mother and the police, but no one gave him any fluid until it was too late and he died. His urgent need had not been recognised.

What a picture this gives of so many people suffering undiagnosed spiritual thirst. Many try to find satisfaction from other sources but can die without knowing the saving life support of the Spirit of Jesus. Yet just as the young man could have been saved by a correctly balanced infusion, so the living water Jesus describes is there for the asking when thirsty spirits connect up with his Spirit. He offers to revive and refresh them for the rest of their lives, changing despair to relief and dryness of soul to total renewal – and never considers them a nuisance.

Why are we waiting?

When God says, 'Wait,' he often plans a surprise. About ten days after Jesus had left them the apostles were waiting and wondering, together with his mother Mary, other women and, more surprisingly, his brothers. In his earthly life these men had not believed Jesus' message and at one time thought that he was out of his mind, [9, 10] but his brother James had been given a personal visit from the resurrected Jesus and in time would become a leader in the early church. [11, 12] Peter, taking charge, organised a replacement for Judas, but the restored Twelve were still at a loss about what to do next. They waited and prayed until suddenly it all became clear. God always has a purpose in keeping us waiting until his right time has come.

Fifty days after that eventful Passover, Jerusalem was crowded with godly Jews who had come from many places to celebrate harvest at the feast of Pentecost. Then, in the second chapter of the book of Acts, Luke vividly describes how the Holy Spirit came in a powerfully transforming way. The disciples had been obediently waiting for they knew not what but when the Spirit of Jesus suddenly came, as he had promised, they were filled with a new power, acting like the heavy rain of a thunder storm that ends drought and encourages new growth. This is what happened in a spiritual sense.

A new language, a new authority and fresh courage

The crowd of visiting Jews spoke a variety of languages between them but to their amazement found that everyone heard and understood what the apostles were saying. They spoke with a new authority, no longer the panic-stricken men who had once deserted their Lord. Peter took the lead again and explained to the huge audience the meaning of Jesus' life and death, resurrection and ascension. He told them how the Old Testament prophecies had been fulfilled, including one about this impressive arrival of the Holy Spirit. [13] He boldly told the crowds how, in spite of being responsible for his death, they could now repent, be forgiven, and know the gift of this Spirit themselves.

Peter knew that the first believers would be Jews but added that all who had been afar off from God and were repentant would be forgiven, regardless of status or culture. Dry outward religion could be transformed into wonderful newness of life. His message was so powerful that at once 3,000 people believed it and joined the company of the newly energised apostles. [14] The Twelve had seen for themselves the resurrected Lord Jesus and now spoke of him with the great confidence that marked their new spiritual power. This is the story that some of the convinced Jews would take back home with them and so the best of news would start to spread.

New energy for all who believe

Paul later told the Ephesian believers (and us) that the mighty power used by the Father to raise his Son from the dead (and transform his disciples) is the same as that still offered to all believers.[15] The Holy Spirit still strengthens and energises those who have entered into a new relationship with God through his Son, Jesus Christ, bringing about a kind of personal resurrection. Our old lives, ruled by self and sin, are made new as we ask Jesus to be Lord of all that we think, say and do. His Spirit immediately comes in to give the fresh life and energy to our spirits that is experienced physically when dehydration is corrected. He helps us to understand the new standards given to us as children of God, renews our spirits and helps us as we learn to live responsively. [16, 17]

This is the help we need, not just to strengthen our own willpower but to change the set of the mind altogether and give us a completely new attitude. [18] Instead of aiming to meet our own standards, however high these may be, we now want to find and to do the will of our heavenly Father, energised by his Spirit at work within us.

Why baptism?

At the end of the long sermon recorded in Acts 2, Peter assured his listeners that if they were to repent and be baptised, they too would receive the gift of the Holy Spirit. We have already thought about repentance and learned of the Holy Spirit, but what did he mean by baptism? In some churches, parents bring infants for baptism but make promises on the child's behalf that must later be confirmed in person by that child. A ritual baptism by itself does not make an infant (or anyone else) a Christian. Rather it is like a promise awaiting fulfilment. Peter was speaking to adults, able to make up their own minds when they understood baptism's true meaning.

One sunny Sunday afternoon about a hundred of us from our local church gathered in the vicarage garden where four adults waited to be

baptised in a small pool of water made ready there. In turn they told
how they each wanted to take this step as a public witness to their new
life in Christ. Baptism is an outward sign of an inward change; it does
not bring about the change.

The first person told us how she had been brought up with a religious
label, but had only recently discovered and accepted the Lord Jesus as
her personal Saviour. She exchanged formal religion for a new and
wonderful relationship with him. The three men who followed spoke of
very different experiences. One had been addicted to pornography, but
those chains had fallen off when he asked God for forgiveness, freedom
and a new inner life. Another had followed an Eastern religion for years
but received no support when in personal trouble. In contrast, he had
found a warm welcome in the love of Jesus and those who shared it.
The last man into the pool was paraplegic after an accident, but his
smiling face shone as he told how the power of God had enabled him
to overcome the many troubles of his life. Two of the four had been
baptised as infants when they had known nothing about it, but all four
wanted to make a public confession of the new spiritual life they had
found through belief and trust in their Lord's promise of forgiveness.

After openly declaring their faith in Father, Son and Holy Spirit each
was firmly held and lowered briefly under the water before being
raised up again. This was a visual aid demonstrating the fact that their
old life is dead and buried and they have been raised up to a new life
supplied by the Holy Spirit. [19] After their public confession of belief,
baptism sealed the commitment each of them had already made
personally. The great news is that this same Spirit and strength will
come into each life that surrenders in gratitude to the offer of a clean
new start made by our Lord Jesus Christ. We thought about that in
the last chapter, and if you have decided to open your life to him
he has already come in, in the person of his Holy Spirit.

Not just a religious custom

To confess Jesus as our Lord when being baptised is to testify that he
has saved us from our old selves. [20] Where water is scarce, it may not
be possible to be 'buried' in it, but instead to have a little poured over

the head. The importance lies in the public statement of faith being made by a dedicated follower of the Lord Jesus Christ. In some countries, to confess openly to Christian belief is an offence punishable by death so secret believers need our prayers for courageous wisdom in the choices they make.

Between 1967 and 1990 the atheistic leader of Albania vetoed religious teaching and worship so that those who broke the rules suffered severely for it. Then a freer regime came in and in 1991, on my first Sunday in Albania, eleven young people were publicly baptised in the local lake. All of them told what it had meant to them to learn for the first time about Jesus and his love and to accept him as Saviour and Lord. One had been dumb, but had been wonderfully given a new ability to speak.

Some years later, a young Albanian student heard about this event. She had already learned more about the need to commit herself to the Christ who was now clearly calling her to follow him. On a day to remember she said: 'Last night I had a dream, at least I think it was a dream.' Referring to the Lord Jesus, she went on, 'He came to me and took me to the water. Then he asked me, "Why don't you give the rest of your life to me?" So can I be baptised now?' After more teaching about the meaning of this step, she was baptised and has never gone back on her commitment.

For further thought

- Did you know that by accepting Jesus as your Saviour, you also receive his Spirit? Is it news to you that Christian baptism is not a formality but a confession of faith?
- Is this a step you have ever thought about for yourself?

Further resources

- Stott J. *Baptism and fullness: the work of the Holy Spirit*. Leicester: Inter-Varsity Press, 2006.

References

1. Matthew 28:18-20
2. Acts 1:4
3. Romans 7:19-20
4. John 14:25-26, Romans 8:5
5. John 14:3, 16-19
6. Acts 1:10-11
7. John 7:37-39
8. John 4:11-14
9. John 7:5
10. Mark 3:21
11. 1 Corinthians 15:7
12. Acts 15:12-13; 21:17-18
13. Joel 2:28-32
14. Acts 2:40-41
15. Ephesians 1:17-20
16. Romans 8:11-16
17. Philippians 4:13
18. Ephesians 4:22-24
19. Romans 6:3-5; Colossians 2:12
20. Romans 10:9

Chapter 20
More from God's own correspondents

There is a regular BBC programme called 'From our own correspondent'. As its title suggests, the Corporation's reporters send in their observations, made in various parts of the world and usually offering interesting little pictures of life in different, often war-torn, countries. Sometimes they analyse how the situations they describe came about and may include powerful interviews with people still living through them. The correspondents all know that the BBC is behind them, making sure that their pieces come over as clearly as possible for those properly tuned in. Tuning in is so important if we are to hear a message clearly.

The New Testament correspondents give us clear reports about some aspects of the gospel of Jesus Christ. They tell us how it was first received and what a difference it made and will still make, when its truth is properly heard, understood and acted on. We are told how the good news spread as far as Europe, but we also read of the riots, arrests, storms at sea and shipwreck that could have hindered the work without the workers knowing the enabling of the Spirit of Jesus. The reporters were very conscious of the Holy Spirit's inspiration and overruling, making sure that what they wrote was clear enough for a tuned in and serious reader to understand.

Messages from Paul

The major New Testament correspondent was Paul, who wrote 13 of the letters we find there. Besides his great letter to the Romans, he wrote eight more to other young and growing churches as well as three pastoral letters in which he gave kindly advice to two young church leaders, Timothy and Titus. He explained to them how leaders should behave and what they should teach others about Christian belief and behaviour. The shortest of his epistles was to a man named Philemon whose runaway slave had been converted to faith. Paul asks the man's old master to take him back, not as a criminal but as a new brother in Christ.

Paul's frequent use of the messianic title 'Christ' (for example throughout his letter to the Ephesians) means that this academic rabbi had no doubt about Jesus being the Messiah. He had not come as the freedom fighter many had hoped would be sent to liberate Jews from Roman rule. Regardless of race, gender or status, the kingdom brought in by Jesus, the Christ, is the kingdom of God, not man. Its citizens are united as those who had trusted in his Son's sacrifice to release them from their bondage to sin. [1] By making Jesus their Lord they had entered his kingdom and found a new life.

Just as Jesus had said that the Spirit gives birth to spirit, calling this 'being born again', so Paul speaks of believers becoming a new creation, their old life replaced by a new life and way of living. [2] Instead of physical circumcision being the mark of commitment to God, as under the old covenant, the new life should be marked by full agreement from the heart to cut off selfish priorities and, in gratitude and love, to worship Jesus as Lord. [3] It will be he who finally judges how people have lived their earthly lives. [4]

Paul spelt this out very clearly when writing to the Galatians, who had been tempted to think that they needed to keep some parts of the old law as well as simply trusting that Jesus had done all that was necessary to save them from the consequences of sin. We can do nothing to save ourselves but, once committed to him, his Holy Spirit will enable us to bear good fruit instead of bad. [5] Unlike demonic spirits whose objective is to cause hatred, distress and destruction, the Holy Spirit produces very different fruit in our lives, the first and foremost being self- giving love. He teaches us more about following God's ways and will never lead us away from following Jesus as demonic spirits would try to do, using the instruction of false teachers.

Jesus had promised his disciples that one day he would suddenly return. In his letter to the church in Thessalonica Paul warns us all to live each day as if this could be the day he will arrive, preparing to welcome him at any time. In this way we shall look forward with confidence to his coming, when even the dead will be raised. All those who have put their trust in him will go to be with him for evermore. [6]

Other New Testament documents

Among the eight letters of the New Testament not written by Paul, the one to the Hebrews is a major book of uncertain authorship, written, as its name suggests, to newly converted Jews. It complements the gospel story by explaining more fully how the old covenant has given way to the new one. It would be more fully understood by those already familiar with the Old Testament books of the law of God, from Genesis through to Deuteronomy, with all the detail that these books give about the hundreds of former religious and ceremonial laws. Instead of thinking it is by struggling to keep these old laws that we will be made right with God, Hebrews shows that we have wonderfully free access to him made possible by the work of Christ Jesus. There is no more need for the annual Day of Atonement, when the high priest made ritual animal offerings to cancel out everyone's sins. Jesus became the highest priest of all when he offered himself to God to pay for the sins of the world, not just for one year but for all time. Faith in his sacrifice frees those who trust him from the burden of sin. On that basis there is now no further need to depend on any other priest's intervention for us.

Because of Jesus' mediation each of us may now have confidence to approach God and find a gracious response. [7, 8] The old covenant has given way to a new one although there are still laws to be kept, summarised by what Jesus called the greatest of them, the twin commands to love God completely and to love neighbours as we love ourselves. [9] His other rules for life harmonise with these two and we'll take a closer look at them now and go into more practical detail later on.

To love is to relate

The words 'love' and 'relationship' are often narrowed in our culture to refer to sexual partnerships, but all those who love and serve God are being restored to his image, not blending in with that of the surrounding culture. We relate to a three-in-one Godhead, each of the three being knit together with the others in self-giving, interactive and creative love, made visible for us in the life of God's Son, Jesus. This other-centred love models the way we should love God and each other.

Loving God

In one of his letters, the apostle John, says very plainly, 'This is love for God: to obey his commands.' [10] John had seen for himself how Jesus had done this to the end of his earthly life, whatever it cost him. His resurrection had won a great victory over sin and death, a victory he now shares with those who love him. [11] Love of God is shown in action, not just by a declaration in words. [12] When we start to love God through his indwelling Spirit, our consciences are sensitised to recognise clear right from definite wrong as we find that he has written his laws into our minds and hearts. [13] Yet we are not robots, simply doing what we have been programmed to do, and there will be times when our choices are less clear cut.

Matters of medical ethics illustrate this when sometimes a decision seems to hang on a choice between two less than good options. Is the risk of serious handicap implicit in prolonging the life of an extremely preterm infant worth the physical cost to the baby, the emotional cost to the parents and the cash costs to the service provider? Does the value of a life made in the image of God mean that all stops must be pulled out? How would we decide what to do in an economically impoverished country? We need to be alert to the Holy Spirit's promptings, coming often, but not only, as we read God's word or seek to act on the principles he gives there. Praying with those who understand the issues may help to alert us to actions that would either fall short of his perfect purposes or move towards their fulfilment.

Bridging the gap

Years ago a ferry was sinking close to land but still just too far for many people to make the leap to safety. One of the passengers, a big tall man, stretched himself across the gap to make a human bridge and so saved a number of lives. How grateful those people must have been. This is a little picture of God's loving answer to the dilemma created by sin and its deadly consequences. Jesus laid down his life to bridge the gap between us. As rescued and forgiven sinners, we should be more than grateful, responding to his love with ours. This commitment to self-giving love should mark our approach to ethical dilemmas, but is much costlier than making a snap decision.

Whatever our work setting, such problems may be resolved as we ensure that creative inter-relationships are well guarded both for the one who is often at the heart of the dilemma and those within the surrounding circle, be this made up of family, professionals or other team members. A list of pros and cons can be helpful but will need wisdom to balance out, and there we have access to the mind of Christ. [14] When possible, a personal encounter is always better than bald messages or heated phone calls. Jesus came in person.

His love at work in us will encourage us to keep his commands, though when (not just if) we fail and confess the fault, he will forgive. [15] Love, the first attribute of the Spirit's fruit mentioned by Paul, continues to act as the bridge between us, keeping the relationship alive. It comes full circle when it includes others. [16]

Loving our neighbour

Other people, whether living next door to us or not, count as our 'neighbours'. We should also aim for other-centred relationships with them, from business contacts to babysitters, cleaners to consultants. In a medical setting, professionals will relate to patients as whole persons, with names, minds and spirits as well as bodies, instead of just calling in 'the next case'. To be treated personally puts the cared for at ease and improves the carer's job-satisfaction. Building relationships creates a better way of life, an approach modelled by Jesus and formed in us by our three-in-one God. We are made in the image of God and the inter-relational love shown within the Trinity shows us the on-going attitude we are commanded to hold with our varied 'neighbours' near and far. We'll return to this later.

Other letters, found towards the end of the New Testament, are written by our old friends Peter and John, with two from *James* and *Jude* who were brothers of the incarnate Jesus. The last book of the Bible describes an amazing vision of John, his *Revelation*. Despite the very different style of writing from John's Gospel this is generally thought to be the same author, now a very old man. He was exiled to the island of Patmos to curtail his missionary activities, but his spirit roamed free. Revelation was written at a time of increasing persecution for the young churches so first John warns and encourages seven of them. He then takes off in strange and visionary language to tell of revelations made to him about events still to come before Christ returns to reign over a new heaven and earth. [17] Those who love Jesus will be with him to worship, serve and even reign with him for evermore. [18] Our finite minds cannot quite grasp all this but the great reality is that we are promised that we shall arrive in the presence of our Lord Jesus, and will then be made like him. [19, 20] Until then, while we look forward to that day, we are committed to following in his steps, guided and strengthened by his Spirit, and loving him whom we have not yet seen.

The Bible ends with a clear prayer for our Lord's return, and for the grace of the Lord Jesus to be with God's people. To the words 'Come, Lord Jesus', the appropriate response must surely be a resounding 'Yes!'

In his letter to the Colossians, Paul spelt out the purpose of his ministry:

'My goal is that they may be encouraged in heart and united in love, so that they may have the full riches of complete understanding, in order that they may know the mystery of God, namely, Christ, in whom are hidden all the treasures of wisdom and knowledge.' [21]

We shall see next whether we can find for ourselves that hidden treasure to which Paul refers though, like all treasure-seekers, we need to be serious about it.

For further thought

- When we need a guidebook we choose one with a reliable reputation. The Bible is a reliable spiritual guide. Have you started to read it yet?
- Different translations of the Bible are available in bookshops and via websites such as *www.biblegateway.com*.

Further resources

- Wyatt J. *Matters of life and death (2nd edition)*. London and Leicester: Christian Medical Fellowship & Inter-Varsity Press, 2012
- Schluter M, Lee DJ. *The R option*. Cambridge: The Relationship Foundation, 2003.

References

1. Galatians 3:28
2. 2 Corinthians 5:17
3. Colossians 2:9-12
4. 2 Corinthians 5:9-10
5. Galatians 5:16-26
6. 1 Thessalonians 4:13-18
7. Hebrews 9:11-15
8. Hebrews 4:15-16
9. Matthew 22:36-40
10. 1 John 5:2-5
11. 1 Corinthians 15:56-57
12. 1 John 3:18
13. Hebrews 8:10-13
14. 1 Corinthians 2:16
15. 1 John 1:5-10
16. 1 John 4:16-17
17. Revelation 21:1-4
18. Revelation 22:3, 5
19. 2 Corinthians 3:18
20. 1 John 3:2
21. Colossians 2:2-4

Chapter 21
Am I whole-hearted or half-hearted?

The British healthcare service (among others) regularly undertakes cost-benefit exercises to decide whether the usefulness of a new therapy, for example, outweighs the expense of providing it. In the same way, sensible people who are about to build a house, buy a car or perhaps take a holiday, have to decide first whether the price involved will be greater than they are able or willing to pay.

A few years ago a group of doctors travelled from overseas to offer a few days' biblical and medical teaching to students in a largely non-Christian country. They used the New Testament letter by James as the basis for thinking about how belief should affect behaviour and pointed out the difference between reality and pretence. For example, counterfeit coins often look like the genuine thing but are exposed as imitations when they fail to pass certain tests, such as being much softer than the authentic coinage. After one of our studies a group member said, 'If I become a Christian I would want to be real, not counterfeit.' He meant that he would not simply apply the Christian label to his life, but would want to be authentic.

A trend is developing for putting a misleading label onto a very poor quality garment or accessory, making it look as though it has come from a famous and expensive fashion house. Some shoppers will be deceived, or want to deceive others, glad not to have paid more for what they see as a status symbol. Others will realise that the item is counterfeit and will soon wear out, belying the name on the label. There are many people in the world who are labelled as Christians but do not behave in a Christ-like way. They do not wear well under pressure for they have never invited Christ into their lives to reign there as Lord, changing their lifestyle and strengthening them under trial. The difference is made clear with the onset of testing.

There are also those who deliberately pretend to be Christians in order to deceive others. In one police state today, true followers of Christ are sometimes invited to a prayer meeting, but should they innocently attend they find it to be a fake. Those who should be welcoming them into fellowship turn out to be counterfeit, using the name of Christ but acting well below his standards and ready to betray them. We need to pray for those who face such deceptions, that they will be wise enough to avoid them. At such times the Holy Spirit sometimes gives an uneasy sense of danger ahead, warning his own and keeping them safe. Some who do suffer for their faith often show remarkable endurance and courage under testing. They are real and not counterfeit so they wear well, and the name that they bear rings true.

Counting the cost

It is possible to accept the Lord Jesus' offer of forgiveness and the promise of new life, even to know something of the presence of his Spirit and enjoy being with other believers, and yet to hold back from full commitment. When Jesus was here in person some of those he invited to follow him began to make excuses when they saw that going further would cost more than they wanted to pay. He had resolutely set out for Jerusalem, knowing what awaited him there, but these half-hearted followers drew back, claiming other priorities. [1] There is a difference between being a believer and becoming a whole-hearted disciple.

Not all called Christian are genuine disciples

We have already started to think about the great spiritual benefits and blessings to be found in trusting the Lord Jesus to change us from being self-centred to Christ-centred, and to enjoy the new life he gives. Yet when Jesus was in Jerusalem at the time of the Passover some presumably Jewish Greeks, there for that feast, asked to see him. Some years later we learn that although some Grecian Jews had evidently joined the young church in Jerusalem, others tried to kill the newly converted Paul. [2] Perhaps those wanting to see Jesus had mixed motives. He would know whether they were spies, genuine seekers or just curious but still gave them no encouragement to join him. Instead he immediately spoke of the need to die to self, as was his own set purpose and clearly one that called on all his resolve. In this he was greatly encouraged by his Father. [3] To follow him would not be all miracles and Hosannas, but could cost true disciples their lives and for many today this is still so. To accept the lordship of Christ needs more than recital of a creed or an impulsive emotional response. It involves complete commitment for life, come what may.

Putting theory into practice

We are all aware that there is a difference between knowing the value of a healthy diet and having the determination to keep to a stricter regime. More seriously, when deciding whether or not to take a stand as a believer in Jesus as Lord, there will be some kind of cost to face. The new life is freely offered because our Lord Jesus paid the price for us to have it and what wonderful consequences follow when we trust him to deal with our old lives and give us new ones. Yet unless he is allowed to be lord of all he is still less than 'Lord'. It has been said that the entrance fee into his kingdom is nothing, for he has already paid it for us, but the annual (daily) subscription is everything. We need not be afraid to hand ourselves over to him for he loves us and is able to meet *all* our needs. The benefits far outweigh the cost. [4, 5]

Early attempts at a power cut

The Bible gives many examples of the opposition that arises when believers act in new and challenging ways that upset unbelievers. Some will only be teased or laughed at while others experience more severe attempts to suppress them without their opponents knowing that the power within them is from God and can never be cut off. This was made clear in the events recorded in the first few chapters of the book of Acts. The wonderful power newly given to the apostles convinced thousands of people about the truth of their challenging message. The Holy Spirit also helped them to bring healing to the sick and suffering, as their Lord had done before them. You would not think that anyone could object to that, but they ended up in court for it.

When I lived in Uganda many years ago, beggars would sometimes gather hopefully outside a church door on Sundays and on the steps of a hotel during the week. Some were badly disabled, perhaps from birth trauma or damage later in life. One was a polio victim who could only crawl to the hotel steps, although he had refused the offer of a wheelchair made by the hospital's orthopaedic department. He thought that he would receive more money by appealing as a disabled beggar. We never saw one of these crippled people miraculously get up and walk, but that is what happened to a man lame from birth who met Peter and John as they went into the temple. Like the Ugandan beggars, he clearly hoped that supposedly religious people would give him money.

Instead Peter said, 'In the name of Jesus Christ of Nazareth, walk' – and he did! A cripple all his life, at the age of 40 this man walked, jumped and praised God, and to everyone's amazement hurried along with Peter and John into the temple courts. Jesus might well have passed the man many times as he entered the temple, but in his name and the power of his Spirit the apostles had the joy of bringing about complete healing.

Like so many of Jesus' own recorded miracles, the healing very obviously dealt with the needs of body, mind and spirit. A thoughtful reading of the story makes it clear how downcast and weary the man must have been after a lifetime of being able to do nothing but beg, and that with mixed success. No wheelchair was on offer for him – but after his healing, what a transformation! His whole being was at once made whole. Others who knew him before and after the miracle were amazed that two such ordinary men had been given such extraordinary power. Only the religious authorities objected and, still denying the power of the risen Jesus, they arrested the two apostles. Yet in the end they could not very well punish such an effective act of kindness, warned Peter and John to stop such activities, and let them go. [6]

Free will or God's will?

Many would have thought it wiser for these followers of Jesus to have obeyed the authorities and kept quiet but instead they went out to speak even more boldly in the power of the Holy Spirit. In our own lives there may be times when we fail to respond to the urging of the Holy Spirit, whether because it is inconvenient, embarrassing, or even dangerous. We are still given freedom to choose between his will and self-will, to respond or to turn a deaf ear.

There is a smoke sensor in my home that makes a piercing noise if something is burning. If it goes off, I neither sit back, hoping for a fire engine to appear, nor do I switch it off and go back to my book. I search for the source of the smoke and deal with it. The Holy Spirit acts as a sensor, warning us to pay attention and not just turn away. Better than that, he comes to our aid as we identify whatever he is warning us about and helps us to put it right.

Unlike my smoke alarm, the Spirit of God sometimes uses a 'still, small voice' to alert us. We need to stay tuned, and then rely on him to help. This was Elijah's experience in 1 Kings 18 and 19, when after a spiritual 'high' came fear, flight and depression before God lovingly gave him comfort – and correction. In contrast, Peter and John, so recently filled with the Holy Spirit, had no doubt about what he wanted them to do, and that he would deal with the consequences of their obedience to bring praise to his name and, in the troubles that followed, all necessary courage to his servants.

Unstoppable power

Following their reaction to the miracle that had made the lame man whole the authorities made other attempts to cut off the power that had healed him and stop the preaching that still went on. Open followers of Jesus were badly beaten and imprisoned, and it was not long before one was stoned to death. [7] Yet despite such growing persecution, the wonderful new power was not cut off and the church continued to grow even when forced to scatter. [8] Believers were finding that the benefits of faith in Christ outweighed any cost men might make them pay. The eventual dispersion of many of them to other regions meant that in time many millions (including us!) would hear about the love of Jesus for the first time.

The missionary traveller Paul gave a catalogue of the sufferings he had endured on his travels. [9] How he was helped to bear them without complaint would show that the power to do so came from God.

Others would be inspired to thank and praise him while Paul himself was renewed day by day as he thought of his final arrival in the very presence of his Lord. That would make up for any trials he had met on the way [10] and by then he would have been transformed into being more like Jesus. [11] Meanwhile the grace of God was helping him to stay strong enough to serve and to suffer faithfully. [12] All who have served and possibly risked their lives for the Lord Jesus Christ can trust him to keep his promises. With him, this present life is richer than without him and his never ending life starts here and now, to continue beyond physical death. [13]

Looking to Jesus

Despite the persecution endured by members of the early church they did not sit down feeling sorry for themselves, but even rejoiced 'because they had been found worthy of suffering disgrace for his name.' [14] Their focus was on their Lord, who had gone through so much for them and called them to be his witnesses. In this they encouraged each other, and we, too, can find strength when with fellow-believers we share the word of God and pray together. The Scriptures are so precious that there are still those ready to risk their lives to own and share a hard-won copy as a source of strength and encouragement to keep on keeping on.

A good passage to read when hard pressed is in the practical section of the book of Hebrews:

> *'Therefore, since we are surrounded by such a great cloud of witnesses, let us throw off everything that hinders and the sin that so easily entangles. And let us run with perseverance the race marked out for us, fixing our eyes on Jesus, the pioneer and perfecter of faith. For the joy that was set before him he endured the cross, scorning its shame, and sat down at the right hand of the throne of God. Consider him who endured such opposition from sinners, so that you will not grow weary and lose heart.'* [15]

This tells us that when we are committed to following Jesus he gives strength, courage and endurance for whatever may be thrown at us. To keep looking to him will remind us of his amazing love, and the grace that strengthens perseverance for this life and gives hope for the next. When we consider his costly love for us our problems will seem proportionately smaller. Peter assures us that after suffering a while we shall enter into his glory, renewed and made strong again. [16]

A young woman once shared her experience of running the London marathon. After she had run for a few miles, despite her deliberately light clothing she had 'hit the wall', the point when runners feel like giving up. Then she heard her trainer's feet close beside her and was helped to keep running. Friends lining the route cheered her along until finally she saw what marked the final goal, the clock face of Big Ben, and she ran triumphantly to the finish. She used this as a perfect illustration of the above passage from the letter to the Hebrews. By fixing our eyes on the crucified, resurrected and ascended Jesus as our example and goal, we put aside whatever would hinder our progress as we run our race. Our trainer, the Holy Spirit, is always there to help and encourage us, while seen and unseen witnesses cheer us on our way, through their presence or by their prayers.

A dying Christian doctor friend said to his wife, 'I want to run the last lap well'. He had been well known as a greatly respected senior physician and in much demand as a faithful teacher of the Bible. Now he was dying of leukaemia with only limited time left to live. This was his 'last lap' as he compared his life to a race that he wanted to complete, as he had lived, to the glory of God. This is what happened as his Lord and his friends helped him to keep going, faithful to the end.

Perseverance in spite of many trials

Other problems beside tiredness or illness can act as a runner's 'wall'. Various difficulties may arise that tempt us to take our eyes off the goal and give up. It has to be faced that to be known as a Christian disciple can result in mild or major hostility, ranging from loss of friends to loss of life, just as it did for the incarnate Christ. This is particularly so in cultures where other gods (or none) are revered and feared.

Elsewhere instead of dangerous opposition we may feel tempted to keep quiet by simply going along with other people's opinions, moral

standards or doubtful ethics even when contrary to what we have
learned to be God's mind on such matters. Our loyalty to him can
be tested when tempted to complain or doubt God's plans, another
form of attack on our faith. In any and all opposing circumstances,
'You need to persevere'. [17]

Just as in the Garden of Gethsemane our Lord struggled to line up his
will to his Father's, so we too will sometimes need courage to face up
to and decide to do the will of God even when we find it hard. Yet we
are strengthened daily by his Spirit and sometimes by the great comfort
and encouragement of other understanding believers. It is easy enough
to sit in safety and write such thoughts, but the reality can be very
testing. In many parts of the world, violent crowds hostile to Christian
teaching have recently killed both adults and children and wrecked
their property, including church buildings.

Western believers sometimes think such opposition is confined to
Christians living somewhere else, and much of it is, but whether it is
small or great there will be a cost to true discipleship. A number of
British health professionals have been in trouble for sharing their faith
and although such sharing should only be done sensitively and with
consent it could contribute to the well-being of the whole person without
the abuse of professional relationships that is sometimes claimed.

Wherever in the world they are, those with open Christian
commitment are likely to experience some form of opposition whether
by simple leg-pulling or much more serious, even lethal, hostility.
When writing to Timothy from his prison cell, Paul warned that
anyone who wants to lead a life devoted to the Lord Jesus will suffer
persecution. [18] As far as possible we need to be sure that none of it is
because of our own unworthy speech or action. [19]

Has all this made you worried?

This chapter has contained some challenges and may have given you
second thoughts about being a genuine disciple after all. Take heart!
Paul, who suffered far more for his discipleship than most of us will
ever be called to experience, wrote to warn the Corinthians against

over-confidence coming before a fall. Self-reliance will not be enough to keep us steady or hold us from the temptation of putting something or someone else (including oneself) before obedience to God. He likens that to idolatry and heading for serious consequences, but he went on to say that to stand firm we do not trust to our own strength of mind but depend on God for, 'God is faithful; he will not let you be tempted beyond what you can bear. But when you are tempted, he will also provide a way out so that you can endure it.' [20]

Paul knew what he was talking about because after he had faced his first trial in a Roman court he wrote that no one at all had come to his support but, 'the Lord stood at my side and gave me strength'. He gave Paul words to use in his defence that effectively proclaimed the gospel to a new audience. He was also 'delivered from the lion's mouth', his possible fate if he had been found guilty. This gave him confidence to trust all future troubles to the Lord until he went to be with him. We have notable models for our learning. [21]

It would be through such experiences that Paul was enabled to say that he had learned in all things and situations to be content because he would be given strength to cope. [22] Perhaps he recalled the assurance of Jesus that preoccupation with troubles of any kind is unnecessary when we are in his Father's care. Jesus had said, 'Do not worry' – a command as well as an encouragement. Like Paul, our prime focus should be the promotion of God's kingdom by the way that we live and he will see to the rest. [23]

In many of Paul's trials and temptations, including specified and unspecified physical problems, he had repeatedly prayed for release. Instead he was given a promise that cheered and sustained him and has strengthened many others since: 'My grace is sufficient for you, for my power is made perfect in weakness.' [24] News from thousands in today's persecuted church still bears witness to this truth and how the grace and joy of the Lord is strengthening their endurance. In spite of the hardships, new followers are being drawn in by their witness. Two of my imprisoned Christian friends enduring unfair sentences have each had this joy – just as Paul did, in spite of his chains. [25]

Still wearing L-plates

Those wanting to be true disciples should know that the word has its origin in the Latin word for the follower of a teacher or leader – that is, a learner. We are still wearing L-plates! As we go on in the Christian life, following Jesus, our greatest leader and example, we keep learning more from past experiences and how we are to face those still to come. Whenever we fail to act on past lessons or falter in the face of tougher ones, all is not lost – it simply means that we need a refresher course in repentant confession, forgiveness and fresh enabling. We should never give up.

Faith strengthened through adversity

Years ago I met someone who had known many trials, the last and longest affecting her youngest son, Sam. When in his twenties Sam's car was hit by the van of a sleeping driver and he became so seriously mentally and physically disabled that he would need lifelong care. He and his mother were greatly loved by our church family, Sam radiating noisy but mostly wordless joy and at least one of his attendant carers has found faith in Christ. Unwittingly, by means of his wheelchair, he acts as a missionary. Not all missionaries go overseas.

Then Sam's mother developed cancer and after a relatively short illness, died. Yet in her last illness she remained uncomplaining and other-centred, quietly trusting her Lord with the tasks she could no longer finish. Towards the end she said, 'You know, it does strengthen your faith not to be worrying about anything.' Her serenity matched her words and showed her faith to be genuine, not counterfeit. The love she inspired lives on and we still see (and hear) Sam when his latest carers bring him to church. Let us thank God – and take courage. His strength is perfected in our weakness.

For further thought

- Had you realised that commitment to Jesus may involve problems and pains?
- Can you give examples of these, either from your own or other people's experience? What good things can outweigh the difficulties?

Further resources

- Brother Yun, Hathaway P. *The heavenly man*: Oxford; London Hudson, 2000
- Maiden P. *Discipleship*. Milton Keynes: Keswick Ministries and Authentic Media, 2007
- Bonhoeffer D. *The cost of discipleship*. London: SCM Press, 1959
- Brother Andrew and Al Janssen. *Secret believers*. London: Hodder and Stoughton, 2007
- Carey G and Carey A. *We don't do God*. Oxford: Monarch Books, 2012.

References

1. Luke 9:51, 57-62
2. Acts 6:1; 9: 29
3. John 12:20-33
4. Philippians 4:19
5. Romans 8:18
6. Acts 3:1-10; 4: 1-22
7. Acts 6:12; 7:54-60
8. Acts 8:1, 4
9. 2 Corinthians 11:23-29
10. 2 Corinthians 4:7-16
11. 2 Corinthians 3:18
12. Acts 16:22-34
13. John 17:3, 24
14. Acts 5:40-41
15. Hebrews 12:1-4
16. 1 Peter 5:4, 10
17. Hebrews 10:36
18. 2 Timothy 3:12
19. 1 Peter 4:14-16
20. 1 Corinthians 10:12-13
21. 2 Timothy 4:16-18
22. Philippians 4:10- 13
23. Matthew 6:31-34
24. 2 Corinthians 12:8-9
25. Philippians 1:12-14

Chapter 22
God's great intention

Years ago when I had just moved to a new area a family with young children welcomed me, their latest arrival being a pretty little girl. A few decades passed and she then introduced me to her own little girl – the image of her mother at the age when we had first met. We sometimes see a young boy whose ways of standing, walking or talking reminds us so much of his father. Perhaps this brings home two of the sayings of Jesus: 'I and the Father are one', and, 'Anyone who has seen me has seen the Father'. [1, 2] Jesus was God-made-man and in him we are shown the divine image. For those who have decided that, whatever it costs, we want to follow him whole-heartedly we'll now take a closer look at God's intention for us as shown in Jesus.

Made in the image of God

Right at the beginning of the Bible story we are told how, as the climax of his creation, God made both men and women in his own image and until they disobeyed him they had walked and talked with him as his companions. [3, 4] We have read how the honest but disturbing record goes on to report how generation after generation repeatedly failed to live up to God's image. He still loved his people and wanted to restore that original harmony, but they kept disobeying, resisting his warnings, choosing other gods or worshipping idols they had made for themselves. Finally Jesus, God-made-man, opened the way to restore that broken relationship.

In previous chapters we have seen how, between them, the Father and the Son planned and perfected this offer of restoration. Jesus gave himself in our place as a ransom, paid as the price of our sin, his resurrection confirming our justification (remember chapter 15?). By trusting him we are given a fresh start and strengthened by his Spirit to live a completely new life as children of God. [5] The intention is for us to be restored to the original image and as our knowledge of our creator and obedience to him increase, the likeness to him will increase as well. [6] As all things were created through the one made in the image of God, his firstborn and only Son, [7] his coming to live on earth has provided the perfect picture of the future likeness intended for us.

The great intention

The flesh and blood model expressed by the Son of God helps us to understand better how the Father longs for us, his adopted children, to grow up enabled by his Spirit to become like his firstborn. Whatever it may cost, the result will be worth it. [8] Yes, *God actually wants us to become like Jesus!* – transformed into his likeness, our minds changed to think and will as he does. [9, 10] What an intention – and, we may add, what a hope! Yet what God intends he is also able to fulfil. Earthly parents plan lovingly and patiently for their children and so does our heavenly Father.

In that last reference from Paul's second letter to the Corinthian church, when he spoke of transformation he chose the Greek word *metamorphosis*, meaning a total change of shape or character. It is the same word as that used scientifically for the astonishing change in shape undergone when a tadpole slowly turns into a frog or a caterpillar into a chrysalis, out of which will struggle the butterfly. The struggle is what strengthens the fly's wings but can also attract the attention of a hungry bird. In the same way a developing tadpole can meet its end, even when already showing a shadowy frogginess. Many a medical student has been shocked to see how a legally aborted foetus is already recognisable as a baby on the way, so unlike the dividing cells of only a few months ago. At each progressive stage there are threats to normal development for all living things and some never complete it.

Examples from natural history give a picture of the great change Paul was thinking of when he spoke of our spiritual development being a metamorphosis, with all the associated changes and challenges involved. Unlike caterpillars, tadpoles and developing babies, the Christian's metamorphosis is not to bring about a physical change but a spiritual one. The intention is that we change from being egocentric to Christocentric, gradually starting to reflect the image of Jesus here on earth. We are also assured that our future resurrection body will be like his. [11]

As a shadowy likeness to him is developing, our spiritual enemy the devil is always greedy to put a stop to further progress at any stage and by any means. [12] The Holy Spirit within will strengthen resistance to his tactics and help progress towards maturity. In addition when others become aware that a young Christian's growth is threatened and faltering, they need to stand alongside, in person and through prayer.

Giving up or toughening up

Threats and difficulties are part of normal experience but the way that we face them can either hold up development or encourage it. Paul gives examples of both reactions in one of his letters from prison. There he had at first been well supported by a man called Demas, but later wrote sadly to Timothy that Demas had left him 'because he loved this world'. The enemy had attacked his weak point, his desire for an easier life. In his place, Paul sent for Mark 'because he is helpful to me'. [13, 14]

Yet there had been a time when the young Mark also deserted Paul, possibly culturally shocked by the goings on in Cyprus and homesick (and seasick?) on his first venture from home. [15] His cousin Barnabas had taken him along on that trip and, as a great encourager, stood by him in the crisis that later arose despite what that would eventually cost him.

Being an encourager

We'll take a little diversion to think more about Barnabas for a few minutes. His name means 'Son of Encouragement' and he first appears in the book of Acts as a sacrificial donor from Cyprus. [16] When the church had heard about Paul's Damascus Road experience Barnabas believed in the reality of Paul's conversion when others doubted. [17] Seconded to Antioch there was so much to be done there that he went to track down Paul in his Tarsus hideout and took him back for a gap year of teaching experience in Antioch (where the name Christian was first used). From there the Antioch church commissioned them, first to take aid to famine victims in Judea and then to act as missionaries in Cyprus. [18] It was after this Cypriot mission that Mark left them while Barnabas and Paul went on further. The Jewish hostility they met, including near lethal stoning, would surely have put off young Mark even more but was the start of Paul's mission to the Gentiles, a move blessed by the Jerusalem church leaders. All this is reported in Acts 13-15.

Barnabas must have encouraged Paul immeasurably as he helped him to develop an appetite for future missionary journeys and see the start of the outreach to Gentiles. It is therefore sad that when Barnabas suggested giving Mark a second chance to travel with them again, Paul vetoed the idea. They had such a sharp disagreement over it that they split up, Paul's still dominant spirit probably overriding Barnabas' gentler disposition. [19] Cousin Barnabas then took Mark back to the place where his courage had failed (not a bad principle, like riding the horse that threw you) and no doubt continued to be to him the encourager he had been for Paul. Apart from a passing reference in Paul's first letter to Corinth, the New Testament makes no more mention of Barnabas. Yet we have a whole Gospel written by Mark! He had been kept from dropping out by someone faithful and humble enough to take a back seat. [20] When eventually imprisoned in Rome it is good to read that Paul sent for Mark, evidently realising how much he had matured, as by then he must have done himself. He was even willing to give Mark the testimonial he sent to Timothy with the request.

As we grow up spiritually we too will learn to rely on God's strength, supplied by his Spirit at work within us. We need not shrink from whatever kind of growing pain we may experience as, like Mark, this can lead to greater maturity and works of service. The pain of a surgical operation should lead to greatly improved health. In the same way we gradually learn to trust that God's creative hands are at work in our times of stress to bring about his perfect plan for our lives.

We can resist change but God has purpose in it

I live in an area of Britain known as the Potteries, made famous by the renowned English potter Josiah Wedgwood and others. I once took some overseas visitors to see a potter at work. As he rolled some dull looking clay into a ball he started a running commentary:
'I first have to work on the clay to soften it up before I can shape it', he began.

One of the visitors asked, 'Do you already know what you want to make?'

'Yes', said the potter, 'but some clay is rather hard, or still has bits of grit in it, and that all makes it more resistant. I can't go on until it is softer'.

We watched him squeeze and knead the clay, just as a baker might treat a lump of dough before it goes into the oven. Then, with both hands firmly holding the softened lump on his spinning wheel, he skilfully started to mould it into shape. It was fascinating to watch, until he suddenly took the clay off the wheel and began to knead it again.

'It isn't coming right yet,' he explained. 'Sometimes, it doesn't go to plan, and I can't make the special thing I had in mind. I may have to make something plainer, though it will still have a use. It depends how the clay responds to me'.

This time, though, we watched in wonder as the original lump of clay slowly changed in his hands to become a beautifully shaped jug, attractive as well as useful.

'I'm just going to put my initials on its base, and then it will be ready for firing,' said the potter, 'It will be the only one of its kind and people will recognise it as my work, but it will have to go through the fire to firm it up. If it stayed soft it would be no use for anything at all.'

As we watched and listened, I could no longer keep quiet. 'You know', I said, 'You are reminding me of something in the Bible about God being like a potter and we are like the clay in his hands'. [21] Our earthly potter looked up at me with a twinkle in his eye, but said no more. I realised that he had perhaps deliberately been giving us a parable that needed no more comment.

The Master Potter knows what he wants to make of each one of us but has to overcome our resistance and sometimes accompany us through painful times before he can finish the work. His plan is to shape us into the unique models he has intended, unmistakeably marked with the Maker's name to identify us as his workmanship. A young man suffering badly from unrequited love was reminded of the potter's intention as he handled the clay. He burst out, 'That's just what it's like. I'm like a lump of clay with feelings!'

There is, of course, a big difference between a lump of clay and a human being. The clay has no say in what is going on, it feels nothing, and its resistance is something intrinsic to its nature. In contrast, we can choose to resist or resent what is happening to us, forgetting that whatever the immediate cause God has allowed it. As we slowly learn to lay down our resistance we find that in our Lord's loving hands the painful pressures of life have shaped us into something better fitted for service – if only to have grown more of his Spirit's fruit of long-suffering.

We left the potter and his wheel with newer insights about the possible creativity at work in some of life's difficult patches, once committed to God's purposeful hands.

Growing pains

As children mature some things have to be unlearned as well as learned. It is a rare child who has met with no painful times as they grow and develop and a rare adult who manages to avoid such times later on. Yet even should they include the fires of persecution our Maker does not desert us. [22] As we all learn to respond more trustfully to our heavenly Father's firm but loving hands he gradually helps us, through his Spirit, to become more like his Son, the Lord Jesus Christ. In time his mark on us will become clearer. His greater goal is for all his followers to be recognisable as his united body on earth. [23] This is not always easy.

Our natural reaction to any discomfort is to moan and groan even when we might have brought the trouble upon ourselves. I sometimes think that such reactions are like the squeaking and squawking of musical instruments in an orchestra before a great performance gets under way. Of course we do not always enjoy being moulded or tuned in to God's purposes, but with his help we slowly learn to endure even unjust suffering with patience, trusting the end result to him. In this we are following our Lord's own example. [24] As his crucifixion was followed by resurrection and the final return to his Father, giving us hope of full salvation, something very good came out of something that had seemed so bad. In time we may look back and see how this has become true in our own experience.

Tracing the family likeness in others

The outstanding cheerfulness and unfailing helpfulness of a supermarket worker made me think that he was serving God as well as the customers and in conversation he readily admitted that we shared the same faith. As he said, it was likely that we would recognise the family likeness in each other, being brother and sister! There are more members of the family around than we often imagine. We should look for clues and then encourage each other to keep our spiritual mirrors polished so that each of us will reflect a better image of our loving Lord. [25] As we slowly grow to be more like him he is likely to show something of himself through us.

Dr Paul Brand was a distinguished surgeon, internationally famed for the advances he brought to the care of lepers by reconstructive surgery to their deformed hands and feet. His skills had been developed when working in London dealing with injuries sustained during the dreadful bombing raids of World War 2. A time of great danger and destruction had been overcome to produce a new and far reaching development.

Years later, during a teaching ward round at the Christian Medical College of Vellore, South India, Dr Brand watched his junior examining a patient. As he did so the young doctor showed great competence and kindness but 'the boss' looked puzzled. He said, 'The way that you are doing that reminds me so much of my old teacher in London. Your whole approach is just like his, but you have never met him.'
To his surprise the watching students looked at each other and started to laugh.
'What's the joke?' asked Paul Brand.
'Why, sir,' they replied, 'He is looking just like you.'
As a Christian junior doctor in London Paul Brand had unconsciously absorbed some of the mannerisms of his old tutor and was now

handing them on to his own students in India. Some of those students would realise that not only was he handing on the likeness of his old teacher but their teacher was also giving them a glimpse of someone even greater. In his care for their outcast patients was something of the loving likeness of his indwelling Lord and Saviour, Jesus Christ.

Learning to look for good coming out of what had seemed so bad
Although Jesus knew the purpose of his coming to earth, and that it would mean extreme suffering before he achieved it he still went ahead, knowing that his Father would finally fulfil their shared will. As we grow up in our relationship with him we, too, learn to look beyond any present hardship and trust God to work for good through it. Looking again at Paul Brand's surgical skills, they had developed out of the horrors of war at a time he had also needed to trust God with his very life – and how greatly used that eventually became.

I once attended a meeting of a small group of junior hospital doctors, mostly from overseas, including our host and hostess. They were both members of staff at the local hospital and there was a hush in the room as they told of a crisis that had hit their busy lives about a couple of weeks before. They were just about to settle down for the night when our hostess, already half asleep, suddenly had two convulsions out of the blue, the second being very severe.

Most unusually our host's brother was staying overnight and, as a general practitioner, was an immediate source of strength and help. Although brought up as an atheist he told me later, 'It was God who arranged for me to be there that night.' Those at the heart of the episode quietly told us that this was also their assurance, helping them to trust that despite the troublesome implications of a diagnosis of epilepsy, their Lord had been with them and they could trust him with the outcome. They were already seeing how this had acted as a wake-up call not only for the visiting brother. Together they had been made to take stock of their married and professional lives, realising that excessive commitment to their jobs had taken the time needed to sustain and strengthen bonds with each other. This is a risk for so many hardworking couples.
When difficulties or outright suffering come our way, we need to recall first that God's aim is to train us to become more like Jesus and then

remember how the suffering of our Lord Jesus Christ led to his resurrection and our salvation. In the same way we may later be able to see how much good God has brought from something that at the time seemed so very bad.

The next chapter will suggest ways in which Jesus' lifestyle could affect our own, remembering that we have the promise of his Spirit to help us and keep us hopeful. [26]

For further thought

- Do you know people who make you think that they are members of God's family?
- It may be interesting to hear the experiences used by God to bring that about.
- Had you realised that life's painful times can also be very productive?

Further resources

- Wilson DC. *Ten fingers for God*. New York: McGraw-Hill Book, 1996
- Brother Andrew with Verne Becker. *The calling: a challenge to walk the narrow road*. Grand Rapids, Michigan: Fleming H Revell, 2002

References

1. John 10:30
2. John 14:9
3. Genesis 1:27
4. Genesis 3:8-9
5. Romans 8:11-14
6. Colossians 3:10
7. Colossians 1:15-16
8. 2 Corinthians 4:17-18
9. Romans 12:2-3
10. 2 Corinthians 3:18
11. 1 Corinthians 15:49
12. 1 Peter 5:8-9
13. Philemon 23-24
14. 2 Timothy 4:10-11
15. Acts 12:25-13:13
16. Acts 4:36-37
17. Acts 9:27
18. Acts 11:19-30
19. Acts 15:36-40
20. 1 Peter 5:6-9
21. Jeremiah 18:1-6
22. Isaiah 43:1-2
23. Ephesians 4:15-16
24. Hebrews 5:7-10
25. 1 Corinthians 13:12
26. Romans 15:13

Chapter 23
Sorting out priorities

Words can hurt or heal. A badly behaved twelve year old told how, six years before, his father had left for work with a cheerful, 'See you tonight'. Sadly the child added, 'But he never came back'. He blamed the abrupt departure on his quarrels with his sister, the sense of guilty responsibility affecting his behaviour. The retrospective memory was made worse by the father's untruth. In contrast, an uncomplaining little girl with leukaemia recalled her mother saying, 'I love you, darling'.

One memorable word can linger for years. How much more significant over the centuries have been words spoken by Jesus, who was himself known as the Word of God. [1] How may his words and ways affect us as we follow him today?

Jesus lived and died for others

The cross of Christ is the best known Christian symbol, reminding us of Jesus' great sacrifice as he offered body and blood in order to present us back to God, cleansed and renewed. The truest symbol is when the cross is empty, for he rose again from the dead and through his Spirit is still alive to strengthen and inspire us.

The logo of the International Christian Dental and Medical Association (ICMDA) is an empty cross with a bowl and towel in the foreground. The empty cross speaks of Jesus' sacrificial love for all, its horizontal bar reminding us that if he is truly to be our Lord, our capital 'I' will need to be crossed out. Like his, our arms should stretch out in compassion, ready to serve others. 'Service' and 'worship' have the same Greek root and in his letter to the Romans Paul defines worship as the sacrificial offering of our whole selves in response to God's great mercy. [2] Although many may consider our church services to be our major acts of worship, at the exit of the church I go to there is a notice facing us with the reminder, 'You are now entering a time of worship,' that is, all the time there is!

Jesus worked hard, became famous but stayed humble

For most of his first 30 years Jesus probably did the heavy, creative and valuable work of a carpenter in the family business at Nazareth, no doubt doing it well, and reminding us to be loyal to our earthly families. When he later returned to his home town as a popular teacher and healer, instead of being proud of him the locals took offence, so he quietly took his teaching to the villages. [3] Later, on his last night with his disciples, he set an example of humble service by washing their feet. [4] His help is still on hand whatever our occupation, reminding us to do it humbly and whole-heartedly as a worshipful offering to him. [5] Humility is not always the first impression given by some who hold important positions, including a variety of health professionals. The bowl and towel of the ICMDA logo is a reminder that however hard working and even famous the members may be, they should be marked by the same humble attitude as was their Lord's.

Jesus knew and loved God's word

As a child, Jesus would see the scrolls of ancient Scriptures unrolled in the synagogue and listen to the readings, learning the timeless stories and singing the Psalms. Mary and Joseph would no doubt help their little son to love and learn the Scriptures by heart, so that later in life he would quote relevant verses, as when answering the tempter in the wilderness. [6] Some of his words from the cross came straight out of Psalm 22, drawn upon to strengthen him in his agony. To hide God's word in the heart gives any of us a source of strength and encouragement for life, and also in death.

In her youth a senior nurse I knew had been made to learn by heart passages of the Scriptures, sometimes rather unwillingly. However, many years later she became a respected Bible teacher as well as an outstanding leader in her profession. Just ten days before she died, by now almost 90 years old and seriously demented, she could still complete verses of much loved passages as they were read to her. We, too, need to get to know and love our Bibles and to teach young people to do so. Thought patterns and attitudes will be shaped for the rest of our lives when we prayerfully digest a daily portion, perhaps with the help of a new translation or study notes. God's Spirit speaks through his word, often with a thought exactly right for the needs of that day.

Jesus practised the presence of God through prayer

As well as meditating on the written word of God, Jesus was nourished at all hours by two-way conversation with his Father. He taught disciples (then and now) to address God as 'our Father', and encourages us to be specific and persistent in prayer, trusting our heavenly Father to know the best answers. [7] When we find ourselves lost for words, the Psalms offer a great resource and often remind us to put praise and thankfulness ahead of a list of requests. We need to approach God with proper reverence. Some find it helpful to structure prayers using the mnemonic ACTS, standing for Adoration, Confession, Thanksgiving and Supplication. Keeping a little notebook will help to remind us of individuals or concerns needing special prayer and is a place to record the outcome. The Lord's answers often surprise and encourage us.

Many of the Psalms model honesty in prayer, giving us words when feeling confused (Psalm 73), depressed (Psalms 42, 43), rejected (Psalm 74), at the end of our resources (Psalm 77), grateful (Psalm 18) or just filled with praise (Psalm 136). Sometimes we will just keep silence before God as we contemplate his greatness. His Spirit will put into words what we find it hard to express. [8] Like Jesus, we always need to keep our prayer line open as we practise the presence of God by quick prayers at any time. Prayer with others is especially encouraging for Jesus has promised to be with us and answer prayers made in his name- that is, by praying as he did, seeking God's purposes and not trying to bend his will to ours. [9, 10]

In the years when Albania was officially an atheist country religious practices were forbidden, so the believing grandmother of a troubled eight year old told her that she could pray to God but must do so secretly to avoid trouble for them all. The child went to her bedroom, prayed in a whisper, and found that her prayers were answered.

Jesus regularly attended a place of worship

It is good to establish the habit of attending public worship when duties (and regimes) allow. Like Jesus, some will be able to take part in the service. Even the way that a lesson is read can show that the reader knows and loves the author.

When Albania eventually opened up, the girl who had learned to pray came to Britain. Now a teenager she was asked to tell her story at her first ever church service.

Someone was present who was ashamed to have neglected so often what for her was so precious. He mended his ways and found out how much he had been missing. It can be hard to go into a new church alone, so it is good to join or take a friend and when possible find a smaller home group to attend during the week. When I was in training and outside activities were cut back by a heavy on call rota, others would join me for coffee and Bible study, first in my hospital room and later at home. Some who came were not churchgoers and a few held different beliefs but we all found those times valuable as both faith and friendships grew stronger.

Jesus enjoyed the company of others

Jesus gladly entered into social occasions, such as a wedding or dinner party, using every opportunity to honour his Father in deed and in word. [11, 12] At one of these parties a much despised gatecrasher showed him such gratitude and devotion that he openly drew the contrast between her actions and those of his neglectful host. There is a time for speaking out about injustice or prejudice, whether in private or public places, even if it brings the unpopularity that Jesus often faced. [13] He had a better welcome at a home in Bethany where he could both relax and be a great help to the host family. [14, 15] Whenever possible we too need to find friends in whose company we are refreshed, remembering other lonely people who may need our support. Jesus knew the importance of a quiet break [16] and with his companions must often have walked, talked and no doubt laughed together.

The companionship of like-minded friends is a priceless treasure, even more so when united in faith. [17] Jesus found companionship with friends, not in marriage but he also knew the pain of being let down by his inner circle. [18] It would be good if we can have (and be) the kind of friend Paul had found in Philippi where some shared his troubles in practical ways. [19] Wherever in the world we go there are Christian brothers and sisters to be found who will offer mutual support and shared prayer in times of pleasure, problems or pain.

In a residential care home near me some of the carers are from different ethnic backgrounds. The work is not well paid and often hard. Two have Indian and African origins and one of them told me, 'It makes such a difference being with another Christian, even if we don't talk much. It's not the same as being with friends who don't believe – you have a different level of fellowship.'

Jesus not only saw needs, he also met them

The prime aim of health professionals is usually to restore and maintain physical health, whereas Jesus brought healing to the whole person. He also cared about those whom others despised or neglected, a point made by his asking for a drink from a woman of doubtful reputation and segregated race. The same principle held in his story of the Good Samaritan's great kindness to a Jew in trouble. [20, 21] In our turn, to buy a sandwich for a beggar could be wiser than to give money likely to be spent on drugs and certainly better than looking the other way.

It seems that Jesus had no spare cash but as his life was one of self-giving, we too can give to our local church or other agencies that show the love of Jesus in practical ways. All that we have is God's gift to us anyway. Young people often need teaching, perhaps by example, to work out priorities and give what they can, even if it means buying fewer cups of coffee (or more).

A doctor friend of mine has a calling to visit orphaned children in her homeland. One day she went to a remote place and was immediately surrounded by dirty, smelly children with runny noses and head lice.

She was at first revolted but sent up a quick SOS prayer and was amazed to be filled with Jesus' love for little children, clean or not so clean. [22] She was also able to try and find practical help for them. Those of us who live more comfortably need to remember Jesus' simple lifestyle [23] and ask him to share with us the grace of giving. [24]

Jesus' delays were always for a purpose

There are several recorded occasions when Jesus seemed to delay over something that others thought urgent. Jairus was no doubt very frustrated when Jesus stopped to attend to a chronic invalid instead of hurrying to his dying daughter. When accused of being slow to help his sick friend Lazarus, Jesus later amazed his critics by miraculously bringing the dead man back to life. Over the centuries countless others have learned to trust God's timing despite his delays.

Most of us have times of uncertainty in life but as we put our trust in God the way can eventually clear. After leaving Uganda I searched for a settled home in Britain for over a year and began to wonder whether I was in the wrong place. Then at last I found a house that said 'Yes!' Confirmation came from a framed verse left on one of the walls saying, 'The Lord shall guide thee. Isaiah 58:11'. Over 30 years later, I still live there! Tested faith grows stronger as we hold on in faith for his promises to be fulfilled. His timing is perfect.

Jesus always demonstrated the fruit of the Spirit

As the Holy Spirit is the same as the Spirit of Jesus, it is clear that our Lord must constantly have shown the Spirit's fruit. In our busy lives we regularly need to ask for his help to stay gracious, loving and fruitful, as Jesus was.

A friend and I visited a famous church that was about to close over lunchtime. A churchwarden with a big bunch of keys hurried us out and there, in pouring rain, stood a photographer. He had come from a distance so had made an appointment for this precise time to photograph the inside of the church. 'Well you didn't speak to me', retorted the warden coldly, locking the door in the visitor's face. It is easy to criticise without knowing the inside story, but those who are Christ's learn to ask for more of his love and long-suffering, even under pressure. He said quite clearly that the kind of fruit we produce shows up our relationship to him. [25]

Jesus had a missionary heart

Jesus' last instructions to his disciples sent them into the world as his ambassadors, making and teaching new disciples. Wherever we live and whatever our work, we will regularly meet spiritually hungry and thirsty people whose greatest need is to know him. As in Jesus' day, some will make a direct approach, but more commonly we'll need to stay tuned, ready to speak a word for him. We'll be thinking more about this in chapters 28 and 29.

I'm not up to all that!

We have been looking at just a few of Jesus' priorities to point to ways in which we may follow in his steps. If you are left thinking that this is beyond you, take heart – on your own, it is! Help is at hand, though, for Jesus not only said, 'The Spirit of the Lord is on *me*' but he also promised the gift of that same Spirit to all his disciples. [26, 27] We need not look anxiously at a checklist, for he will lead us to what is ours to attend to and give us all needed wisdom, strength, sensitivity and supportive friends as he does so.

Remember, too, that Paul said how he *had learned* the lessons he was handing on. [28] As with other kinds of learning, some lessons can be hard, or take a long time to sink in and even longer to put into practice. Yet the end makes it all worthwhile.

For further thought

■ Are you inspired or discouraged to think about Jesus' priorities?
■ Try looking at your own priorities and see how closely they match up with his.
■ Where you know they don't match up, ask for Jesus' help in becoming more like him.

Further resources

- Martinez P. *Praying with the grain: how your personality affects the way you pray.* Oxford: Monarch Books, 2012
- Yancey P. *Prayer: does it make any difference?* London: Hodder and Stoughton, 2008 (new edition)
- Stott J. *The grace of giving: ten principles.* Oxford: International Fellowship of Evangelical Students, 2012.
- Sider RJ. *Rich Christians in an age of hunger: from affluence to generosity.* Nashville: Thomas Nelson, 2005

References

1. John 1:1, 14
2. Romans 12:1
3. Mark 6:1-6.
4. John 13:2-17
5. Ephesians 6:4-9
6. Matthew 4:1 -11
7. Luke 11:1-13
8. Romans 8:26-27
9. Matthew 18:19-20
10. Luke 22:41-42
11. John 2:1-11
12. Luke 7:36-50
13. Matthew 9:9-13
14. Luke 10:38-39
15. John 11:1-6, 14, 41-44
16. Mark 6:30-32
17. John 1:12-13
18. Mark 14:32, 37-42
19. Philippians 4:14
20. John 4:9
21. Luke 10:29-37
22. Mark 10:13-16
23. Matthew 8:20
24. 2 Corinthians 8:7
25. Matthew 7:20
26. Luke 4:18-19
27. John 14:25-26
28. Philippians 4:11

Chapter 24
How to have a fruitful life

I n my garden is a young plum tree. One year it produced a good crop of juicy fruit and the following year there was so much early blossom that I was hopeful for a repeat performance. Then we had an unexpected frost, the flowers died and with them most of the hoped for fruit. To be fruitful is how things were meant to be for all living things. Among the saddest couples in a medical practice are those wanting children but who never have any of their own despite all the help now on offer.

Yet there is a kind of fruit that any of our lives can produce when handed over in gratitude to God for what he has done for us and wants to do through us. This is the work of the Spirit of Jesus, who comes to live within us when we open up to him in answer to that patient knocking. Jesus once promised to give his followers a completely full life. [1] This can happen even when something was at the time a dreadful disappointment, seeming to empty life rather than to fill it. Yet by waiting on him (again!) we sometimes look back and see that he has brought a greater good than the earlier lost hope would have given, often bringing benefit to others as well. Jesus' disciples must have found much the same thing when Good Friday gave way to Easter Sunday, with all that followed to bless them and so many others, including us.

Father, Son and Holy Spirit: our three-in-one God

When still with his disciples, Jesus promised that when he left he would ask the Father to send them his Spirit, and we have already seen how that promise was dramatically fulfilled at Pentecost. The way that Jesus foresaw this is interesting. First he said of the coming Spirit that the world would not accept him (just as it had rejected Jesus). Jesus added, 'But you know him, for he lives with you and will be in you. I will not leave you as orphans; I will come to you.' So far, Jesus was the one who had been living *with* them, the Spirit already acting in and through him. When he left them the Spirit would come to be *in* disciples, sent by the Father in the Son's name to remind them of all his teaching. [2]

In the New Testament, the Holy Spirit is also variously spoken of as the Spirit of Jesus, or of Christ, or of God. [3, 4] The Spirit had descended on Jesus as John baptised him, remaining with him as the source of his authority and giving the seal of his Father's approval. [5] Father, Son and Holy Spirit are thus inseparably intertwined in our three-in-one God. We have the privilege of approaching our Father God through the way opened up by his Son, Jesus, and our prayers and progress are assisted by the Holy Spirit. [6] Although the idea of an indivisible Trinity may be hard to take in, a sign following will be the Spirit-given assurance that through Jesus we are truly God's children finding daily spiritual strength and guidance.

Fruit is grown, not manufactured

Opposition, or disappointment, can hit the lives of those who have committed themselves to serving the Lord Jesus Christ. Faith in him is not an insurance policy against future troubles but instead we are assured of his constant presence and power as we meet them. Sadly, some find the difficulties too much for them and the early promise of a fruitful spiritual life is cut off, just as the frost cut off hope of fruit from my little tree. Yet fruitfulness does not depend entirely on us, or our circumstances, for it is the result of the Holy Spirit's work in our lives. Jesus compared himself to a vine, and vines are intended to bear grapes, just as my plum tree was intended to bear plums – but he was referring to spiritual, not literal, fruit. [7] His message was that to be fruitful we need to abide in him, to stay close to him. The results of our own unaided efforts would quickly die away or receive a frosty reception and then, discouraged, we could be tempted to give up altogether. The secret is that his Spirit is the one who works through us, guiding and helping us with day to day tasks and giving perseverance and endurance for whatever comes our way. How does he do this?

A fruitful life depends on the work of the Holy Spirit

There may be those known to us who have little idea of what is spilling over from their lives. Focused on and devoted to serving God and others, despite their trials, they may quite unconsciously show evidence of the love, peace and patience that are all different attributes of the one fruit of the Holy Spirit. Paul gives us a full description of the fruit of the Spirit in his letter to the Galatians:

> 'The fruit of the Spirit is love, joy, peace, patience, kindness, goodness, faithfulness, gentleness and self-control... Since we live by the Spirit, let us keep in step with the Spirit.' [8]

Paul's decision to send what was a corrective letter to the Galatians was because they risked being side-tracked in spite of at first running their race well. [9] Others had cut in on them, teaching that they needed more than to fix their eyes on Jesus in faith but should also be ticking a few legalistic boxes (such as the rite of circumcision) before being genuine disciples. This still happens whenever it is said that faith alone needs an add-on extra to make us acceptable to God. In effect, this would mean tying on counterfeit fruit, not that produced by the Spirit.

Paul reminded the Galatians that the old covenant has been replaced by a new one (see our earlier chapters 7 and 8). Centuries before the law was given to Moses, Abraham had received a promise that still held – it is faith alone that saves (not faith plus something else). [10] Paul's readers had been accepted into God's family by faith in the atoning work of his Son, Christ Jesus, and had been baptised to bear witness to that faith, so why on earth were they (or we) going back to laws that no longer held? Ritual circumcision, for example, was no longer needed. They believed that they loved God, this being the expression of the faith that puts him first, the rest of the law summarised in the all-embracing command, 'Love your neighbour as yourself.' [11]

Love should make the world go round

The first aspect of the fruit of the Spirit is love. Wouldn't it be wonderful if everyone in the world obeyed the command to love their neighbour as they loved themselves! It is so evident that this is not so. Perhaps it is all too easy to sing or say, 'All we need is love', but not to clarify which of the many uses of the word 'love' we have in mind.

When a junior doctor says, 'I love orthopaedics,' does he (usually 'he'!) mean that he loves the idea of straightening crooked children (the original meaning of the word) or that he loves working out the mechanics of repair for disordered parts of the skeletal system? He may even mean that he favours the variety of old and young patients who come for help, but he would be saying something quite different if instead of loving orthopaedics he had spoken of his love for his girlfriend. Is love just a mental exercise, a thrilling feeling, or a decisive costly commitment?

Self-giving love

There must be some standard to show us what true love should involve, and the remark of a young mother probably comes close to it. Speaking of her new baby she wrote, 'I now know what it's like to be willing to give up my life for someone else'. Such selfless love is rare, but is the kind that heads Paul's description of the fruit of the Spirit. In one of his last conversations with his disciples, Jesus had conveyed the same thing when he said, 'Love each other as I have loved you. Greater love has no one than this: to lay down one's life for one's friends.' [12] Jesus went on to put belief into practice, giving his life for enemies as well as for friends. His love was (and is) so selfless that all over the world ever since, much enmity has been broken down by it. As he and the Holy Spirit are one, this is the kind of love that can be expected to grow when the Spirit is allowed to bear his fruit in our lives. It makes an interesting Bible study to find how Jesus' own life illustrated all the other aspects of the fruit of the Spirit. [13]

Lack of fruit

Before telling us of the fruit of the Spirit to be expected in a committed life, Paul listed the open sins we hear of daily in our media and also the hidden attitudes others do not always know about, such as secretly held hatred, jealousy or selfish ambition. [14] Those who have gratefully invited the Lord Jesus to forgive their sins and give them a new start should have no further desire for such things and find them wholly unattractive. Instead we have the offer of a new attitude of mind. [15]

Yet just as a surgeon is upset when his operation proves unsuccessful, or a gardener finds that the expected bunches of delicious grapes are small and sour, so we can grieve the Spirit. This happens when supposed believers act unkindly, without compassion or forgiveness, or still hang on to some of those secret sins that hurt other people. We who have been forgiven so much should be ready to forgive each other. [16] Even so, all of us must know regrettable moments when things were said, done or thought that we should not have allowed so we need to ask for forgiveness from God and from others we have offended.

Keeping in step with the Spirit

The secret of continued fruitfulness is to walk in step with the Spirit, tuning in each day as he helps us to pay special attention to something we read in the word of God or are reminded of in some other way. When we do get out of step we feel uneasy until we identify what is wrong and ask for help to put it right. When Jesus took the burden of our sins on the cross, we died to them with him and now find that his resurrection life is ours as well. [17] He gave us a new nature with his Spirit, but unless we co-operate with him our old nature tends to keep popping up again – dead but it won't readily stay down all the time.

For our comfort, all gardeners know that weeds need constant attention and that growth and fruit-bearing take time. As Jesus said in his parable of the vine, pruning improves fruitfulness. When discomforts great or small come our way it may help to think of them as being like the gardener's shears, designed to cut out useless, unproductive parts of our lives and to encourage more fruit to come. [18] Most busy people find it hard to cultivate patience, long-suffering or, at times, kindness, but that means lots of opportunities, with the Spirit's help, to practise and produce them!

As fruit grows, it shows

Christians have sometimes had a reputation for being killjoys but as part of the fruit of Spirit is joy that too should be growing in us. Having been taught this, a young Christian medical student started to take one attribute of the Spirit's fruit from Paul's list each day and pray that it would grow in her. One 'joy day,' another student unexpectedly said, 'You look happy today'. Without her being aware of it the Holy

Spirit was quietly at work (though his joy is deeper than happiness, so often dependant on happenings).

Years later, as a young doctor, the same person struggled to put up an intravenous drip into a small baby's tiny vein. As she finally succeeded, the assistant nurse accidentally dislodged the needle and the whole process had to start again. With a quick SOS prayer, tongue and temper were controlled and the job completed. The relieved nurse commented, 'You are so patient, doctor,' and the doctor thanked God that his Spirit had helped her to exercise self-control and kindness, and to learn more patience. Peace and joy would return later, but if instead she had snapped out an angry rebuke, to keep in step with the Spirit would have meant an apology, both to the Lord and the nurse. Sometimes that prospect holds back the outburst in the first place – but there are better motives. The fruit is to bring glory to God, not merely to add to our reputation.

For further thought

- When you can, read John 15 and 16, and make a note of some aspects of the fruit that the Spirit of Jesus wants to grow in our lives.
- Have you seen these growing in the lives of others?
- What do you think stops them growing in you? Surely not lack of opportunity?

Further resources

- Drummond H. *The greatest thing in the world*. Grand Rapids, Michigan: Fleming H Revell, 2002

References

1. John 10:10
2. John 14:16-18, 26
3. Acts 16:7
4. Romans 8:9
5. Matthew 3:13-17
6. Romans 8:16, 26
7. John 15:1-10
8. Galatians 5:22-23, 25
9. Galatians 5:7
10. Galatians 3:11-14
11. Galatians 5:6, 14
12. John 15:13
13. Galatians 5:22-23, as shown by Jesus eg: love (John 13:1); joy (Luke 10:21); peace (John 14:27); patience (John 14:9); kindness (John 8:10-11); goodness (Luke 23:41); faithfulness (John 17:4); gentleness (Mark 5:41, 43); self-control (Matthew 26:62-63)
14. Galatians 5:19-21
15. Ephesians 4:22-24
16. Ephesians 4:30-32
17. Galatians 2:20
18. John 15:1-2

Chapter 25
Gifted lives

At least in most of the western world birthdays are traditionally a time for presents. This is especially true for young children who eagerly look forward to their special day, often with increasingly heavy hints. My brother once remarked that the older we get the more birthdays we have, but the other side of that truth is that the older we grow the fewer the remaining friends and the smaller their gifts. In any case, enough is enough.

The coming of the Holy Spirit at Pentecost is sometimes spoken of as the birthday of the church and the amazing gifts given to the young church then have stayed on offer ever since, the selection and distribution depending on the Holy Spirit. Fruit-bearing will take time but both gifts and fruit are the result of faith in the atoning work of the Lord Jesus Christ and a relationship with him kept fresh through his Spirit.

Naturally gifted

Perhaps most of us have known people whose particular skill has made us exclaim, 'What a gifted surgeon, mathematician, athlete!' and so on. Natural talents seem to be distinct from spiritual gifts in that they can be evident early on, as with a child I knew who showed when she was about six years old that she was a born and determined organiser. Another Ugandan schoolgirl loved to share what she had learned that day by teaching other children whose parents could not afford school fees. Although aptitude for administration, teaching, leading and helping others are also found among the gifts of the Spirit, the natural gifts are enriched when a gifted person asks God to use for his glory what in any case came as *his* gift in the first place.

What are spiritual gifts?

The Holy Spirit's gifts to believers are sometimes recognised better by others than by the gifted people themselves. Whereas the *fruit* of his

Spirit should be growing in each life dedicated to God and in relationship with him through his Son, the *gifts* of the Spirit are given 'just as he determines', suggesting that not all receive all, but each will have one or more of them. [1] In three of his letters, the apostle Paul gives several overlapping, possibly incomplete, lists of more than twenty gifts of the Spirit. [2,3,4,5] They include the more spectacular but intermittent gifts that we have already seen demonstrated at Pentecost and used by the apostles and some disciples since, namely speaking in a previously unknown language and miracle-working. [6] Some will have the ability to interpret the new language or to deliver a direct message from God by prophesying (that is speaking out a revealed truth from God). [7] Gifts of teaching, encouraging, giving generously or just being helpful and merciful are less conspicuous but more usual gifts. Paul points out that all these are truly *gifts*. It is for the Spirit, the Giver, to decide how to distribute them. Gifts will differ, but that is their beauty.

The purpose of gifts

The purpose of spiritual gifts is to prepare God's people for works of service and to be used for the common good as they work together and support each other. [8,9] 'God's people' means a company of believers, his 'church', whether or not they meet in a special building. Obviously, works of service will be much more effective if everyone is pulling together, acting as a healthy, united body.

Less obvious gifts are still vital to the wellbeing of the whole

Church members have sometimes made one gift of greater importance than another, some even teach that speaking in an unknown tongue is the passport to joining the fellowship at all. In one of his letters to a young church, Paul taught otherwise by stressing the unique but important and integrated functions of the different parts of our physical bodies. [10] I once heard an African preacher comment on this passage suggesting that if we all went around with our brains or livers on display, vital as they are, that would not just be unsightly but in Paul's blunter word it would be to reveal something 'unpresentable'.

Able-bodied people with more obvious gifts need to realise that the frail little old lady in her wheelchair can still function as a gifted member of the body of believers. Whatever the more obvious gifts she might once have had she may now have been given the powerful but inconspicuous gift of encouragement, or of one-to-one teaching about the spiritual life. In turn she should be encouraged as a loved and valued church member. Paul says that, whatever they look like, the different parts of Christ's body should have equal concern for each other. We should humbly remember that the Spirit is the one to decide which gifts to give and when to give them.

Working together like parts of a body

Medical or physiotherapy students who study anatomy and physiology learn how the human body is made up of many parts, all working together in a balanced way under the direction of nerve centres in the brain. The system fails badly if messages from the brain cannot get through. To maintain balance, some muscle groups normally act in the opposite way from each other, so that a finger or arm can bend or extend, though not at the same time. This gives a picture of the way that each member of God's church, his body on earth, is designed to work together, united in acknowledging the Lord Jesus as the Head, submitting to his central and essential control for their individual and different functions.

In Paul's letter to the Ephesians he explains how different parts of the church should find their different gifts interacting in peaceful harmony. The final goal is for the body of believers to become as mature and complete as Christ himself. By definition, maturity takes time to develop but will come as we trust in the Son of God and learn more about and from him. He must have possessed all the gifts as well as the fruit of the Spirit in order to give them to us. [11]

Without the Spirit's fruit, the gifts could cause division, not unity, but the intention is for us to be bound together by Jesus' self-giving love. As we speak the truth in love, each of us can encourage others to practise gifts that they might not have known were theirs, so helping the whole body to work more effectively together. A company of believers, despite their differences, should act like the body of Christ on earth, more widely available than the earthly Jesus could be when limited by time and space. [12]

Gifts are not status symbols and they differ. By remembering that the Lord Jesus Christ remains at the head of his spiritual body on earth [13] each member of that body should learn to be humbly responsive to him so that our gifts can work together to his glory. As with spiritual fruit, there is no place for conceit or envy. [14] This will still hold in the workplace, for his fruit and gifts are not left at the church door when we leave for home. His Spirit goes with us everywhere, helping us not to be like children, jealous of other people's gifts, or even like members of certain committees who join battle with those of other departments, thinking that the others have been granted more privileges than they have.

When things go right with the body

When the Olympic Games are celebrated and we watch the performance of a trained gymnast, it shows how the different parts of our natural bodies can work together as one. Yet to reach this standard has taken many years of hard work with a professional trainer or coach. The Holy Spirit is ready to act as coach to believers, keeping us one in spirit and functioning well as the united body of Christ on earth. Any success will not gain us an earthly gold medal but should bring glory to God. On his last night on earth, Jesus prayed for us to be united in that goal. [15]

When things go wrong

Sadly, it is all too evident that Jesus' prayer for unity is not yet answered. God's intended work of witness is spoiled as a result and the root cause is likely to be loss of connection with the Head, our spiritual nerve-centre. Self-importance cuts off an adequate supply of the selfless love that only comes from him. [16]

Years ago there was a popular advertisement for a certain make of shoe. It read, 'If your feet aren't happy, you aren't happy, so walk the

Barratt way'. Similarly, any imbalance within the body of the church spoils its walk, work and witness, acting like a sore heel or dragging leg. When this is happening it would be wise for members of the local fellowship to meet to pray, asking whether some in that body need more help to keep in step with the Spirit. Silent suffering should not be necessary in a loving church family. Christians known to be isolated, or forbidden to gather together, need much prayer support and often practical help, even from afar.

Use and abuse of gifts

God's gifts are given in love and are to be neither abused nor neglected but we need to know that, sadly, false claims are sometimes made about them. Mass rallies to witness the exercise of someone's supposed healing powers can leave behind disillusion and even loss of faith among those who had been led to expect a miracle but were disappointed. Sometimes sufferers with ills based on emotional hurt do receive a boost to their spirits that relieves their symptoms at least for a time but we also need to remember Satan's way of pretending to be other than he is and that he will always try to spoil any work of God. [17]

There is, though, a great difference between the obvious need of a self-proclaimed 'miracle worker' to see results and the gentle, prayerful response to the Spirit's prompting by some who have been given the genuine gift of a healing ministry. They exercise their gift much more quietly and personally and use it entirely for the glory of God, not for self-promotion. Even then, the healing can be inner rather than the total cure of an advancing disease but because we are made up of minds, emotions and spirits as well as bodies, to bring relief to one is likely to ease all.

We should remember that a successful response to medical management is as much God's work as ours. Skill and wisdom are also his gifts and whether consciously or not, a medical team is in partnership with him. Although not always acknowledged, the glory of success is not primarily theirs but God's, for he allows and encourages the discoveries that promote health and healing. Best of all is when medical therapy and prayer go together

Do genuine miracles still happen?

We sometimes hear people say, 'It was a miracle that I found it,' or, 'You've really worked miracles on that old thing,' using the word in a much more casual way than is meant when speaking of supernatural intervention. Jesus' miracles were what first drew the crowd's attention to him but we are told that this was not his main reason for doing them. He was always moved by infinite compassion but also expressed two main purposes for his miracles. Firstly, he showed that he really could forgive sins when some doubted. After assuring a still paralysed man that his sins were forgiven, well aware of the watchful doubters he went on to heal him physically so showing his divine authority to act in both areas of need. [18] Secondly, his miracles revealed his divine glory and encouraged people to trust him. [19] Any miracles reported today in largely secular societies should share these two effects.

Jesus and the apostles brought about total and remarkable healing of body as well as mind and spirit. This is still sometimes seen, predominantly (though not solely) in places where there is inadequate medical aid. As in the days of the early church, healing then is 'in the name of Jesus Christ', to give glory to God. [20] The healing can sometimes be total, but may be of someone's attitude to their failing powers rather than complete disappearance of the disease itself. We can confidently take our requests to the Father, but it is up to him how he answers.

Inventions or discoveries? - God's other gifts

Inventiveness is not often seen as one of God's gifts to mankind, although the universe speaks of an imaginative Creator and we are made in his image. Yet the honour for successful human inventions usually goes to the inventors, not their Maker. Some even claim that their discoveries make it unnecessary to believe in him at all, not asking who had first created what they have now discovered! The finding of the Higgs boson particle in 2012 was celebrated as a great scientific breakthrough, as indeed it is. Yet to call it 'the God particle' because it is thought to hold mass together does not exclude a divine creation, it just reflects the truth expressed in God's inspired word.

Speaking of the Son of God, made in his Father's image, Paul writes: '...all things were created by him and for him...and in him *all things hold together*' (emphasis mine).[21] Our creator still has secrets to be discovered, and some receive the gift of enough intelligence to find them, his Spirit inspiring human creativity of many kinds.[22]

Giving God the glory

In the mid 19th century two new practices transformed the progress of surgery from then on. The first was general anaesthesia. Chloroform was especially favoured by James Simpson, professor of surgery in Edinburgh, and also by Queen Victoria for its use for her deliveries. The other advance was reduction in post-operative infection. Joseph Lister, from the Glasgow chair of surgery, introduced carbolic acid as an early form of surgical asepsis and immediately cut the post-operative death rate (even though he operated without gloves and in his street clothes!). Clearly, more refinements have followed both these advances and although each pioneer is still celebrated it is rarely acknowledged that both men were professing Christians. At a public lecture about anaesthesia Sir James Simpson was once asked what had been his greatest discovery. He humbly replied: 'I discovered that I have a great Saviour.'

All who rely on God's Spirit will learn to think God's thoughts after him without always knowing that this is what they are doing.

Gifts are given in love and should be exercised in love

Failure to develop an intended gift is as limiting to God's service as when a gift is misused. Yet at the end of one of Paul's gift lists a whole chapter is used to make clear that it is worthless to practise any gift without love, the essential first aspect of the fruit of the Spirit. Gifts will no longer be needed when we meet the great Giver, but love will outlast them all.[23] Although we have not yet seen him, we love him and nothing, not even death itself, will separate us from his love.[24] Love will reach its pinnacle when we meet our Lord face to face and are made like him, who is self-giving love in person.[25]

For further thought

- Be thankful that Christ remains Head of his body, the church, and that both fruitfulness and giftedness come from his Spirit.
- Have you recognised anyone's spiritual gift – including your own?

References

1. 1 Corinthians 12:11
2. Romans 12:6-8
3. 1 Corinthians 12:7-10
4. 1 Corinthians 12:27-31
5. Ephesians 4:11-13
6. Acts 2:6, 43
7. Acts 21:10-11
8. Ephesians 4:11-16
9. 1 Corinthians 12:12, 14
10. 1 Corinthians 12:16-26
11. Jesus had gifts of revelation: knowledge (Matthew 12:25); wisdom (Luke 5:22-25); discernment of spirits (Mark 5:2-8); speaking gifts: prophecy (Matthew 24:29-34); doing gifts: his many acts of healing (Mark 5); and his miraculous power over nature (Mark 4:37-39). I owe this classification to notes prepared for his congregation by Rev Nigel di Castiglione. Other examples await your own study.
12. John 14:12
13. Colossians 1:18
14. Galatians 5:26
15. John 17:20-23
16. Colossians 2:18-19
17. 2 Corinthians 11:14-15
18. Mark 2:9-12
19. John 2:11
20. Acts 3:6-10
21. Colossians 1:16-17
22. Exodus 31:1-6
23. 1 Corinthians 13:13
24. Romans 8:35-39
25. 1 John 3:1-3

Chapter 26
Growth and development

It is self-evident that we were all children once but with health and help most of us have, as was hoped, grown up. When my brother and I were children, our mother used to measure our annual growth in height with a little mark on a back room wall. Today paediatricians use more formal charts for measuring growth in both height and weight, checking results with the normal range for age. It can be harder to evaluate some other forms of growth although simple observation may show some of them, if only approximately. We could say that someone behaves very immaturely for her age, or that some great preacher is a spiritual giant, occasionally with the added comment that this is just like (or unlike) that person's corresponding parent.

Growing up takes time

It takes time to grow up physically and in the same way, spiritual maturity does not happen overnight. Those who watch the growth of young children know that much teaching and training are needed before they mature into adolescents and then adults. The saying, 'You can't put old heads onto young shoulders', is true for physical, emotional and mental growth, yet at each stage the inborn family characteristics may stand out. The same is true of spiritual growth. As soon as we put our trust and hope in Jesus as our Saviour and ask him to be Lord of our lives, his Spirit starts to change us. Although it will take a long time for the full *metamorphosis* to happen, others may soon start to notice that we have come under new management.

It is comforting that we have so many examples in the biblical records of people who eventually became famous and revered for their faith in God but had needed to grow up to get there. To name only a few, Abraham, Moses and David in the Old Testament and Mark, Peter and even Paul (when Saul) in the New had each fallen short of the behaviour expected of servants of God. Yet after saying a sincere

'Sorry', with the intention of doing better and learning from past mistakes, they continued to grow in experience and knowledge. We now think of them as not quite perfect but still giving us notable examples of godliness.

Of all of these great men, Paul and Peter most clearly put into writing the idea of growth. Peter compares to newborn babies those who are hungry for what he calls 'spiritual milk'. [1] In a similar phrase, Paul refers to 'mere infants in Christ', not yet ready to feed on anything more solid. [2] Milk is an excellent food for babies, but later on will not produce adequate growth on its own. Paul explained that by infants he meant those who had believed in Christ (were 'born again') but whose spiritual growth had scarcely begun. Their appetite for the right food was being spoiled by a preference for the junk food of the world they lived in. They argued like children about which leader to follow when the aim of all of them, leaders included, should be to grow up to be more like Christ.

Child development and spiritual growth

As children grow up they often want to match what they see others doing but may not get it exactly right. Copying from someone else's picture book onto the sitting-room wallpaper will cause big trouble, but some things matter more than others. For a nearly three year old to object to eating tomato is not worth a confrontation but she will need to be firmly told that a working computer is not a toy. Strong and even forceful expressions of self-will can mark a child's emerging independence (sometimes continuing to old age) but a persistent cry of 'I want' needs correction at any age, as does refusal to share. Well-informed youngsters often develop a heart for those worse off, both at home and abroad, but whether or not full maturity of thought is ever reached will depend on the standards set by teachers and the responsiveness of those taught. Some lessons are harder to take than others but will be more effective when explained patiently, not harshly hammered home.

There are parallel spiritual lessons. We are not told how well Peter and Paul knew young children, but the 'milk' they spoke of as being essential to young believers is the pure word of God. When regularly read, inwardly digested and applied by the Holy Spirit, it brings growth in grace and the knowledge of our Lord and Saviour Jesus Christ. [3] Just as a child's progress to greater understanding is taught stage by stage, so the indwelling Holy Spirit enlarges spiritual wisdom over time, producing an asset so very different from the wisdom of the world. [4] James illustrates this when he says that the wisdom from God is humble, peace-loving and considerate, not boastful, envious or selfish. [5] Early on in spiritual development the Spirit points out the universal tendency to 'look after number one first'. He will also clarify the not uncommon dilemma over which things are permissible and which are not. [6] The twin goals should be to glorify God and do no harm to someone else, another expression of our love for God and neighbour.

Steer clear

There are some activities that the people of God are told clearly not to do. Moses warned the Israelites not to follow the evil practices they had seen in Egypt and would see in Canaan. God said, 'Do not do as they do...You must obey my laws'. [7] The Lord Jesus gave the same warning when speaking of the proper practice of prayer made improper by those who had turned it into a public show. 'Do not be like them' [8] These two warnings were intended to steer away those who are his from copying the norms of the surrounding culture or sharing in what are only empty religious performances.

Each of us will need to examine ourselves to see how this applies to us, but being obedient to such instructions will often mean separation from activities that others regard as normal. Paul reminded the Romans (and us) that to set self aside in order to please God is the essence of true worship and will involve refusal to be moulded by worldly standards. [9] We all need the wisdom of the Holy Spirit to keep us out of these pitfalls. What has been called a 'Christian counter-culture' does not go with the flow and is prepared to be different, shining like a light in a dark place. [10] Material idols of all kinds surround us, urging a consumer society to spend, spend, spend, acting out the childish cry of 'I want,' with the addition of, 'must have'.

We have the warning left us by Demas, once Paul's supporter in prison but led astray by his greater love of the world he left Paul behind. [11] Each of us is open to obvious temptation along these lines. We must be sure before God that we are not rationalising as a real need what is really the wish to keep up with other people or, at heart, simply greed. When Jesus washed his disciples' feet he was reminding them that it was by walking on the dusty earth that they had been soiled, and as we walk every day in a world contaminated by evil we constantly need him to make us clean again.

The young church in Philippi lived in a proud and prosperous city, but Paul needed to warn them to let the peace of God guard their hearts and monitor what they put into their minds. [12] Spiritual food is not usually to be found in popular diversions or many status symbols, and we are warned off any that disturb that peace.

There is need for patient endurance as we learn to grow up

Children sometimes have to learn painful lessons as they grow up, and we may find the same on our way towards spiritual maturity. Unless already mature, or blessed with a relaxed temperament, most of us know how badly we can react when upset, even by as small a matter as a rainy day. On a visit to Australia some years ago I learned that the British are known there as a nation of whingers, always complaining. This is far from Paul's state of contentment whatever the circumstances [13] and even further from the maturity of the crucified Christ who so patiently bore insults, abuse and injustice as he entrusted himself to the most righteous judge of all, his Father. [14] Yet his is the image that God wants to reproduce in us and to be realistic it is going to take time – a lifetime – to accomplish but what a wonderful prospect, to be made like him.

In Florence, there is a large and lifelike sculpture by Michelangelo of David, the shepherd king. It began as a big block of marble but when the sculptor studied it, he knew what he could create from it. Perhaps in the same way God can see what he wants to make of us and uses our many trials as his tools to chip away at our stubborn self-wills. He wants to bring out the beauty of Jesus in lives given to him but still not yet mature. Some of those tools could be in action in the lesser stresses of life. How do we react to the intrusive ring of the telephone, the frustrating traffic jam, the cancelled train or an overbooked clinic? There are many other unfulfilled expectations of various kinds, known to us all. Do we take it patiently? If not, we are likely to be given lots more practice in exercising the endurance that will make us more like Jesus. Again, this is not natural to us, but comes as a fruit of his Spirit whose long-suffering will fortify our weakest points until they are weak no longer. Yet to arrive there takes conscious co-operation and repeated practice.

We are not asked to chase after suffering or to tolerate it in others

Victor Gollancz was a Jewish publisher who became a Christian. Writing to his young grandson he said: 'Suffering, though never to be sought, should be regarded, if it comes to ourselves, as an opportunity; but in the case of another we should...endeavour to experience the sum total of it, by a compassionate sympathy in our own person, and then, made active by imagination, struggle with all our power to relieve him of it.' The 'opportunity' he mentions is one of trusting God to use the upsetting circumstance as one of his tools for making us more like his image.

The stresses under discussion in this chapter are those that come to us without our wish or plan, but are allowed and used by God to develop his image in us. Our part is to trust him, even when we would prefer the lesson to end. Later, a more objective view may show what good things he had been doing in and around us that would probably not have arisen if life had been easier.

Followers of a popular Eastern religion say that 'Life is suffering', as though all we can do is to bear it. There is even a misguided school of Christian thought that says, 'If God uses our sufferings for good, let's bring them on'. Some may even tell those in the depths of misery that their trouble is doing them good. Paul had a better approach in his second letter to the Corinthian church. God himself will comfort us in all our troubles so that later we can share that comfort with others. [15]

Theory followed by practical experience

Many of us will remember student days when a lecture explaining a theory, say in physics, was followed by a practical session. It was so when writing this, as after theorising about God's possible use of our trials and his support in them, plenty of opportunities arose that put theory to the test. Within the space of a few days important telephones were found to be out of order, a key worker resigned without warning or replacement, I was handed round to various other people in turn who did not hold the information I needed (so tempting to call them 'clueless') and it had all come about when trying to help someone else. As the week wore on, 'You have need of patience' (or perseverance) became abbreviated to YHNOP [16] and at times was (regrettably) muttered very *im*patiently.

Then in our midweek communion service we read Psalm 116 – a good meditation for those bothered by troubles great and small as well as a necessary reminder that the Bible, the word of God, is there for our continued comfort and learning. We suffer when we neglect it, for it holds just what we need to hear. A few hours later, there was a breakthrough as a particularly clued up young man answered my queries and the way ahead became clearer, though not all the problems were completely solved. For the present, though, 'Return to your rest, my soul, for the Lord has been good to you'. [17] Such peace is one part of the Spirit's fruit, often following a storm but also present as it rages. [18]

Compared with the major setbacks, hardships and life-threatening events faced by so many others worldwide this is but a tiny, though not unusual, example of how patience is regularly tested in ordinary life but grace, peace and strength are on offer as we learn to develop Christ-like endurance. Refresher courses, or further tests, may well follow to ensure that the earlier lesson has been well learned.

Effect on bystanders

Following Jesus' example, persecuted believers, too, can – and do – learn to entrust themselves to the one who judges justly, but who alone sees the desired end product. By witnessing hardships patiently borne, others may dimly see something of the Lord's own likeness. I wonder whether the fanatical heart of Saul had been somewhat stirred as he watched the stoning of Stephen. Perhaps on the Damascus Road, before he met the risen Lord Jesus for himself, Saul (later Paul) had tried to blot out the memory of hearing the dying man pray so movingly for his murderers to be forgiven before he committed his spirit into the hands of his Lord. [19, 20] Stephen still died but his suffering bore fruit. Paul would soon be challenged that in his enmity towards Christians he was in fact persecuting their Lord, and with that insight the fight went out of him. He became as intense a follower as he had been an opponent. Sometimes this same effect on their persecutors has followed more recent martyrdoms.

Each experience of God's grace gives more assurance that he will be there to support us through the next trial. We will find fresh encouragement to keep going as we look to the Lord Jesus Christ, God-made-man: 'Consider him who endured such opposition from sinful men, so that you will not grow weary and lose heart.' [21]

For further thought

- Over the last year do you think that your spiritual development has advanced at all? Had you realised that God may use life's little annoyances to train you in patience?
- Do you pray for persecuted Christians and their witness to their persecutors?

Further resources

- Stott J. *The message of the Sermon on the Mount: Christian counter-culture*. Leicester: Inter-Varsity Press, 1992
- Gollancz V. *My dear Timothy*. Harmandsworth. Penguin Books. 1969.

References

1. 1 Peter 2:2
2. 1 Corinthians 3:1-4, 11
3. 2 Peter 3:18
4. 1 Corinthians 2:12-16
5. James 3:13-18
6. 1 Corinthians 10:23-26, 31-33
7. Leviticus 18:3-5
8. Matthew 6:7-8
9. Romans 12:1-2
10. Matthew 5:14-16
11. 2 Timothy 4:10
12. Philippians 4:7-9
13. Philippians 4:11-13
14. 1 Peter 2:21-23
15. 2 Corinthians 1:3-7
16. Hebrews 10:36
17. Psalm 116:7
18. Mark 4:37-39
19. Acts 7: 54- 8:1
20. Acts 9:3-5
21. Hebrews 12:1-3

Chapter 27
I've never thought of that before

Long ago and far away there was a Greek mathematician named Archimedes who had a moment of inspiration when taking a bath. Although his bathtub would be different from ours, he sometimes filled it too full so it overflowed when he got in, and he (or more likely a slave) had to clean up the floor before anyone slipped and fell. One bright day as he lay there soaking and thinking, he had a flash of illumination. He was so excited that he leapt out, forgetting his towel, and with a great and memorable cry he ran through the streets calling out, 'Eureka!' which is Greek for 'I have found it!', or as we might say today, 'Got it!'.

What he had realised was that a body immersed in a fluid (like Archimedes in his bathwater) is subject to an upward force equal in magnitude to the weight of the fluid it displaces (like the messy overflow when he sat in the water). He would have been amazed to know that this mathematical equation would for evermore be known as 'Archimedes' principle', and that for centuries, mathematicians and physics teachers would try very hard to get it into the heads of their pupils. The students had probably never thought about it before either and even after these lessons, however many puddles on the bathroom floor they made, would probably never cry 'Eureka!' We do not always think things through.

Most of us have probably had 'Got it!' moments. One of mine came in the middle of an examination, clarifying another principle of physics that I had never before understood. At the time, it was important to pass that test before continuing as a medical student and I was grateful for the inspiration, even at the last minute.

New life new lifestyle

One important illumination comes when we realise that the Lord Jesus Christ was not just a remarkable figure in history. To take a closer look at the meaning of his life, death, resurrection and ascension is to recognise the selfless outpouring of his love and to realise that it had been for all time and all people, including you and me. Some have gratefully asked him to become Lord of their lives and want to show responsive love to him by changed attitudes and behaviour. Yet old habits of thought and deed are slow to die away until more 'Eureka!' moments come with a fresh understanding of the role of the Holy Spirit. He is the very Spirit of Jesus whose long-term aim is to make us more like him as he grows his fruit in us and helps us to find the special gifts on offer to each committed believer.

In his letter to the Ephesians, Paul wrote to encourage the young church to live this new kind of life. The whole letter has so much in it to lift our spirits. He begins with the reminder that the Holy Spirit lives within us and, as we co-operate, the same power as raised Jesus from the dead will transform our lives. [1] Once we were aliens, out of God's family and under the reign of self-rule, but we have been welcomed into a different kingdom, founded and governed by the Lord himself. [2, 3] We now live to inspire praise for his glory. [4]

Living to the glory of God

When we were students, a friend of mine came to faith in Christ as her Saviour. As she started to read her Bible she often came across that word 'glory' and asked me, 'What is glory? What does it mean?'. We knew what a glorious sunset looked like, and could enjoy a glorious piece of music. A dictionary would offer many extra shades of meaning, but the overall picture is of something or someone having such splendour as to inspire wonder and praise. Living to the glory of God is to live in such a way that our lives please, praise and give total credit to him. It does not make us better than other people to live that way because we know all too well that we are among the 'all' who have sinned and come so far short of God's glory. [5] It has only been by admitting our past failure and accepting the love and forgiveness of the Lord Jesus Christ that we start on the changes he wants to work in us, through his Spirit. It is all of God's grace, namely his generous favour, so all thanks and honour go to our Lord as his work goes on in us. We make it our goal to please him, [6] to give him pleasure in our restored relationship, as we will find pleasure in discovering a new lifestyle.

A changed attitude

Looking back to Paul's letter to the Ephesians, it is from the middle of the third chapter onwards that he gives practical advice about ways in which we should live in response to the 'wide, long, high and deep' love of Christ for us, that is so far beyond our understanding. He reminds us of what we considered in chapter 25 that, as newly gifted members of the earthly body of the resurrected Christ, we are intended to work together just as the parts of our physical bodies do when we are in good health. This will often mean that members of his body learn to hold a different attitude from the body of popular opinion, so acting as a Christian counter-culture. [7]

Like any other form of learning, we may only gradually come to recognise the great extent to which we need to be renewed in our thinking. This is where it helps to be able to discuss and pray about these things with others in the same kind of work, who also desire to represent their Lord in the workplace. (This is as much a place of worship as anywhere else, for true worship is the offering of our whole selves in his service.) In student or professional life, it is all too easy to take as the norm what we learn from our teachers, or to accept certain practices because everyone else accepts them. Yet with minds renewed by the Holy Spirit we are made more alert to ways in which our loyalty to Christ's teaching will be expressed through very different attitudes and behaviour.

In medical practice, for example, our views can become very different from those of our teachers or colleagues, as when considering abortion, euthanasia, genetic manipulation or even protracted but futile intensive care. We may find ourselves drawn to specialties found unexciting by others such as differing addictions, or chronic disability of mind or body. Some may aim to work overseas or serve the poor nearer home. There will be many areas when the belief that we are all made in the image of God gives us such a different outlook from that held by those who have never met, or already rejected, this idea. We need to think and study more deeply to be ready when asked to give an intelligent explanation of our ideals and ethics, our aims, attitude and practice. Thankfully we also learn to send up SOS prayers and find that the Spirit of God helps us with the answers.

Guarding the tongue

Both Jesus and James in turn emphasised the need to tame our tongues. [8, 9] In his letter to the Ephesians, Paul gives a detailed list of areas where Christian behaviour can stand out as being different. [10] It is popular to speak of being 'economical with the truth', but Paul would probably call this plain *falsehood* or lying. Truth may best be broken in stages, as when breaking really bad news, but it should always be told in love, so very different from 'telling a few basic home truths' or 'giving it to him straight'. In this letter, Paul warns about *unwholesome talk*, including *bitterness, rage, anger, quarrelling* and *slander*. Each of us will know our own weak points. Gossip is a very favourite activity in many workplaces and even in church circles. A spicy bit of news grows spicier with the telling. It can become *malicious*, too, something else to avoid. Paul's mention of unwholesome talk would also include *obscenity, foolish talk*, or *swearing*. All these are to be 'put off' when we have 'put on' the new self and thankfully the Holy Spirit will help us to see and to drop any such bad habits, perhaps helped by a friend prepared to 'speak the truth in love'.

It is very easy for people out of their own culture to pick up words, stories or local ways that they do not really understand but accept as normal because others use them so freely. Bad language is like measles, easily picked up by the unprotected. A Christian Hungarian doctor became very fluent in the use of both good and bad English phrases and needed to have some of them interpreted as his form of verbal immunisation! God's name is so frequently misused by the general public, the media or in different languages that it is easy to forget that this breaks a commandment. [11] Paul also cites the need to *forgive* one another, and this will sometimes involve *apologising* (again, lovingly) when we have caused offence. It is better to clear the air than to nurse a grudge and spoil a relationship.

A tired doctor was woken up to go and see a baby in the middle of the night but considered the call to have been unnecessary, and said so. She could see that the night Sister was offended, and after going back to bed felt the Holy Spirit prompting her to go and apologise before

Sister went off duty. Later in the day, she was so glad that she had done so. As she had left the ward and before the belated apology, another doctor overheard the remark, 'What else can you expect of those Bible-bashers!' Hospital staff are among those who love to gossip, so he took some pleasure in repeating the comment to the offender. It was a relief that an apology might not have been part of what was expected but it was also a reminder to pray for control of her lips, even when tired.

Not stealing and *working hard* come into Paul's list of the different attitudes that are expected of Christians. The first needs a tender conscience (are pens, paper or phone calls really 'on the house'?). The second is difficult for the unemployed, although when in a paid job it would be stealing not to be a conscientious worker. On the other hand, it is easy for doctors and other professionals to overfill the diary with non-essentials, even to enjoy looking busy, but to rob the family of time together. A good chairman will ensure that 'meetings' are not unnecessarily long and chatty. Paul's list ends with the need to avoid personal *immorality*, *impurity*, *greed*, *obscenity*, *foolish talk* or *coarse joking* and *drunkenness*. The first two on this list can tempt people of mixed gender who are expected to spend long hours away from home as part of the job. Sometimes the long hours are solely undertaken for extra pay, not only to meet pressing needs. It can be all too easy to pick up other people's bad language or enjoy smutty stories (better to keep stocked up with clean ones!), or overindulge at the bar after work. What a minefield awaits anyone who allows attention to wander and feet to stray!

We are again grateful that the best mine detector is the Holy Spirit, who will help us to walk prayerfully in step with him, sensitive to his warnings and ever grateful for his help. When dealing with things that offend us or make us uneasy we need to act with firm politeness. Fellowship with others will help us not to dwell on our difficulties but to keep a song in our hearts, 'always giving thanks to the Father for everything'. Other Christians in the same kind of work could enlighten and encourage each other, seeking together to honour our Lord. That is our truest goal, not merely keeping a list of rules, and in time we will not even want to do things that we are here warned to avoid. [12]

Should we be tempted to step off the right paths and tread on an emotional or spiritual landmine, we must remember that turning back to him, broken and ashamed, will be to find that he still loves us overwhelmingly enough to forgive us and put us together again. [13]

Finding fellowship with others

It is an enormous benefit to be able to meet others who share the same faith in the Lord Jesus and urge each other to keep going straight. It is also a command that we should do so. [14] In some cultures where the open gathering together of God's people is not allowed, believers still try to meet in secret. Those in a freer world should be grateful for open access to places where we can hear the word of God read and preached, praising him together in spiritual songs of various kinds. To be over-critical, or to say, 'I can worship God anywhere – I don't need church, especially that one,' misses opportunities for inspiration, fellowship and further instruction that many others long for. Where there is choice, we should look for loyalty to the word of God as a priority, and a missionary spirit. We hope to share the love of Jesus wherever we are, in attitude and the way we act, for love is the first attribute of the fruit of his Spirit.

It can be harder to find other believers in the workplace but it can be so strengthening to do so. Doctors love to 'talk shop' and fellow-Christians are likely to hold similar views on medical ethics, and to show a more respectful attitude than some for even the most off-putting patients. To hear someone hum or whistle a Christian song or mention a book or church can alert us, or to notice a significant badge or tie, or a head bowed in thanksgiving before a meal. All these can act as signals, given and received, for the like-minded. More public identification such as advertising an openly Christian meeting, formal or informal, can of course arouse unsympathetic interest and name-calling ('Bible-bashers!') but also draws in others, often from overseas, who will welcome more personal fellowship.

Careful use of money

Jesus spoke a lot about money. Total commitment to God must include giving him our pockets and purses. At first sight this can look more like a cost than a benefit and a few may say, 'God richly provides us with everything for our enjoyment [15] so that must include my money, to enjoy as I please', rather than 'as he pleases'. This is a matter for each to decide individually, but careful reading of the Bible tells us that giving support to others is part of giving ourselves to the Lord.[16]

I know someone who delights to tell how God supplied all he needed when he had offered himself for special training on a minimal grant. Another wrote from India to say that a small sum sent by airmail had arrived on the very morning that the exact amount had been needed. A group of young people hoped to leave for a Christian camp later that day, but had not been able to raise the fee. Then at the last minute the gift arrived, precisely meeting their expenses and enabling them to go. Our Father may keep us waiting up to the last minute but such evidence of his care encourages both giver and receiver to stay strong in faith.

I once saw a news story of refugees in their thousands, fleeing from a destructive army to an already overcrowded camp, yet the local people welcomed and fed them as much as their poor resources allowed. Richer people can speak of compassion fatigue, but this is put to shame by stories and pictures of starving men, women and children dying by the roadside, or arriving at a feeding station to find supplies running out. It is heartening to read of relief teams, such as Tearfund, fuelled by Christian compassion and providing emergency relief. After that, to avoid cash falling into the wrong hands they aim to teach poor people better ways of managing their own affairs.

The smaller the income, the more costly it can be to give – yet the poorest people are often the most generous. I recall a church service in South Africa where the congregation, although far from rich, literally danced up to the front to give their offerings and did so again when they heard that the gifts already given had not met the current need. Paul encourages sacrificial generosity by reminding us of the costly self-giving of the Lord Jesus Christ 'that you through his poverty might be rich'. [17] Wanting to share the love of Jesus, lover of justice and mercy, is to shift our focus from a 'me-centred' lifestyle to help those who could well have felt forgotten. They may meet God's love in action through our gifts, whether financial or as assistance in person. A little prayerful research will lead us to people or organisations most likely to benefit from our various offers.

Appreciation of the natural world

There can be no doubt that Jesus walked for miles in the countryside, and many of his parables and illustrations came from his observation of nature (the flowers of the field, bird life), rural activities (sowers of seed, ploughmen) and the weather. He well knew that the natural world is among the 'all things' that our creator has given us to enjoy and care for.

A young city dweller had not had any such interests before she became a follower of Jesus. Another person, having had a first rare sight of a badger on a lovely summer evening, was so delighted that she said, 'I wish there was someone to say "Thank you" to!' – and, of course, there is!

Many of the Psalms, such as Psalm 66, are songs of praise for all the wonderful works of the Lord. He detailed some of them himself when at last addressing suffering Job. [18] Publications of various kinds tell of the wonderful interdependence of different flowers and animals, insects and birds, if they are to survive. Sadly, the thoughtless or greedy acts of humanity have already threatened some of them with extinction. Taking timber from forests that give homes to chimpanzees, for example, is threatening them with extinction. Long ago, Paul spoke of how creation is groaning to be liberated from decay [19] and there is a growing awareness that such decay is accelerating. More education and action are needed to halt the process. One Christian who has received a personal challenge about how we are mistreating God's beautiful world is David Bookless. As a result, he and his family decided to keep a strict watch on their own use of resources and also aimed to increase other people's awareness of environmental issues. The earth is the Lord's, but we share responsibility for looking after it.

Single-mindedness

Loyalty to godly principles will affect private as well as public choices. God's word warns against making alliances with those who hold no allegiance to him. [20] The reference Paul makes to an unequal yoke is a vivid one, referring to the days when two oxen would be joined by a bar across their shoulders as they pulled a plough. By combining their strength the yoke improves their efficiency, but if one pulls away from the other the very thing that should have doubled their output becomes a big problem.

This can apply in business partnerships, but is particularly relevant in marriage, where a promising relationship may have to end if it is clear that the prospective partner has very different goals in life. Such choices can be painful for both parties but when handed over to God he is able to use disappointment in ways probably seen best some time later.

Too much to ask?

In case this seems like an impossibly long checklist to be solemnly worked through, everything on it is something that the Holy Spirit will gradually work in us as we accept his gentle guidance. There may be an occasional sudden illumination ('Eureka!'), but more often it will be a new sensitivity to something not much thought about before. Becoming like Jesus is a lifetime process and because his service is perfect freedom we are not intended to go about with a frown, desperately afraid of putting a foot wrong. Instead we have the great assurance that we are in this together with him and it is his power that will work in us, helping us 'to will and to act in order to fulfil his good purpose'. [21] As we co-operate with his Spirit, he will, in time, change us into what he wants us to be. Remember that joy, not despair, is placed second in the list of his Spirit's fruit. [22]

For further thought

- Have you had many 'Eureka!' moments?
- Was there anything in this chapter that gave you such a moment?
- What do you plan to do about it?

Further resources

- Bookless D. *Planetwise: Dare to care for God's world*. Nottingham: Inter-varsity Press, 2008

References

1. Ephesians 1:13-14
2. Ephesians 2:19
3. Ephesians 4:19-24
4. Ephesians 1:6, 12, 14
5. Romans 3:23-24
6. 2 Corinthians 5:9
7. Ephesians 4:22-32
8. Matthew 15:18-20
9. James 3:8-10
10. Ephesians 4:25-32, 5: 3-21
11. Exodus 20:7
12. Hebrews 8:10b-12
13. 1 John 1:8-9
14. Hebrews 10:24-25
15. 1 Timothy 6:17-19
16. 2 Corinthians 8:3-5
17. Corinthians 8:9
18. Job 40:15-24; 41:1-34
19. Romans 8:20-22
20. 2 Corinthians 6:14
21. Philippians 2:13
22 Galatians 5:22

Chapter 28
Sharing the good news where we are

Have you ever known someone recently engaged to be married? Somehow, the name of the beloved keeps coming up whatever the subject under discussion. Whether talking about food, literature, music or sport, 'Oh yes, Daryl always likes, recommends, or plays, that', says Daisy. Eventually we start to think of the unknown Daryl as a real person, someone Daisy not only loves but also loves to talk about. Her words are truly the overflow of her heart.

At this stage, I hope that you know Jesus as your Saviour and Lord of your life and, like Daisy, long to share the good news with all comers. Some live in a culture where open confession could risk family hostility, if not worse. Yet it does not take long to realise that Daisy's heart is fixed on Daryl, even though some perhaps wonder what she sees in him. Even so, some of her unattached friends may feel a little envious of Daisy's obvious happiness. In the same way, those who (perhaps without realising) hunger to know God for themselves may try to find out more when they see the changed priorities of a newly committed life.

It is true that good news is worth sharing. Those brought up in a formally Christian environment perhaps think of faith as a creed to be carefully recited from memory, or certain rituals to be followed, rather than knowing the newness of life made possible when lived in daily fellowship with a loving God. They may think that religious belief is either just a formal affair or too private to talk about in any depth. However accurate some creeds might be, the Bible indicates that belief should stir the will and affect behaviour; lives and lips together should confirm what is so often being automatically recited. We are not merely offered membership of a formal religion but a personal relationship with our creator God, made possible through the mediation of his Son. The same offer holds for those who so far have belonged to other faiths.

Living the life

Many people were first attracted to the Christian faith because of the difference they saw in friends, fellow students or work colleagues who knew, loved and followed the Lord Jesus Christ in the strength of his Spirit. Such lives are different because they are given over to him and have started to reflect God's great intention by showing some features of the divine image. [1] This process does not happen by our own willpower or by orders of anyone else, but by personal commitment to finding and following the loving purposes of our Lord and Saviour, enabled by co-operation with his Spirit.

The more we get to know about God's intention the more we realise how far there is still to go before we truly reflect the likeness of Jesus. Just as a maturing tadpole begins to develop little limb buds, hinting at frogginess to come while not yet ready to live out of water, so our earthbound lives will start to be changed by his Spirit within. At first, there will only be a shadowy, immature likeness to the one into whose full image we are intended to grow. As long as believers in Jesus live here on earth this will always be a work in progress, a truth we realise more and more the older we grow. Yet his desire is for us to inspire others and help them to know him too. [2]

Enthusiastic believers can sometimes cause embarrassment by feeling it a compulsive and uninvited duty to force their beliefs on others. Yet this could simply be a turn-off rather than a natural overflow of the love of God. One way to introduce the all-important subject is to 'raise a flag', that is, to mention something to do with Christian things without coming across as a preachy know-all.

Putting up flags

I have Norwegian friends, and when in Norway with them I have noticed how the Norwegian flag flies openly outside so many houses, including theirs. During long years of enemy occupation this was forbidden, so now a raised flag signals their freedom. My friends make no fuss about their national loyalties and although obviously more at ease with those who speak the same language they still give a great welcome to others, ready to say more about their flag if anyone asks. In the same way, as we quietly indicate our own loyalty and love for God and enjoy being with others of the same mind, we will welcome those who may want to ask us more. Perhaps they will borrow a relevant book, or in time start a deeper conversation about the freedom we now enjoy as members of God's family.

Building bridges

We possibly have little spare time or energy when the working day ends (if ever!) but there could well be others, perhaps on their own, who are in the same position. Ways of building bridges could be to invite one or two people for a meal, a match, a bike ride or a concert. On a day off a country walk together would blow away the cobwebs and it is easier to talk side by side. We'll all have ways of discovering shared interests that help friendships to grow, even when busy lives limit opportunity. Hopefully our new friends will gradually realise that our main purpose and pleasures in life are significantly different from those of many other people. Even if they do not always go along with the crowd, they can still be curious about some of our own activities and raise flags of their own to say so.

For many, Christianity may just be one of the great religions and it could be a totally new idea that we are invited to have a personal relationship with God, opened up by his Son, the Lord Jesus Christ. (For some it may even be news that the very name 'Christian' comes from his.) Add to that the promised presence and power of his Holy Spirit to teach, strengthen and guide believers day by day, and what better news can there be? – except that this will never come to an end! Clearly, like any good newscaster, we would hope to attract attention with a headline (the 'flag') and as more interest develops, go into more detail about our faith. In any case, we will keep praying for our friends and hoping to stay friendly.

Allowing the Scriptures to speak

In what were once thought of as Christian countries, increasing numbers of those who live there are no longer familiar with the basics of Christian belief. Many do not own a Bible, or only a very ancient one. Otherwise intelligent people can show great ignorance about biblical matters, whereas others have a real hunger to learn more but don't know where to look for answers. Some seekers after truth try out one or more of the many world religions, diverted by the 'spirituality' sections in bookshops or on the internet. Others could find their search comes to rest when they meet Christians who are prepared first to listen, share their good news or perhaps study a Gospel together.

A teenager in once-atheistic Albania had been brought up with no knowledge of God. When the country at last opened up and he heard of Jesus' love and what he had done for him, he was so thrilled he immediately wanted to tell others. He was by nature an outgoing boy, so set out to share the good news with all his school friends, giving each of them one of the Bibles newly brought in by missionaries. He also began to visit a school for blind children, telling them of the way that Jesus could open their spiritual eyes because of his love for them. His boyish enthusiasm spoke volumes about what his new relationship with God meant to him and he did well to introduce his friends to the Scriptures so soon.

Help in sharing the good news

Most of us are probably not as bold as that schoolboy, and in conversations that may follow our flag-raising we sometimes feel a bit lost as to what to say or how to say it. There is help on hand. As well as thinking about studying a Gospel together by using *Uncover*, there are some Christian Unions, professional bodies and churches with 'just looking' groups. Interested friends could be invited to these, assured that their questions would be taken seriously. The Christian Medical Fellowship runs *Saline Solution* courses, designed to show how to be sensitive when sharing our good news in a professional setting. Through the Holy Spirit, God will be gracious about backing up sincere but stumbling efforts to introduce others to him and will speak in powerful ways beyond our own understanding. Nothing is hidden from him, including thoughts and attitudes. [3]

Some of our friends may later be willing to join in a more concentrated time of reading and learning, perhaps at a day conference or a residential weekend. Developed with this sort of audience in mind are the courses *Christianity Explored* and *Alpha*. CMF also runs local and regional conferences for health professionals. My university roommate and I met on our first day at medical school and she became a Christian a year or two later. Her doctor father paid the bill for the two of us to go to a CMF student conference over a weekend where we had good teaching and a lot of fun. Both played their part in opening up her mind, heart and will to entrust her life to the love of Jesus. Our existing friendship had taken us both to the conference but later we had even more in common and remained lifelong friends.

What if I do believe, but what if I don't?

This is one of the questions our newer friends may ask. In answer, one tested and tried mnemonic can be useful: 'God, man, God; what if I do and what if I don't?' When unpacked, this covers God's plan for mankind, made in his image but spoiled by human self-will. The coming of Jesus offered the way to restore the broken relationship, that offer having consequences whether accepted or rejected. We would prefer not to talk about the second set of consequences but it is too important to ignore. It is easier to speak of the forgiveness, joy, new life and spiritual growth that can all follow the handing over of our lives to our Lord Jesus Christ.

Yet Jesus also made it plain that to count him out carelessly or deliberately will mean to suffer the eventual knowledge that more has been rejected than was ever thought possible. His aim was not to frighten people into belief but to draw them to himself by his love. Even so he warned them of the consequences of refusal to be drawn. We touched on these in chapter 18.

Most of the relevant biblical references using the English word hell refer to *Sheol*, or *Hades*, meaning simply the place of the dead. Jesus made an unusually full and direct reference to it as a place of torment in a story he told about a rich man who ended up there. In life he had lived very comfortably, but regularly walked past poor sick Lazarus at his gate with no offer to help him. In the hereafter the poor man found comfort and the rich man endured fiery suffering. Behaviour towards others in life affects what we face in the afterlife. [4, 5] Some have used the description of the rich man's agonies as the literal expectation of all who have rejected Jesus' offer of forgiveness. Yet when Jesus spoke of Dives and Lazarus it was in the context of a story evidently intended to bring home the serious message that repentance can come too late. For some death will bring everlasting joy, for others eternal separation from God. In his book *The Great Divorce,* CS Lewis makes the point that to have chosen to live apart from him in life will be to experience more of the same after death.

The Gospels show how Jesus was obviously happier to speak of the joys of heaven [6] than the alternative of needless perishing. He taught that 'eternal life' starts now as we come to know God through his Son. [7, 8, 9] We need to keep praying for our friends, and in this we have Jesus' example. Right at the end of his earthly life, he prayed for those who were putting him to death or were watching how he bore his sufferings. At least one repented of wrongdoing, right at the last hour. [10]

To miss out on the joys of the new life on offer brings needless loss and hopelessness here and now yet, sadly, there are still those who turn their backs and deafen their ears to the divine invitation to trust and follow Jesus, God's Son, and find newness of life. Perhaps they mock the whole idea of his existence, or turn to other gods. We also have to leave with our loving, just and merciful God the full meaning of Bible passages that perhaps we find it hard to understand. A picture that helps me to get a glimmer of what could happen is that of the abandoned babies I saw years ago in Eastern European orphanages. At that time, they had been separated from love by its having been withdrawn from them, and some of them died of the deprivation. It is the other way round for people who choose to reject the love on offer but whose souls may undergo the same process of failing to thrive to the point of death.

As in so much else, including the destiny of those who have never heard the good news on offer, we have to be confident that our Lord, who knows all, will only do what is right. [11] To be left uncertain and uncomfortable about exactly what will happen to those who do not believe makes it more urgent to tell our positive story. It is wonderfully possible to experience the power of Jesus' resurrected life through the presence and power of his Holy Spirit. He changes lives, and any who believe can know this. To turn the back on such a wonderful offer would indeed mean great loss, but how can people believe unless a convinced messenger sets out to tell them?

Confidence in God's help grows as we experience it and find that seeds can take root in unlikely ground when watered with prayer and then looked after. By tuning in to God's voice we become open channels of his love. Our lives and lips should give the same message but the work of convincing someone of the truth of the good news we share is entirely the work of the Holy Spirit, however persuasive we may hope to be.

Making sure of a refill

Years ago, I listened to Dr Paul Brand, the great leprosy surgeon, give a talk in which he illustrated an important point. He took a very full glass of water, walked across the stage with it and then deliberately tripped so that some of the water spilled out. He used this to show that what fills our hearts will be made obvious when we experience some of the stresses of life, a point sometimes made in film versions of bad-tempered surgeons in action. When we meet something unsettling, we would hope to be so filled with the Holy Spirit that some telling evidence will overflow. For a glass, a cup, or a life to run over, it must first be filled. A very real test of whether others will find our message convincing is how we respond to life's different circumstances, whether good or not so good.

The filled heart overflows. One bright sunny day a flock of ducks flew up just as a stranger and I were crossing a canal bridge at the same time. The lady was from Singapore so lacked British reserve as she excitedly turned to me and joyfully exclaimed, 'Praise God! Isn't he wonderful?' Of course, I had to agree! – and she is still a good friend. Yet she could equally have been showing something of her overflowing joy in the Lord to someone who had never met that before. So that our spirits can overflow so helpfully we need to stay open to the touch of the Holy Spirit through prayer, absorbing God's word regularly and when possible sharing these activities with one or more others. In busy lives, opportunities for fellowship can be hard to come by but it is so encouraging to find a teaching church (and get there) and to meet and know other believers, either there or in the workplace. Jesus promised that when we meet he would be there as well. [12] The pieces of hot fuel on a barbecue go cold unless they stay close together, a risk also for those who face isolation from Christian fellowship. If visits are not possible, friends need to warm each other by their prayers, phone calls or correspondence.

The family of God

At gatherings for the Olympic Games, those chosen to represent their countries feel honoured to take part and carry their national flags with pride. We, too, are honoured to raise the flags that tell of our citizenship of a different kingdom, the kingdom and family of God. [13] The only passport needed to enter this kingdom is the equivalent of a birth certificate to confirm that we have been born again, through faith in the work of his beloved Son on our behalf, and are now the children of a heavenly Father. [14, 15] The complete family record is kept in God's great books. [16, 17] Until he opens these at the last day we do not know what other names will be found there or what deeds are recorded. How wonderful it would be to find that some in the book of life had been those we had helped to enrol. They too will reach our Father's home as accepted family members, all sins wiped from the record by the mediation of Jesus, our loving and beloved older brother. As we pass beyond death to the next stage of our eternal lives, we shall at last be fully restored to the image of the Lord Jesus Christ, God's great intention fulfilled. [18]

For further thought

- If you are a new Christian, have you told anyone else?
- Did you realise that life and lip should be saying the same thing?
- Could you explain to someone else God's great intention and how he fulfils it?

Further resources

- Pippert RM. *Uncover Seeker Bible study guides*. Oxford: University and Colleges Christian Fellowship, 2012
- Lewis CS. *The great divorce*. London: Geoffrey Bles UK, 1945.

References

1. 2 Corinthians 3:18
2. Romans 10:9-15
3. Hebrews 4:12-13
4. Luke 16:19-31
5. Matthew 25:31-46
6. Luke 15:7, 10
7. John 3:16-18
8. John 6:40
9. John 17:3
10. Luke 23:33-34, 39-43
11. Genesis 18:25
12. Matthew 18:20
13. John 3:3, 5-6
14. Ephesians 2:19-20
15. John 1:9-13
16. Revelation 3:5
17. Revelation 20:11-12
18. Philippians 3:20-21

Chapter 29
Sharing the good news with those from further away

When waiting in the aisle of a plane I was once moved aside by someone who wanted to spread his prayer-mat in the same space. He needed to face in the right direction for his prayers, due at that time. He probably had quite wrong ideas about what Christians believe, perhaps never having met any as prepared as he was to make such a public demonstration of faith. He could also have thought that race and religion went together, as they would normally do for him. That was not the moment to try to enlighten him but instead to stand respectfully aside. The position of the body in prayer is secondary to whether the praying heart is in the right relationship with God.

At a more convenient time and under more relaxed circumstances those of other faiths are often very ready to compare their beliefs with others and Christians should be ready to listen as well as expecting others to do the same. All too often, this kind of exchange never takes off and each side continues to have mistaken ideas about the other. Some find it surprising that the God worshipped by Christians is a Trinity of Father, Son and Holy Spirit united as one, not three separate gods, and that the third person is not Jesus' mother, Mary, but his Spirit.

Mistaken thoughts from abroad

Some of those coming from overseas may believe that a once Christian country still practises that faith and everything they find there expresses normal Christian standards. If this judgment holds, then when they are greeted by certain prominent advertisements at one of our airports or other public places, they will find some of them very shocking. In the homeland of many, alcohol, semi-nakedness and certain forms of entertainment are taboo. Starting off with this bad impression of supposed Christianity, things do not necessarily get much better as they become more deeply involved in the culture, either as workers or travellers. Some continue to feel isolated, if only by the language barrier of a regional accent. A Polish doctor friend had an adequate command of English until he went to Scotland and worked in a Glasgow hospital where, for a time, neither he nor his patients could understand each other. It would be natural then to look for friends among fellow nationals only.

This kind of displacement is now recognised by some organisations, but not all will be known of or trusted by the incomer, even if easy to find. Students can fare better and may respond to the invitations now issued by many university Christian Unions and others, giving a special welcome to any from overseas. Some professional bodies do the same and it can be by meeting real Christians for the first time that poor first impressions start to fade. For some, this will be to hear the familiar language of faith that they knew in a church at home and, possibly for the first time since arrival, they can relax and make new friends in an otherwise foreign land.

Yet there must be many more outside such welcoming circles, or in jobs too busy to give time to look for them. These are often the very people whose greatest need is for someone to show a little personal concern as they struggle with new systems. An Albanian doctor friend, on call for different parts of the hospital, found each ward's protocol very different and confusing but, as he went around, it was such a help to meet other Christians on the staff. He even married one of them! Together they began to invite others to meet in their new home. It can be so worthwhile for the locals to notice people who look like foreigners and to start a conversation, even if it is only to discover that they were born and bred in our own country. Some turn out to be members of our spiritual family. This was so with a Nigerian lady I once greeted when she was sitting on a wall near my home, cheering herself up by listening through earphones to what she told me were Christian songs. She turned out to be another doctor and a sister in the family of God, to our shared benefit.

The Great Commission

Before he died, Jesus spoke to his Father about his disciples saying, 'As you sent me into the world I have sent them into the world'. [1]

Then, just as he was about to leave them to go back to the Father, he gave them what has become known as the Great Commission, his mission statement for the church. [2] It began, 'Go and make disciples of all nations'. They were to baptise new believers in the name of the Father, Son and Holy Spirit – the true three-in-one Godhead – and teach them to obey Jesus' teaching. He finished with the promise that (through his Spirit) he would always be with them.

For many, the word 'mission' creates a mental image of a delegate or ambassador sent overseas from one country to another, and at root the word does hold the idea of being sent somewhere. A missionary is someone commissioned for a specific mission and can be any one of us just where we are, not fitting one popular image of a flushed person under a palm tree, with a Bible in one hand and the other ready to swat flies. The mission for those early disciples, and for later ones, too, is to be compelled by his love to become ambassadors for Christ. [3] This does not mean that he forces us to do this whether we like it or not, but in the same way as someone in love cannot help talking about the beloved, so when we delight in his love we may feel compelled to share (sensitively) with others that he extends this love to the whole world. [4]

After Jesus had returned to his Father, the disciples obediently waited in Jerusalem until his promised Spirit came to them. Then they began their mission just where they were. At the time many thousands 'from every nation under heaven' had gathered in the city to celebrate Pentecost and a great number believed their message straight away. [5] What an encouraging start to their mission!

Taking opportunities where you are

It is probable that our own first outreach will be where we live and work and wherever that is we are likely to find a variety of listeners. Until we detect a real interest, we will probably start simply by being friendly, raising a few 'flags', and taking it from there. No one becomes an overseas missionary by taking a sea voyage or spending a few hours in the air. Like charity, mission begins quietly at home and for some there may never be a call to go further. Then, sometimes a new door opens.

In 2012, the Olympic and Paralympic Games in London attracted many thousands of athletes and supporters from across the world. Some were welcomed into local homes, some placed with Christian families who were able to give reasons for their faith, helped in this by simple literature already prepared in many languages. A special 'sports edition' of the Bible was given to the athletes and those who took this literature to share at home would become missionaries, whether they knew it or not.

Prepared hearts

We only know a few of the stories that followed this outreach, but it seems that some who received the good news had already been on a spiritual search. On their return home with the new Bibles and booklets, perhaps hungry for further teaching, some would find help through Christian broadcasts, often to be picked up even in unsympathetic countries.

When Albania was still under an atheistic regime, the officer appointed to check the media for subversive channels became captivated by a Christian station that he would have been expected to block. Taking a great risk, he continued to learn from its messages and eventually gave his life to Christ. Many other Albanians had listened in secret for 20 years before there was a change of government, when the Christian broadcaster received 200 letters from those whose lives had been changed through learning, through his messages, to have faith in Jesus. At times, airwaves reach places that other missionaries cannot reach.

The Holy Spirit uses many other routes to touch hearts and change lives. Soon after Albania opened up a thoughtful teenager saw an advertisement nailed to a tree. It recommended a correspondence course of teaching about the Bible, a previously banned book, so she took note, wrote off and joined up. Later, through an unexpected series of events, she met Christian friends who helped her to find a personal faith in the Lord Jesus. It had started by keeping eyes and heart open, then following that unusual first lead. The Spirit of God had been at work all the time.

Looking further afield

There are still parts of the world that are quite unreached by the good news of Jesus and his love. Some of us will be called to take that news to them in person, but before changing countries we need to be clear of our calling. For various reasons, including gifts and responsibilities, others of us may have to help from a distance. Unseen numbers have been convinced of the truths they first heard on the airways, and someone has to prepare such programmes! In whichever way our help is to be channelled, acting on impulse is unwise without more assurance of God's guidance.

Seeking and finding God's will

In the mid-19th century, a man named George Muller set up a number of orphanages in the English city of Bristol. He had complete faith that God would supply all he needed and never asked for money to support the hundreds of orphans in his care. It always came and they never went hungry. Then, one morning the children sat down to an empty breakfast table. Muller had just given thanks for the non-existent food, trusting their heavenly Father to supply it, when they heard the local baker arriving with a load of bread. It was surplus to his needs but exactly matched theirs! The Father must delight to honour such simple faith and supply genuine need.

Aware of his need for daily wisdom, George Muller made a dependable checklist to use when facing decisions great and small and that can still help us, so here it is: First, he said, our hearts must be completely ready and willing to obey God before he will normally show the way forward. This openness to him is an absolute priority.

Then, feelings are poor guides but God's word and the Holy Spirit together form a reliable combination, neither to be taken as the last word without support from the other, for the Spirit's guidance will always agree with and illuminate the Scriptures he inspired.

Thirdly, circumstances can act as pointers but all these checks and balances need to be thought through in prayer until our hearts find peace. We may add to Muller's list that when taking major decisions

we would be wise to ask others to join their prayers with ours.
(For further discussion about God's methods of guidance, see chapter 30)

These pointers [6] can be helpful when wondering whether our Lord is
calling us to go to a different part of the world to fulfil his commission.
We will need clearer ideas about where and when to go, what training is
needed and what to do when we arrive in a foreign culture with a new
language to learn. Sometimes we have to go ahead, trusting that God
will bless what we think is his path without many very obvious signals,
though he is often merciful in giving a clearer sense of direction.

For varied reasons some will not be called to such work but the rest
of us should strongly support those who go, perhaps especially those
already known to us.

If we do feel drawn to work in a particular country, we need to find
more about the needs and customs of that place before we set off. In
many countries, the job description of missionary is unacceptable,
as is the open teaching of a different faith, so those doors will not open
without added professional qualifications. Foreign teachers or doctors
can still be refused entry or expelled after some kind of national crisis.

In countries opposed to Christianity growing hostility towards them is
affecting the believers who live there, increasing as well as decreasing
their numbers. Unable or unwilling to leave their homeland, some are
ready to suffer and sometimes to die for their faith. Some of these
countries are being torn apart by war, but an increasing number of
residents previously opposed to Christians have been so touched by
their steadfastness and willingness to help other sufferers that they
have decided to follow the Lord Jesus with them. In a recent message
from members of one persecuted church, they said how touched and
grateful they were to feel supported by the prayers of brothers and
sisters elsewhere. We must not fail them.

Closed doors can mean diverted routes

Most regular road users are likely at some time to come across a notice
saying, 'Road closed: follow the signs'. When needing God's fresh

guidance and looking for more signposts it will be helpful to recall that many believers in the early church were driven by persecution to find refuge elsewhere, and it was in this way that they spread more widely the good news about the Lord Jesus. [7] This is how we eventually came to hear it, as well as the many others in the world. God is never at a loss and will overrule when our plans are changed for any reason. Many have found that failure of a job application has brought an uncertain interval holding a lesson in faith, often to be strengthened by the final outcome.

When in the last century missionaries were expelled from China, they did not all go home but moved to other parts of Asia where the work grew and is still effective. The Holy Spirit must love to touch previously unreached people and often does so through God's uprooted but willing and obedient servants.

Why go overseas at all?

Before we engage in sharing our faith, whether with those from abroad who now live in our midst or when planning to go overseas, there are people who will probably ask, 'Why go and impose your views on people who are happy enough with their own beliefs?' Yet so many, especially in developing countries, are poor, malnourished or downtrodden, and are not at all happy to be living in fear of local violence or national warfare.

The work of organisations such as Tearfund or Wateraid shows how the life of a poverty stricken community can be transformed through a relatively small cash gift plus training in how to use it well. A supply of clean water will save lives and more sensible farming offers better nutrition. Preventive medical care is less dramatic than treating acute illness or doing heroic surgery but, apart from those called to be specialists in major centres, doctors often need to be generalists. To immunise all children in a village would eventually pay for the cost of the vaccines by preventing so much disease and death. Teachers, too, will cover subjects more likely to have relevance to the local community, unlike the recitation of Wordsworth's poem, 'Beside Westminster Bridge', that I once heard in an African village!

Of course, many kind-hearted people go out as teachers, or to help physical or mental illnesses, without knowing anything about relieving spiritual sickness. They still do valuable work, and all credit to them for that. Yet when workers are inspired to share the love of Jesus in creative, practical and life-saving ways, people sometimes ask, 'Why are you doing this for us?' The door is then wide open to explain how much more satisfying life could be for those whose spiritual awareness is often directed elsewhere, such as to costly worship of idols. It is a double blessing when those providing a well for a village also tell of Jesus' offer to quench spiritual thirst. It is a joy when some then learn to put their trust in him and find life transformed by a new hope. [8] It certainly seems fairer for those with such life-changing news to go and share it with people who never heard it before.

Culture shock

Whether we stay close to home or go much further away, the Great Commission will not be fulfilled without his followers knowing and obeying our missionary Lord. We should not then be dismayed if we encounter and experience a degree of discomfort or suffering as we leave behind the comforts of home. Whether expecting it or not, culture shock will still be shocking until the newcomer learns to adapt. The different climate, strange language, new customs, sights, sounds and smells can together be overwhelming and will be viewed either as an exciting challenge or a cause for homesickness. Even the threatening drone of a tiny mosquito can become a disproportionately huge trial.

Experienced and supportive new friends will help to see the newcomer through the early days but to have been first convinced that this is the place of God's leading gradually steadies the emotional turmoil. The daily reading of his word will also bring assurance of his sympathy and support. [9] No culture shock we experience could ever be as great as that of our Lord Jesus when he left heaven's highest glory to live in poverty and die in pain on a cross; yet the resurrection and ascension that followed was the route to our salvation. In our turn, what can sometimes seem like death to self can bring in a changed new life not only for us but sometimes for others.

Death to self

For many persecuted Christians, dying for their faith is a reality. It is also a possibility faced by expatriates working with them. Jim Elliot was an American missionary to South America who was killed by the tribesmen he had been trying to tell of the great love of Jesus for them. Years before, he had written in his journal, 'He is no fool who gives what he cannot keep to gain that which he cannot lose.' Those who did not understand this spiritual truth probably thought that his sacrificial life and death showed that he had indeed been a fool. Yet Elisabeth, his widow, stayed on to continue their work and in time met some of her husband's killers, to find that after all they had taken his message to their hearts. Accepted by God and forgiven for all wrongdoing, they now knew and welcomed the Father's love for themselves, and loved him in return. This would indeed have brought about the joy in heaven described in some of Jesus' stories. [10] No doubt Jim's delighted participation would add to that celestial celebration.

For further thought

- Do you know someone from another culture?
- Have you ever asked them what they believe, and really listened to the answer?
- Do you ever wonder if God may be asking you to share his love in another country?

Further resources

- SGM Lifewords: *www.sgmlifewords.com*
- Bible Society: *www.biblesociety.org.uk*
- Butterworth J. *God's secret listener*. Oxford and Grand Rapids: Monarch Books, 2010.
- Pierson AT. *George Muller of Bristol*. London: James Nisbet and Co, 1899. Steer R *George Muller: delighted in God*. Tuin, Rossdale: Christian Focus. 1997
- Elliot E. *Shadow of the Almighty*. Milton Keynes: Authentic Media, 2005.

References

1. John 17:18
2. Matthew 28:16-20
3. 2 Corinthians 5:14-20
4. John 3:16
5. Acts 2:5-12, 41
6. I am grateful to Dr. Valerie MacKay for sharing with me these guidelines, used by George Muller and preserved in notes made by her husband, Professor Donald MacKay.
7. Acts 11:19-21
8. John 4:13-14
9. Hebrews 4:15-16
10. Luke 15:7, 10, 32

Chapter 30
Where do we go from here?

The question of personal guidance is one that often causes concern to young believers, especially for those thinking about a career or simply looking for work. Asking where God wants me to go is perhaps the wrong question, but to attend to how he wants me to live can open up the next step of his plan for a committed life. He cares for each of his followers individually as well as lovingly linking them together to be his body on earth. Although God will have a different outcome in mind and use different ways of guidance for different people, it can still be encouraging to hear someone else's story.

Rani's story

A few years ago, I attended a congress in Singapore, organised by ICMDA. Many hundreds of people were there, mostly from countries in that region of the world. We met for prayer before breakfast and one morning I felt urged to pray for any at the congress who were burdened but finding it hard to find someone free to listen to them among the many meetings, greetings and languages going on around them. Sometimes God directs us to answer our own prayers and at breakfast I met an Indonesian medical student who told me how troubled he was about his brother. He was a law student, vainly trying to earn money for food and fees by peddling a rickshaw bicycle and I promised to look for funding when back at home. Eventually that chapter would end happily, but in Singapore I also had the privilege of hearing Rani's own story and I have used italics for the pointers God used as he directed his way. Some of them are likely to apply to our own very different circumstances.

Both Rani and his older brother came from a poor but loving Christian family and lived in a village fifteen hours' walk from the nearest bus stop. Somehow their widowed father supported the boys' attendance at the local school where, on the walls of his simple classroom, young Rani saw pictures of nurses and doctors and was filled with an unshakeable longing to become a doctor. He imagined bringing medical aid back to his remote people who at that time had none. This became a *conviction*, although *common sense* might have said that there would never be enough money for such costly training. Yet early in life he had been taught the verse, 'With God all things are possible',[1] and believed that it was from a completely trustworthy God that this desire had come, and he would keep his word.[2] Still a child, Rani put the dream into the hands of this wonderful God and studied as hard as he could.

Rani's father died and with him the hope of more money, but his son's *commitment* still held, based as it was on trust in God's promise. As a *consequence*, another family member offered to pay for him to train as a nurse. Although his hope of studying medicine seemed to have met a *closed door*, he set off on the difficult journey to another island and there enrolled in a nurses' training school. It was not very long before one crisis followed another. The promised cash supply failed, he took on poorly paid jobs but became too sick and weak to work, or even to buy food. Yet *God's care continued*. Unknown to him, some local missionaries noticed the absence of the conscientious Christian sweeper in the market place so asked others about him.

The missionaries were told that Rani was sick, starving and dying. At this major *crisis* in his life, God prompted those *concerned Christian friends* to find him, nurse him and give him a job and a home as their church caretaker. When his health improved one of his new friends, hearing of the interrupted training, asked him what he had really hoped to do. His *circumstances* had now changed so much that he very shyly shared his old longing to be a doctor. The missionaries prayed about it, became assured by the Holy Spirit through the word of God that although not rich themselves they had been given enough to be generous[3] and offered to pay for him to go to medical school. It was during those undergraduate years that we met in Singapore and I heard his story and shared his gratitude to the God who was meeting all his needs.[4]

At that time this still left the problem of his brother because Rani had very honourably felt that the money given to him by the missionaries had been dedicated for his use and he was not share it. Throughout his personal difficulties he had been learning more of the faithfulness of God, and encouraged his brother in that same trust. It was later very moving to hear how the two of them had knelt on their pillows and wept together as they thanked God for the way he finally honoured their faith by enabling the graduation of a young law student and later his medical student brother.

Rani and I met again at another ICMDA conference in Taipei, after his own graduation and just before his marriage to a Christian midwife. Today they and their children live over a clinic in the home they rebuilt after an earthquake. It is close to the remote area where his journey of faith had begun as he trusted God with a small boy's longing to help his own people. They *continue* to look to God for his wisdom and help with many daily problems, and have set up several prayer meetings in their district. Rani does not tire of saying, 'He is the God who understands his children's needs and, in his time, answers prayers. See what God has done in my life. If he can do it for me he will do it for you, too. Whatever the problem you face, he is the God who is always there and never leaves you.'

In the last chapter, we considered George Muller's guidelines when seeking God's will and they broadly match the detailed steps that finally led Rani to the place of God's choice for him. We, too, may confidently expect to find help from the same Lord as we look for his signposts on our way. Each journey will be different, though our goal will be the same- to glorify our God.

Commitment

The first essential is to commit our lives into God's hands and be willing to follow wherever he leads whatever the difficulties. Whether he takes us to work humbly at the back of beyond or to the top of our chosen profession, or even through a time of unemployment, is all up to him. He gave us our gifts in the first place, and will not waste them. Like Rani, we may eventually find ourselves doing exactly the work we had wanted to do, or instead undergo a surprising change of direction. Graduates undecided about which way to go may find help from counsellors, both secular and Christian, or there are a number of helpful books available with various suggestions, including the idea of trying out short term service overseas.

A short term commitment to work overseas may influence longer term plans. Not all our activities involve such major decisions and twice the simple selection of which petrol station to use has led me to unexpected but important encounters. More urgently, a clinician may have to make a quick decision and shoots up an arrow prayer for guidance about what to do or say and only later realises that wisdom had been given.

A clear call

An unexpected telephone can open a new door. This is how I was invited to go to Albania ('as soon as possible'!) to help the desperately deprived children there. That previously closed country had just opened up its secrets to the outside world. Despite an inner 'Yes!' it was better, as Muller advised, to be sure that this was a call from God. Instead of reacting impulsively, it is better to pause prayerfully and see whether enthusiasm grows warmer or cooler. This can be one of the ways that his Spirit leads.

Common sense

God does not write messages in the sky to tell us what to do for each step of our way. By using what has been called 'sanctified common sense' some jobs will be out of bounds for any Christian, or we may lack the quick wits essential for, say, work with accidents and emergencies. Our gifts may be used better in a particular way, such as preventive medicine, administration or teaching. As Rani's story shows, God can remove obstacles in the path and whether or not doors open on all that we had hoped for, he still cares about his trainees as they are given lessons in trust.

Conviction

Our assurance of God's leading grows as we rely on his promises. By walking with him and reading his word, his Holy Spirit will put some of his promises into our memory bank to be recalled when faith is tested, or to act as signposts in times of uncertainty. In a period of doubt, we may read in our daily reading, 'Trust in the Lord with all your heart and lean not on your own understanding; in all your ways submit to him and he will make your paths straight.'[5] If about to take an important decision, it is so reassuring to read a word such as, 'The Lord will guide you always; he will satisfy your needs in a sun-scorched land.'[6] Even when too hard pressed or unwell for much reading, a stored verse may come to mind or the memory be triggered in some other way, acting as God's personal word given through his Spirit.

Muller spoke of the importance of this double leading, the word illuminated by the Spirit and the Spirit's nudge confirmed by the word. Feelings alone are a poor guide but, deeper than both natural anxiety and enthusiasm, we can know the stability of being anchored in God and the promises he sometimes underlines as we read them.

Consequences

Having committed our way to God, ready to trust his word and will, we can expect him to act. He is not in the same hurry as we may be, but in his time he will honour our faith. A friend of mine had finished his training as a general practitioner but, about to marry, no practice had yet accepted him and the young couple did not know where to look for a home but trusted God completely. At the last minute, they were amazed to be offered a practice and a home, both of them accommodated in an English castle! God's provision is sometimes far above all we could ask or imagine.[7] What a unique wedding present!

Closed doors

When we have decided on a particular career, our work will often proceed along an expected pathway, whether it be medical, educational or theological training. The course set is often the direction we will keep although sometimes we start to feel an uneasy sense that it is time to move. Perhaps a job or promotion we had hoped for went to someone else, or we find ourselves out of work. An illness arises in our immediate circle or knocks us sideways and it is difficult to know what to do.

The end result is the same – our set path has come unset. Some doctors have a growing conviction that they are being called out of medical practice to give priority to people's spiritual needs, or to concentrate on work for social justice. It is so helpful at times of uncertainty to look back along the way and be assured with the words of an old hymn that 'he who has led us hitherto will guide us all our journeys through' and will never leave or forsake us. [8] Past experience can fortify future hope.

Coincidences need confirmation

At times of uncertainty we can be tempted to see coincidences as God's way of directing our paths, as indeed they can be, but they can also be organised by the enemy of our souls. He is ever ready to try to distract, dazzle or destroy us. [9, 10] Perhaps a better way to view a coincidence is as a wake-up call to be prayed over, perhaps with a sympathetic friend.

I had already been looking at more senior jobs in Britain when three letters arrived in one day, all suggesting that I look at a post in Uganda. I had recently learned that coincidences can happen without necessarily being God's guidance, so I looked for his *confirmation* or otherwise that this was from him. In my daily Bible reading I also took up a neglected little book of selected verses (*Daily Light*) and that particular day there were so many of 'my' verses, including those quoted earlier, that the Spirit within me said 'This is the way!' (Many can testify to that unmistakable nudge as a verse lights up, so different from mere wishful thinking as it is not always pointing to something that we would have chosen.) I knew little about the country then but the name 'Uganda' kept surfacing in all kinds of connections. Surprisingly, having looked for guidance, instead of being excited I began to feel very apprehensive. Then a visiting speaker preached on Joshua's commission before he entered new territory. In the version that the preacher used the message came to me as well as to Joshua, saying, 'Don't be frightened'! [11] What could I do after that! The initial coincidence had been unmistakeably confirmed by signs following and I applied for the post.

Crossroads and crosswinds

When facing a major decision, the understanding and prayers of
Christian friends can be more important than we always realise. They,
or our senior colleagues, may introduce *contacts* who offer experience
or advice about this or alternative options. Yet a time of uncertainty
may also be a reminder to go back to renewed and honest tuning in to
God's word and Spirit. Are we thinking of giving up the present
position because it is harder than expected, or do we just want a
change? If we believe that this was clearly God's placement from the
start he will help us to complete it. [12] If it is time for a move this will
also be made clear.

At times it can still be hard to go forward, especially when crosswinds
arise that could take us off course. The anchor of that previous
confirmation will then hold us in the face of what could be enemy action
trying to hold us back. After all that build-up of presumed leading
towards the post in Uganda – I did not get it! It took many months for
the Ugandan authorities to explain a misunderstanding and say that the
post was still on offer. By now my enthusiasm had cooled and different
options had come up, but that past leading had been too clear to put
aside. Trust can grow through its testing, and at such times God seems
particularly kind with encouragements to stay obedient and hold on
to him, even should we then head for the unknown land, as I did,
on dragging feet. He had other important lessons to teach me there.

A strange commission

Centuries ago, a rich landowner asked his trusted servant to set off
with a party of a few men and ten camels to make a return journey of
between eight and nine hundred miles across unknown territory, riding
on camelback. He was to find a special girl that he had never met in
his life and whose name he did not know and bring her back to marry
his master's son. It is not surprising that he asked a hesitant, 'What
if...?' before obediently setting off on this extraordinary journey.

Amazingly, he eventually found and identified a young woman with
the right ancestry, and she invited him to stay with her family, taking
all his camels and companions with him. Her parents welcomed him
and gratefully received the many gifts he had taken and, overnight,
with her father's blessing the girl agreed to leave home. No doubt it
was with some excitement and perhaps a little apprehension that she
set off with the party and headed for the unknown. She put her faith
in the messenger and his story, and also trusted his God as she faced
the prospect before her. When you are able, read the whole account
in Genesis 24.

It is worth noting the number of times that Abraham's servant, Eleazar,
prayed for guidance. He did his share in keeping a close lookout for
God's signals, faithfully given, assuring him that he was on the right
path. The journey had started with his commitment, in obedience to
his master, to set out in the confidence that God would direct him, and
ended with a celebration of praise that he had so wonderfully crowned
the journey with success. It is of even greater significance to us that the
bridegroom waiting patiently for his unknown bride was Abraham's
God-given son Isaac.

Together they would become ancestors of Jesus, who is called Christ. [13]
Behind the mini-plan of Genesis 24 was a master plan, to be fulfilled by
an even more remarkable journey as God's own Son came from heaven
to earth to seek and to save us, offering amazing gifts to those who
receive him. He promised that one day he will come again to take those
who love him back to his home. [14] What a wonderful destination, the
greeting from our Lord Jesus in his unimaginable glory far outweighing
any hardship we might have experienced on the way there. [15]

Sometimes our mini-plans meet unexpected delays or disappointments,
but God's overall plan is to bring about something much greater, often
not at all clear to us at the time. He delights in teaching us to have
more trust in him and then he honours that trust. The retrospectoscope
is a wonderful instrument for illuminating his wise and loving ways.
In his summing up Eleazar said, 'As for me, the Lord has led me
on the journey...' [16]

As we finally look back after years of commitment to that same Lord, may we each be able to echo his words, sharing in praise and thanks to God for his faithfulness, yesterday, today, and for evermore. [17]

For further thought

- Are you willing to go wherever God may take you?
- Did you start off like that but have now lost your way?
- There is a way back – and then forward again. Trust him!

Further resources

- Jensen PD with Payne T. *Guidance and the voice of God*. Kingston: NSW Australia: Mathias Media, 2005
- Eccles S, Sanders S (eds). *So you want to be a brain surgeon? (3rd edition)*. Oxford: Oxford University Press, 2009
- Lavy V. *Short-term medical work*. London: Christian Medical Fellowship, 2013.

References

1. Matthew 19:26
2. Psalm 37:4
3. 2 Corinthians 9:11-14
4. Philippians 4:19
5. Proverbs 3:5-6
6. Isaiah 58:11
7. Ephesians 3:20
8. Deuteronomy 31:6
9. 1 Peter 5:8
10. 2 Corinthians 11:14-15
11. Joshua 1:9
12. Philippians 1:6
13. Matthew 1:2, 16
14. John 14:1-3
15. 2 Corinthians 4:14, 16-18
16. Genesis 24:27
17. Hebrews 13:8

Chapter 31
Reaching the final goal: the image restored

n many Christian circles throughout the world, the name of John Stott is likely to bring immediate recognition. Son of a consultant cardiologist, Dr Stott once said that his own first word had been 'electrocardiogram', and that for a time he had wanted to be a paediatrician. Instead he became known worldwide as a leading Christian thinker, speaker and writer of many books. His Bible studies alone are models of clear explanation and practical application. A firm believer in the divine inspiration and authority of the Scriptures, he applied biblical principles to contemporary issues, including medical ethics. Sharing Jesus' concern for the poor and needy [1] he lived very simply himself, a major interest being to support and provide teaching material for struggling overseas church and student leaders. He wrote very many helpful books, some of them suggested in this publication as possible further reading.

In 2007, in his 86th year and only four years before his death, John Stott gave his last address at the great annual convention in Keswick, Cumbria. He urged his audience to consider ways of becoming more like Jesus, highlighting his incarnation, his service, his love, his patient endurance and his mission. Perhaps in our busy lives we tend to focus on present duties but, unless we know what we're aiming at, we'll never hit it!

We are to become like Jesus here on earth

A friend of mine once asked what made Christianity different from other faiths. There are many distinctions, in particular the way our burden of guilt is lifted when sins are forgiven and, through the sacrificial death of Christ, our broken relationship with God can be repaired. Yet ours is also the only faith that worships its founder as God-made-man, whose Spirit lives in believers to make them as fruitful and gifted as was the earthly Jesus. (See chapters 24 and 25) Ours is an incarnational faith. God was in Christ, reconciling us to himself, and now the Spirit of Christ is in us, to make us more like Jesus. He works in us to do more of his work here until the time comes for him to call us home to be with him.

Human disobedience spoiled the intended image of God in mankind and even awareness of it. The coming of the Lord Jesus Christ to live on earth showed exactly what that intention had been. [2] If we are to be made like him, then we, too, should finally reflect that same image.

In chapter 22, we looked at a number of pictures to illustrate this further, such as the possibility of developing a family likeness, or the metamorphosis undergone as one life form matures into another. Of course, the incarnation, the 'enfleshment', of Jesus was unique but in a sense, as the same Spirit lives in those who are committed to him, they should gradually be seen as being in the same mould and mature into a more recognisable likeness. Although we must all be very conscious of how far short we still fall, God looks at the work in progress and longs to perfect it.

When on safari in Africa, Matthew Parris (columnist for *The Times* newspaper and a declared atheist) noticed a difference between traditional African people and African Christians, who seemed to him (rightly!) to have been freed from anxiety, fear of evil spirits and more, and were more direct and open with other people. 'They stood tall', he said, and he felt safer to camp overnight near a mission station than anywhere else. His conclusion was that 'Africa needs God'. This was the title Matthew Parris gave his piece and it was an interesting comment from someone who professed not to believe in God at all. He had unexpectedly seen a glimpse of God's image being restored in the Christians he met.

A preview of what lies ahead

On the Mount of Transfiguration, Jesus was temporarily changed, dazzling the amazed eyes of his disciples. The Father spoke from heaven that *this* was his beloved Son. [3] John's book of Revelation contains word pictures of someone who almost defied description, yet John also spoke of him as a slain but enthroned Lamb. This should remind us of John the Baptist's declaration that Jesus is the Lamb of God who would take away the sins of the world. [4, 5] In his revelation John witnessed great praise arising from people of all nations who had accepted the Lamb's sacrificial offering and were now in his glorious presence. In John's first letter, he said that when we see him we shall be like him. [6] We get an earthly glimpse of this when we see a young child running in delight to welcome a parent arriving home after a day's work, each face reflecting the joyful love of the other. Airports are also good places to witness such moving reunions.

It will be a lifetime before we even begin to reflect the glory of Jesus. For each of us there is always more than a little of 'me' left that is not Christ-like, and does not easily give up the old ways. We (the writer included!) are often surprised by a sudden emergence of self. Like a purring little kitten, all may look good on the surface until someone accidentally treads on its tail and purring gives way to hissing and scratching. We know already that patience and long-suffering are not the easiest aspects of the Spirit's fruit to grow, and self-love so often cuts off the flow of any Christ-like self-giving love. Producing the fruit of his Spirit needs our willing co-operation, and at times an experience of pruning before that lost, intended image can be restored.
Yet there is hope ahead.

The refining process

Most people find it easier to complain when life is hard than to give thanks when all is well. Yet as we seek God's grace to look back we can sometimes see how instructive and creative our difficulties have been. At one point in the old account of Job's many sufferings he reached the conclusion that, just as a goldsmith applies heat to unrefined gold to show up and deal with its impurities, so he could see that he was undergoing a process of refinement from which he would finally emerge like pure gold. [7] Before the gold ore is refined it looks very dull with only occasional sparkles, but afterwards the goldsmith may see in it a reflection of his own face. The last book in the Old Testament, Malachi, includes the same idea. [8] This puts a new slant on suffering, whether minor or major, as not being altogether pointless. Unlike the melted gold, we can choose whether to complain of the heat or trust God to use it to refine us.

We pick up this thought from Paul when he writes of our having only a hazy reflection of God's loving intentions now, but how, through suffering, we may go on to reflect more clearly the Lord's own image. [9, 10]

We shall one day be like him

Before his death Jesus promised that one day he would return to take his followers to be with him in his Father's house. [11] In 1 Thessalonians, Paul describes how he expects this to happen both for those still living and the resurrected dead. [12] As Paul was probably the unidentified person who had once had a remarkable but private visionary experience we may perhaps suppose this to have been one of the insights given then. [13] He also said that until we go to be with him we are gradually undergoing transformation (metamorphosis) into the Lord's likeness. [14]

Keeping our eyes on the goal

Although we naturally draw back from any idea of suffering, yet when Jesus said, 'Follow me', he was on the way to Calvary. He warned against any such turning back once we have started to follow [15] Later, his Spirit came to the disciples to strengthen and sustain them, even in the persecutions they faced because of staying true to him. When trouble came, the Spirit actually enabled them to count it as joy. [16] With more experience and hindsight, James was another who could say that it is best to face trials of many kinds with joy because they gradually produce in us perseverance and maturity. [17] It does help to count our present troubles as not worth dwelling on in the light of the glory ahead. We therefore learn to fix our eyes not on what we can see all too well but on what we cannot yet see at all. [18] We need to adapt to long-distance vision, even if sometimes the lenses are made from our tears.

Not long ago I met someone whose work had often taken him to India. He commented on the contrast between rich and poor observed by thoughtful visitors to such countries and added, 'Yet despite being so obviously impoverished, I never heard anyone complain. They seemed to have such endurance, as if this had actually emerged from their sufferings'. We agreed that it was rather like the way pruning a rosebush helps to grow more blossoms, a similar thought to the final effect on gold of its refinement. Obviously this should not make us tolerant of other people's pain without trying to offer relief, otherwise there would be no health care professionals or aid workers.

Yet there is a spiritual parallel, for it is in the loving hands of the Father of compassion and the God of all comfort that many of his children come to develop more patient endurance, even through distressing experiences. As we win through by keeping our focus on the Lord Jesus, who endured the cross for us to bring such joyful results, [19] so we find that by needing to be comforted ourselves we have gained more understanding for others we meet who are still in need of it. [20] Even so, it is of no help to say to someone, 'I know how you feel.' None of us will have had exactly the same feelings as others but when we have walked through a similar valley and found the comforting presence of our Lord there with us, that is a testimony to be shared. [21]

This positive result must not be turned into a deliberate search for extra suffering, or the foolish idea that this would score more good marks to help us on judgment day. Our salvation is an entirely free and undeserved gift from God. [22] Paul had a much longer catalogue of difficulties than most of us will ever have but, like him, we can hope in our trials to show clearer evidence of Jesus' vitality at work in us. [23] God is faithful and will not allow testing beyond our endurance. [24]

It's not all sorrow and suffering!

Those who mock the Christian faith sometimes call it hoping for 'pie in the sky when you die', but not having much pleasure in life here and now. I must not leave that impression! – for most of those who seek to walk in step with the Spirit of God will already know something of the love, joy and peace he produces. [25] There is a great wealth of friendship among believers that is unlike any other, providing a source of love, joy, fun and fellowship with mutual support in more difficult times.

Wanting to become like Jesus

It is a long process for each of us to be made more like Jesus, yet as we co-operate with him this is the aim of his Spirit within us. What a goal that is! – to recover the image that God meant for each of us at the beginning of time and illustrated for us in our Lord Jesus Christ. [26, 27] In ways that we cannot begin to imagine, his image will be fully reflected in us when we join him in his heavenly home and are made like him. Other tasks await us there but no more tears or pain. [28, 29] God's original intention will have come full circle.

Those who heard John Stott's last great Bible address would think how much like the Lord Jesus the speaker himself had unconsciously become as he neared the end of his long life. Yet with Paul, he would have admitted that he was not yet made perfect but still pressing on. [30] That famous international preacher and inspiring teacher ended his talk with a simple children's chorus, using it as a prayer:

Like Jesus, like Jesus,
I want to be like Jesus.
I love him so, I want to grow
Like Jesus day by day.

Whatever our age or experience, we can add to that our own 'Yes!'.

Am I all that I could be?

Although sin spoiled the intended image in us all, we begin the process of recovery when we ask God's Son, the Lord Jesus, to restore the broken relationship between us. By his Spirit he then starts to refine and transform us until the day when we shall meet him face to face to fully reflect his image for evermore. Until then, like Paul, we press on to take hold of that for which Christ Jesus took hold of us.

For further thought

- What a great privilege and prospect we have, to be changed and made like Jesus. Have you met anyone already so transformed that you are reminded of him?
- To learn of their early struggles may suggest a creative purpose in your own.

Further resources

- Steer R. *Inside Story: the life of John Stott*. Nottingham: Inter-Varsity Press, 2009
- Stott J. *The Model – Becoming more like Christ*. Available as teaching DVD, KESW 009 from *www.iccstudiosandduplication.com*
- Parris M. Africa needs God. *The Times*, 27 December 2008 available at: *bit.ly/1g9A28a*

References

1. Luke 14:12-14
2. 2 Corinthians 4:4
3. Mark 9:2-7
4. John 1:29
5. Revelation 5:6
6. 1 John 3:2
7. Job 23:10
8. Malachi 3:2-4
9. 1 Corinthians 13:12
10. Romans 8:16-18
11. John 14:3
12. 1 Thessalonians 4:16-18
13. 2 Corinthians 12:1-6
14. 2 Corinthians 3:18
15. Luke 9:51, 59, 62
16. Acts 5:41
17. James 1:2-4
18. 2 Corinthians 4:16-18
19. Hebrews 12:2-3
20. 2 Corinthians 1:3-7
21. Psalm 23:4
22. Ephesians 2:8-10
23. 2 Corinthians 4:7-12
24. 1 Corinthians 10:13
25. Galatians 5:22-25
26. Colossians 1:15
27. Philippians 3:20-21
28. Revelation 22:3-5
29. Revelation 21:4
30. Philippians 3:12

Chapter 32
Here are the headlines again

A t the end of a news broadcast it is usual for the main items to be summarised, whether their content has been good or bad, reminding listeners of that day's headlines. Often they are left downcast or anxious about what has happened, or is likely to happen. A newscaster who once tried to give only good news failed in the attempt and was replaced. We have been considering the best possible news and it still applies every day whatever is happening in the rest of the world. To be reminded of the loving purposes of God is to be filled with wonder and thankfulness for the past and great hope for the future. We are given the best of news that will never be withdrawn or replaced.

The image created

So God created man in his own image, in the image of God he created him; male and female he created them. [1]

The image spoiled by enemy tactics

The serpent said to the woman, 'Did God really say...?'
The woman said 'God did say, "You must not eat of the fruit...or you will die."'
'You will not surely die,' the serpent said.
When the woman saw that the fruit was good...pleasing...desirable... she took some and ate it. She also gave some to her husband and he ate it. Then the eyes of both of them were opened and they realised they were naked.
The man and his wife heard the sound of the Lord God as he was walking in the garden, and they hid.
Then the Lord said 'What is this you have done?'
and banished them from the Garden of Eden. [2]
We all, like sheep, have gone astray, each of us has turned to his own way. [3]

The image made visible

[Jesus] is the image of the invisible God, the firstborn over all creation. [4]
'Mary, you have found favour with God. You will be with child and
give birth to a son, and you are to give him the name Jesus...The Holy
Spirit will come upon you. So the holy one to be born will be called
the Son of God.' [5]

The offer of restored relationship...

'Mary...will give birth to a son, and you are to give him the name
Jesus, because he will save his people from their sins...' [6]

...restored at a price

For what the law was powerless to do...God did by sending his
own Son in the likeness of sinful man to be a sin offering... [7]
...the Lord has laid on him the iniquity of us all...He committed no
sin.... [8]
He himself bore our sins in his body on the tree, so that we might die
to sins and live for righteousness; by his wounds you have been healed. [9]

The offer not recognised by all

The god of this age has blinded the minds of unbelievers, so that they
cannot see the light of the gospel of the glory of Christ, who is the
image of God. [10]

The offer accepted by some and their relationship restored
Yet to all who received him, to those who believed in his name,
he gave the right to become children of God. [11]

You are all sons of God through faith in Christ Jesus, for all of you
who were baptised into Christ have clothed yourselves with Christ.
Because you are sons, God sent the Spirit of his Son into our hearts,
who calls out, '*Abba*, Father'. [12]

Enemy action will try to threaten the image...

I am afraid that just as Eve was deceived by the serpent's cunning, your minds may somehow be led astray from your sincere and pure devotion to Christ...for Satan himself masquerades as an angel of light. [13]

...but it can be renewed

If we confess our sins, he is faithful and just and will forgive us our sins and purify us from all unrighteousness. [14]

The full image slowly being restored

...you have taken off the old self with its practices and have put on the new self which is being renewed in knowledge in the image of its creator. [15]

For the eyes of the Lord range throughout the earth to strengthen those whose hearts are fully committed to him. [16]
Do not conform any longer to the pattern of this world but be transformed by the renewing of your mind... [17]
And we, who with unveiled faces all reflect the Lord's glory, are being transformed into his likeness with ever increasing glory, which comes from the Lord, who is the Spirit. [18]

One day the likeness will be complete

Now we see but a poor reflection as in a mirror;
then we shall see face to face... [19]
Our citizenship is in heaven. And we eagerly await a Saviour from there, the Lord Jesus Christ, who by the power that enables him to bring everything under his control, will transform our lowly bodies so that they will be like his glorious body... [20]
And just as we have borne the likeness of the earthly man,
so we shall we bear the likeness of the man from heaven. [21]

In this hope we keep looking ahead

Let us fix our eyes on Jesus, the pioneer and perfecter of our faith, who for the joy set before him endured the cross, scorning its shame, and sat down at the right hand of the throne of God. Consider him who endured such opposition from sinful men, so that you will not grow weary and lose heart. [22]

Not that I have already obtained all this, or have already been made perfect, but I press on to lay hold of that for which Christ Jesus took hold of me. [23]

The image fully restored

...we know that when [Jesus] appears, we shall be like him, for we shall see him as he is. Everyone who has this hope in him purifies himself, just as [Jesus] is pure. [24]

Thought for each day

That is not the end of the news as further reports are expected at any time. Everyone hoping to receive them must remain connected, and stay tuned. It is God's great intention to restore us to his image. With the help of his indwelling Spirit we will gradually come to know more of life to the full, as promised by our Lord Jesus Christ, who lived it. [25]

Perhaps the words of this hymn could shape your daily prayer that God would be continually transforming you to be more like Christ, fulfilling God's great intention for you as you walk with him:

May the mind of Christ my Saviour
Live in me from day to day,
By his love and power controlling
All I do and say

May the Word of God dwell richly
In my heart from hour to hour,
So that all may see I triumph
Only through his power

May his beauty rest upon me
As I seek the lost to win,
And may they forget the channel,
Seeing only him

(Kate Barclay Wilkinson,1925)

References

1. Genesis 1:27
2. Genesis 3:1-5, 6-13, 21-24
3. Isaiah 53:6a
4. Colossians 1:15
5. Luke 1:30-35
6. Matthew 1:21
7. Romans 8:3
8. Isaiah 53:6b
9. 1 Peter 2:22- 24
10. 2 Corinthians 4:4
11. John 1:12
12. Galatians 3:26, 4:6
13. 2 Corinthians 11:3, 14
14. 1 John 1:9
15. Colossians 3:9-10
16. 2 Chronicles 16:9
17. Romans 12:2
18. 2 Corinthians 3:18
19. 1 Corinthians 13:12
20. Philippians 3:20-21
21. 1 Corinthians 15:49
22. Hebrews 12:2-3
23. Philippians 3:12
24. 1 John 3:2-3
25. John 10:10

I keep asking that the God of our Lord Jesus Christ, the glorious Father, may give you the Spirit of wisdom and revelation, so that you may know him better. I pray that the eyes of your heart may be enlightened in order that you may know the hope to which he has called you, the riches of his glorious inheritance in his holy people, and his incomparably great power for us who believe. That power is the same as the mighty strength he exerted when he raised Christ from the dead and seated him at his right hand in the heavenly realms, far above all rule and authority, power and dominion, and every name that is invoked, not only in the present age but also in the one to come.

(Ephesians 1:17-20)

CMF BOOKS

All these and many more are available to order online
at *www.cmf.org.uk/bookstore*

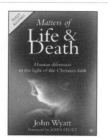

Matters of Life and Death
John Wyatt

Complementary and Alternative Medicine
Robina Coker

At A Given Moment
Graham McAll

Hard Questions about Health and Healing
Andrew Fergusson

Mad, Bad or Sad
M Dominic Beer and Nigel D Pocock

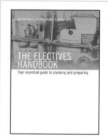

The Electives Handbook
Rachel Perry, Emma Pedlar & Vicky Lavy

Facing Infertility
Jason Roach & Philippa Taylor

Surviving the Foundation Years
Peter Saunders

Short-Term Medical Work
Dr Vicky Lavy